THE

REIGN OF QUEEN ANNE

II.

THE
REIGN OF QUEEN ANNE

BY

JUSTIN McCARTHY

AUTHOR OF 'A HISTORY OF OUR OWN TIMES' ETC.

IN TWO VOLUMES

VOL. II.

LONDON

CHATTO & WINDUS

1902

PRINTED BY
SPOTTISWOODE AND CO. LTD., NEW-STREET SQUARE
LONDON

CONTENTS

OF

THE SECOND VOLUME

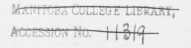

THE
REIGN OF QUEEN ANNE

CHAPTER XXI

'SWEDISH CHARLES' AND CZAR PETER

THERE were at this time two European Sovereigns, either of whom might, were he disposed to intervene on the one side or the other of the great struggle then going on in Europe, have exercised a serious influence on the fortunes of the war. These Sovereigns were Charles the Twelfth of Sweden and Peter the Great of Russia. Neither Sweden nor Russia had any particular interest in the conflict one way or the other. The keenest observer of European politics could hardly have ventured to say, at the opening of the war, whether the inclinations of Charles the Twelfth or of Peter the Great might or might not have led him to this side rather than to that. But then both these rulers had already shown themselves to be possessed by such an adventurous temper, and by such an ambition for extended dominion and influence, that it would hardly be possible to count on their patient neutrality under all the conditions of the struggle.

The war had not gone on for very long before it became evident that it was destined to bring about some material changes in the territorial system of Europe, and at any moment, therefore, new conditions might arise which would be well calculated to inspire a man like Charles or a man like Peter with the hope of obtaining some sudden and substantial increase to his dominion if he were to lend his military support to the arms of the Allies or to the arms of France. The whole territorial system of the Continent on its western side seemed likely to be cast first into confusion and then into reconstruction by the process of events. New divisions of territory were already beginning to be laid out; new States were claiming recognition; new titles for new sovereignties were in process of creation, and an ambitious, adventurous, ruling 'outsider' might at any moment see good hope of some great reward for his direct intervention on either side. Sweden and Russia were alike 'outsiders' so far as the causes of the war were concerned, but how long would either remain an 'outsider' if tempted to come in?

Long before the war had come to a close, and even before the secret negotiations for terms of peaceful settlement had begun, the English Government had made efforts to secure if not the co-operation yet, at least, the benevolent neutrality of Peter the Great and of Charles the Twelfth. Russia was then only beginning to make herself known as a

power in Europe. The policy of Peter the Great
had seemed to be directed, above all things, to the
internal organisation and the economic strengthening of his country, to her improvement in all the
industrial and mechanical arts, and to promoting
whatever trade and commerce could bring out and
employ the natural resources of the country. That
Peter had in his own mind some ambitions and some
projects for the expansion of Russia's territorial
domain, and for the strengthening of his empire so as
to make it formidable in war as well as in peace,
there cannot be the slightest question. But thus far
he had shown no inclination to mix himself up with
the interests and the quarrels of States which had no
direct concern in Russia's affairs.

When the alliance with Germany and Holland
was in process of formation it did not occur to the
English Government that Peter would be likely to
take any part in such a federation, or that his active
co-operation could be of great value to the Allies.
But it had always been thought desirable for England
to keep on good terms with the Russian ruler. Peter
was a great admirer of Marlborough's military
genius, and he sent to Marlborough a Russian decoration of the highest order, which was acknowledged by
the English commander in a letter written for him,
as we may well believe, the epistle being all in grandiloquent Latin. It was addressed to ' Serenissimo
ac Potentissimo Magno Domino CZARI ac MAGNO DUCI
PETRO ALEXIOWITZ,' and much more to the same
effect, in profuse acknowledgment of Peter's title to

the world's homage and reverence. Burton remarks
that the letter was written 'with the grandiloquent
superfluity of courtesies and titles that renders the
recent use of the Latin language in diplomacy so
bewildering a contrast to its severe simplicity in its
classic days.' At present the States of Europe do
not feel bound to transact their diplomatic correspondence in that Latin which Cæsar and Cicero knew
not how to write, and which, we may take it for
granted, Peter the Great knew not how to read.

Marlborough had more direct dealings with
Charles the Twelfth, whose co-operation, if it could be
obtained, was considered by the English Government
much more important than that of Peter. Charles
had been a disturbing influence throughout a great
part of the European Continent since his succession
to the throne of Sweden, and he was looked upon as
a man who might easily be prevailed upon to take
an active and an important share in any dazzling
enterprise which seemed to promise military glory.
At a very critical period in the war Marlborough,
whose presence it might have been thought could ill be
spared from the field of action, was sent on a special
mission to Charles with the real, although not the
avowed, object of securing if possible the co-operation, or at all events the neutrality, of the Swedish
Sovereign.

In a letter which Marlborough wrote to
Harley, he noted his understanding of the mission
entrusted to him as an effort to secure the friendship
of Charles, ' on account of the great advantage the

Allies may reap from him, or the damage he may do us.' In another letter Marlborough tells Harley all about his first audience of Swedish Charles. 'This morning at ten o'clock I had an audience of the king, at which I delivered the queen's and the prince's letters. It lasted till dinner, and was afterwards renewed for a considerable time. The king expressed great tenderness and respect for her Majesty, as well as friendship for his Royal Highness, and seeming to be very well inclined to the interest of the allies; so that hitherto I have had good reason to hope my journey may have all the success her Majesty and the public expect from it.' Marlborough further mentions that he was accompanied by an interpreter during his audience with the King, 'though I always expressed myself in French, which the king understood for the most part himself.' Marlborough appears to have delivered, after the fashion of the time, quite a florid and pompous little discourse to Charles when presenting him with Queen Anne's letter. 'I present to your Majesty,' he said, 'a letter not from the Chancery, but from the heart of the queen my mistress, and written with her own hand. Had not her sex prevented it, she would have crossed the sea to see a prince admired by the whole universe. I am in this particular more happy than the queen, and I wish I could serve some campaign under so great a general as your Majesty, that I might learn what I yet want to know in the art of war.'

There were many difficulties, however, in the

way of any cordial political agreement between
the representative of England and the King of
Sweden. Charles as usual had his mind filled with
all sorts of schemes for securing his crown, extend-
ing his territory, and obtaining triumphs over
his foreign enemies, and at the same time the one
public purpose which then especially occupied his
attention was to obtain full religious liberty for
Protestant communities in all parts of Europe.
Marlborough himself would no doubt have been
inclined to favour all these latter projects, but
when he remembered that England was engaged
in arranging the succession to the throne of a
Catholic kingdom, he felt bound to deal very
cautiously with any plans or proposals which must
bring up in a new form the perplexing religious
difficulty. Nothing of any definite nature came
from the personal interchange of complimentary
speeches and political discussions between the two
great soldiers who had so much in common on
subjects of military interest. After Marlborough's
return to England he wrote to the British resident at
the Court of Sweden, thanking him for the constant
account he had given of his negotiations with the
Swedish Sovereign. 'I see with a great deal of
concern,' he wrote, 'how obstinately the King of
Sweden insists upon the article of religion. . . .
These proceedings cannot but tend to the greatest
advantage of our common enemy at this juncture,
and will be so far from advancing the Protestant
religion in general, that it must, of course, be a

great prejudice to it, and will hinder anything we might do in favour of it at a general peace.'

These comments coming from Marlborough are characteristic alike of the times and of the man. Marlborough's sympathies would naturally go with the cause of the Protestant communities who suffered from religious intolerance and oppression, but he was essentially a man of the world, and his enthusiasm for any particular form of faith was never likely to carry him into even a momentary forgetfulness of the political and military difficulties which might be created by the display of too great fervour for the general principle of religious liberty. They were characteristic also of the times, for we find that every State in Europe was quite ready to make use of the religious question when its use could be turned to the disadvantage of the enemy, and equally anxious to keep it out of sight when its obtrusion might tend to embarrass the State itself. Louis the Fourteenth persecuted the Huguenots, but professed much concern at the intolerance which the English Government displayed towards the fellow-religionists of the exiled Stuarts. England welcomed on her battlefields and in her commercial and industrial life the help of the banished Huguenots, and was herself meantime actively engaged in oppressing the Catholics of Ireland. Statesmanship then had not risen to the height of accepting the doctrine of religious freedom as a common and equitable principle. Each State regarded as religious persecution that very policy in her neighbour which she

insisted on as the just maintenance of religion in her
own case. But, at the same time, the statesmen of each
country felt themselves perfectly free to let the true
religion take care of itself in any instances where an
untimely or inconvenient championship of its cause
might have interfered with projects of a more practical
and worldly order. Charles the Twelfth, therefore,
was able to obtain from Marlborough but little support in his schemes for the protection of the Protestant communities, and the Allies did not gain
much direct advantage from the negotiations carried
on for them by England.

The Allies had before long good reason to
know that Charles was not likely to disturb the movements of the Alliance by any interposition of his own.
The King's mind was bent on other projects. Those
projects Marlborough, during his conversations with
Charles, found it easy to penetrate. Voltaire in his Life
of Charles the Twelfth gives an interesting and vivid
description of the manner in which Marlborough
came to understand that the one dominant passion
in Charles's mind, just then, was his desire to throw
himself into fierce antagonism with the Sovereign of
Russia. When Marlborough mentioned to Charles
the name of the Czar he saw, Voltaire tells us, ' that
the eyes of the King lighted up at the mere sound
of the name; he saw too that a map of Russia lay
always on the table of the room where he conversed
with Charles, and it needed nothing more to enable
him to judge that the veritable design of the King of
Sweden and his sole ambition were to dethrone the

Czar after the King of Poland.' 'He left Charles the
Twelfth to his natural inclinings, and satisfied with
having penetrated them, he made no proposition to
him.'

Voltaire is always anxious in his Life of Charles
to give his readers precise authority for every statement he makes, and he informs us that all the
particulars which he has given concerning the conversations between King Charles and Marlborough
'have been confirmed to me by Madam the Duchess
of Marlborough, his widow, still living.' There are
few chapters in the history of that age more interesting, more curious, more picturesque in the true sense,
than that which illustrates the meeting of these two
great soldiers so much akin and congenial in military
genius, so unlike in the capacity for the practical
business of war—the one filled only by the glamour
of his own personal ambitions and projects, the other
quietly resolved to learn all he could and to give
out in return as little as possible of the policy
and purpose which his own Government had at
heart.

The passages in which Voltaire describes the
meetings and the exchange of ideas, so far as it
could be called an exchange of ideas where so
cautious a man as Marlborough made one of the
figures, is well worthy of further quotation. 'The
King of Sweden,' Voltaire tells us, 'received at that
time in his camp the ambassadors of almost all the
princes of Christianity. Some came to supplicate
him to quit the territories of the empire; the others

would have much desired that he should turn his
arms against the Emperor; the rumour even was
spread abroad everywhere that he was about to join
with France in order to bear down the House of
Austria.' Then we come to Marlborough's part in
the negotiations. 'Among all these ambassadors
came the famous John Duke of Marlborough on
behalf of Anne, Queen of Great Britain. That man
who never besieged a town which he did not take,
or began a battle which he did not gain, was at St.
James' an adroit courtier, in parliament a leader of a
party, in foreign countries the most skilful negotiator
of his age. He had done as much harm to France
by his intellect as by his arms. The Secretary to the
States-General, M. Fagel, a man of great merit, has
said that more than once the States-General having
resolved to oppose some measure which the Duke
of Marlborough was expected to propose to them,
the Duke arrived, spoke to them in French, a language in which he expressed himself very badly,
and persuaded them all to accept his suggestions.'
Voltaire adds that 'Lord Bolingbroke himself has
confirmed me as to the accuracy of these statements.'

It will be remembered that Voltaire, at a period
somewhat later than that which we are now describing, spent some years in England. He was always
getting into trouble with the authorities in France,
had been twice thrown into the Bastille, and on the
second occasion was released only on the condition
that he should take himself off to England. During
his period of exile he passed his life very pleasantly,

and made the acquaintance of many among the most distinguished English men and women then living. Bolingbroke became one of his friends, and by Bolingbroke he was introduced to Pope, and became a familiar figure among Pope's set in the famous villa at Twickenham. He came into association with Peterborough and Chesterfield, with Young, Thomson, and Gay, was welcomed by the Duchess of Marlborough, and dedicated his poem the 'Henriade' to Queen Caroline, who received the compliment most graciously. We can easily understand, therefore, how Voltaire came to be able to confirm so many of his historical statements by the authority of English men and women who were in a position to give them authentic confirmation.

We return to Voltaire's appreciation of Marlborough. Voltaire observes that Marlborough 'sustained with Prince Eugene, the companion of his victories, and with Heinsius, the Grand Pensionary of Holland, all the weight of the enterprises of the Allies against France. He knew that Charles was embittered against the empire and against the Emperor; that he was solicited secretly by the French; and that if the Swedish conqueror should embrace the cause of Louis the Fourteenth, the Allies would be oppressed by such a strength. It is true that Charles had given his word not to mix himself up in any way with the war of Louis the Fourteenth against the Allies; but the Duke of Marlborough did not believe that there could be a prince so completely a slave to his word as not to sacrifice it to his own greatness and his own interest. He set out from The Hague with the purpose of sounding the intentions of the King of Sweden. M. Fabrice, who was then with Charles the Twelfth, has assured me that the Duke of Marlborough on arriving addressed himself secretly not to the Count Piper, first minister, but to the Baron de Gortz, who was beginning to share with Piper the confidence of the King; he even arrived in the carriage of that baron at the quarters of Charles the Twelfth, and there was a marked coldness between him and the Chancellor Piper. Presented by Piper, with Robinson the representative of England, he spoke to the King in French; he told him that he should esteem himself happy to be able to learn under his orders all that he did not know of the art of war. The King replied to that compliment by no civility, and appeared to forget that it was Marlborough who was speaking to him. I know even that he found that the great man was dressed in a manner somewhat too elegant, and had too little the air of a soldier. The conversation was fatiguing and general, Charles the Twelfth expressing himself in Swedish and Robinson serving as interpreter. Marlborough, who was never in any haste to make his propositions, and who had by long habitude acquired the art of thoroughly understanding men and of penetrating the relations which exist between their most secret thoughts, their actions, their gestures, their discourses, studied the King most attentively.'

Then follows the passage to which we have

already referred, telling how Marlborough read in a glance of the King's eyes his determination to assail the Emperor of Russia, and how Marlborough went away well content, with the conviction that the Allies had just then nothing to fear from Charles the Twelfth. Voltaire adds some characteristic observations which are worthy of quotation, if only because of the rather lurid light they throw on the code of political morality supposed to prevail even among Ministers of State at that time. 'As few negotiations finish without money, and even ministers of state are sometimes seen who sell the hatred or the favour of their master, it was believed throughout all Europe that the Duke of Marlborough had succeeded with the King of Sweden by giving with that object a great sum of money to Count Piper ; and the memory of that Swedish statesman has remained tarnished by that report up to this day.' Voltaire, however, is inclined to be charitable, 'for myself, who have gone back as far as it would be possible to the source of that report, I know that Piper did receive a present, mediocre in its amount, from the Emperor through the hands of the Count of Wratislau, with the consent of the King his master, and nothing from the Duke of Marlborough.'

The position of Peter the Great was one which caused considerable anxiety to the Allies during the earlier stages of these negotiations. Times had greatly changed with the Russian Sovereign since the days when Marlborough had seen him in a Dutch dockyard dressed in the dress of a common seaman

and studying the practical art of building ships. He
was at last coming to be recognised as one of the
established sovereigns of Europe. For a long time
he had been treated by Western diplomacy merely
as the Duke of Muscovy, and when the original
Grand Alliance was in process of formation, the
thought had not come into the minds of English
or of German statesmen that he could possibly
be regarded as a fitting personage to take part
in such a federation. Since those days, however,
Peter had asserted and established his position,
and had for some time been admitted to the honour
of representation by ambassadors at the Courts of
the great European Powers. During the earlier
stages of the Russian Sovereign's advancement to this
dignity a mishap had befallen his representative at
the English Court which caused an immense sensation, brought about a dispute between Peter and
the English Government, and actually threatened
an outbreak of war between England and Russia.
The story, although at one time it seemed destined
to have a very serious conclusion, has a good deal
of the comical and almost of the farcical about
it. Even an international war could hardly have elevated the episode which was the original cause of
controversy to anything like the dignity of history.

In 1708 the ambassador to England of the
Russian Sovereign was about to leave London and
return to his native country. It so happened that
the Russian ambassador, like many other statesmen
of the time, had a way of running into debt and

putting off as long as possible any satisfactory arrangement with his creditors. He had bought a large quantity of lace and other goods from certain London tradesmen living in the region of Covent Garden, and these worthy traders, when they heard that he was about to leave the English capital and return to his native land, seem to have come to the conclusion, after a consultation among themselves, that the diplomatic representative of Peter the Great had no other purpose than to abscond without paying his just debts. The tradesmen took measures accordingly, and the ambassador was arrested in one of the streets of London by a party of men who were no doubt duly authorised by a legal warrant to commit an absconding debtor to prison. As everybody knows, the law at that time, and down to a period much later than the days of Mr. Pickwick, enabled a creditor to consign his debtor to a prison cell for an indefinite time, or at least until the legal claim and the charges for costs were fully liquidated. But at the period when the Russian ambassador was stopped in the London street it happened that the metropolis was still overrun by those roystering bands of Mohocks who have been described in a former chapter. The Russian ambassador apparently thought that he understood what Thackeray in one of his ballads describes as 'the ways of this wicked town,' and he took the officers of the law for mere street ruffians bent on robbing or otherwise maltreating him. He offered a vigorous resistance, but the officers of the law were too strong for him; he was overpowered,

made captive, and carried off in custody to a sort of
intermediate station as a preliminary to his incarcera-
tion in an ordinary cell.

The story spread like wildfire over all that part
of the town, and before long an English nobleman
who knew the Russian ambassador came to his
relief, accompanied by a well-known and substantial
London tradesman, and the two by their joint influence
succeeded in bailing out the foreign captive of English
law.   Then, as if to make the matter more complex
and more comical than before, it came to be known
that the Russian ambassador had actually made
full arrangement for the payment of all his debts
before his departure from London.   Here, then,
was indeed an international grievance of a very
serious order.   The Russian ambassador peremptorily
demanded that the English Government should visit
with exemplary punishment the minions of the law who
had dared, in defiance of all the comity of nations and
the rules of diplomacy, to arrest and capture a representative of a foreign Sovereign.   From the language
used by the ambassador himself and by other foreign
diplomatists who sympathised with him, it seemed
as if the scaffold, or at the very least the pillory, could
alone be the fitting doom of the misguided men who
had thus insulted the ruler of a great dominion in the
person of his representative.   Some of the offending
minions of the law were temporarily committed to
prison while the weighty question was under official
discussion, although it does not seem that any reasonable fault could be found with the men, who merely

executed, in the best way they could, the legal warrant with which they had been entrusted.

The whole subject was discussed with much anxiety by the Queen and her Privy Council at several meetings. The trouble was that it did not seem as if any breach of English law, or even of international usage, had been committed. Queen Anne was deeply troubled by the affair, and was most anxious that everything possible should be done to appease the wounded pride of the ambassador. But then, although it was quite clear that the person of a foreign ambassador should be held sacred from inter-ference or molestation, yet it was not altogether so certain that the immunity extended far enough to secure a foreign ambassador against being compelled to pay his just debts by the ordinary process of civil law.

The question was surrounded by perplexing troubles, one of which was the great difficulty of explaining to such a Sovereign as Peter the Great the fact that Queen Anne had no power to over-rule or suspend by her own decree the action of the laws which dealt with the arrangements between debtor and creditor. To make matters worse, the Russian ambassador flourished in the faces of the British statesmen a letter from the Czar himself, in which Peter demanded that the offended dignity of Russia should be at once conciliated by the doom of death to the offenders. What was to be done? Was there to be a war with Russia? Or were British officers of the law to be sent to the scaffold because they had done what it was part of their legal business to do? The matter seemed to Peter to involve no particular difficulty, for if he felt anxious to gratify any demand from the Queen of England, he could have ordered the instant execution of a Russian or a number of Russians without anyone to say him nay, and he probably could not understand why the great Queen of England should not be equally obliging with a number of her subjects. In order to show that something was being done, the Government directed that the men who had captured the Russian ambassador should be prosecuted in due form before the Court of Queen's Bench, and Chief Justice Holt, one of the greatest lawyers of his time, or of any time, had the whole case brought before him. All this had much the appearance of a mere performance for stage effect, seeing that nobody could possibly have expected a judge like Chief Justice Holt to coun-tenance any straining of the law in order to oblige any number of imperial or royal personages, or even to evade the chance of an international war.

The trial dragged on for a long time, but it ended in nothing, and meanwhile the Queen and her advisers were naturally anxious to show that the whole business had given them much cause for regret, and that it was not their inclination to sanction the slightest want of deference to the dignity of the Russian Sovereign and his representative. The Queen's advisers at last hit upon the idea of preparing and carrying through an Act of Parliament the preamble of which could contain a public expression

of regret for the whole incident, a disclaimer of any
intention to disregard the dignity of an ambassador,
and could introduce fitting clauses to guard against
such inconvenient accidents in the future. There was
much discussion among the ambassadors and other
foreign representatives in London as to the terms of
the preamble and the clauses of the measure itself.
The measure was termed ' An Act for preserving the
privileges of Ambassadors and other Public Ministers
of Foreign Princes and Foreign States,' and the preamble of the Bill was itself an elaborate expression
of regret for the insult offered to the Russian
ambassador, a disclaimer of all intention to interfere
with the recognised privileges of the diplomatic
fraternity, and a declaration that measures must be
adopted for the prevention of such irregularities in
the future. The preamble was, in fact, the whole
point of the story, and the Act did nothing more
than put on record the parliamentary recognition
of the privileges extended by international courtesy
and convenience to the persons of those who represent in London the authority and dignity of foreign
States.

No harm of any kind was done by this measure,
and a magnificently emblazoned and bound copy
of it was presented with due ceremonial to the
offended Czar. Nothing in particular came of the
whole episode, but Burton tells us that Peter was not
altogether pacified in his temper even by the solemn
parliamentary homage which was paid to his sovereign
dignity. Burton gives an amusing account of one

illustration of the Czar's still abiding dissatisfaction.
'Two young Russians visiting London and claiming
the title of prince were received at the palace with
great hospitality as royal persons. That they were
in some measure related to the royal family seems
certain. Peter, however, proclaimed loudly that they
had no right to compromise him by accepting courtesies from the sovereign of Britain.'

At no period, therefore, during the progress of the
war was there much chance for any friendly negotiations between Great Britain and the Court of
Russia. Peter had other schemes and projects to
occupy his attention and he did not concern himself
much with the war that was going on between the
Allies and Louis the Fourteenth. The object of
Great Britain throughout the later negotiations for
the restoration of peace went no farther than a
general effort to keep the Czar from any active
interference with the policy of the Allies, and in
these negotiations Marlborough took a frequent
part. This history has little more to do with the
career of the Czar. No other European Sovereign
of his time accomplished anything like the work
achieved by Peter in the extension of his dominions
and the strengthening of his power. He found Russia
a country almost entirely land-locked so far as his
European territory was concerned, but it was his
great ambition and his firm determination to create
for her a way to the sea, and he set the policy going
which was destined before long to accomplish his
object. He found Russia a semi-barbarous and in

almost every sense an Oriental Power, and he succeeded in establishing her firmly as a recognised
European dominion, admitted on equal terms to the
position of European sovereignty.

Peter's reign was indeed a despotism of the
most thoroughly Oriental character, but unlike all
other Oriental despots he had a keen eye to the
advantages of European civilisation and he understood, as hardly any other European Sovereign of his
time could have done, how to build and consolidate
the fabric of national greatness. From the opening
of his career he had no antiquated prejudices to set
him against new systems, and everything in Western
civilisation was so new to him that his mind had a
free choice for the selection of whatever seemed most
suitable for his purpose to imitate and adopt. He
created the Russia of modern days as distinctly as the
French Revolution has created Republican France.
His empire is only yet in its beginning, but we can
hardly doubt that it is destined to be one of the
greatest influences of the coming time. His personal
character was disfigured by many evil qualities and
stained by many vices, but he must ever take his
place among the founders of great empires.

CHAPTER XXII

MALPLAQUET—AND AFTER

THE French were now preparing for a great effort. The spirit of the country was thoroughly roused, and King Louis well knew that, despite all the prevailing hardships and poverty, he could rely upon his people to support him in what he hoped might prove the final struggle. The policy of the French Sovereign was now directed merely to an enforcement of the terms which he had already offered to the Allies, and the abandonment on their part of the conditions which they had endeavoured to force upon him in his hour of extreme necessity. No one knew better than Marlborough how much the population of France had suffered during the exhausting war thus far, and no one felt more certain than he that King Louis was preparing for a decisive and tremendous struggle. Marlborough's policy continued to be just what it was before the futile negotiations for peace had set in. It was the policy represented by the siege and capture of Lille. Marlborough's plan was to force his way into the heart of France, to leave no French stronghold uncaptured which came between him and his line of advance, and to hold his course, until he could dictate terms of peace in the French capital.

With this object in view he used all his influence to convince his Government that he must have additional troops sent out to him, and he succeeded in this demand, although at the time Queen Anne's advisers were already thinking that it might be safe to recall some regiments from the field. The Dutch Allies were also persuaded or coerced by him to send some additional force to his assistance, and he had at last got an army of more than 100,000 men under his command.

King Louis entrusted the command of the French troops to Marshal Villars, the general who had done so much by his military skill and by his generous clemency to bring to something like a peaceful conclusion the insurrection of the Camisards. Marshal Boufflers, who had won the admiration of Prince Eugene and of all the civilised world beside by his splendid defence of Lille, was senior in rank to Villars, but promptly offered to serve under his command, and this action on his part gave one other impulse to the enthusiasm of the French army. There were three strong fortresses which stood immediately in the way of the advance contemplated by Marlborough. These were Tournay, Mons, and Valenciennes, and it was naturally the business of Villars to maintain these strongholds to the last possible moment. Marlborough began his movement by one of his characteristic stratagems. He directed an advance in such a manner as to mislead the enemy. He made as if he contemplated a direct attack upon the main army of Villars, and Villars was deceived by the movement. The French commander apparently made up his mind that, if the first attack were to be directly on him and on his main army, it was his duty to strengthen that army at whatever risk. Accordingly he withdrew at a moment's notice some of the troops from Tournay and with them strengthened his own forces in the field. This was exactly what Marlborough would have wished him to do. The allied forces instantly made for Tournay, and by a night march succeeded in their plan for investing it.

Tournay was splendidly fortified, and its defensive works had long been regarded as the noblest illustration of Vauban's engineering skill. The town was taken in about a month, but the defending forces then withdrew into the citadel, and there bravely held out for yet another month and more. The defence of the citadel was made memorable by the skill, audacity, and pertinacity with which the besieged garrison turned to account the use and the explosion of subterranean mines to destroy successive parties of assailants. All the attempts at defence proved in vain, and there was nothing for it but to surrender. Marlborough, who, like every great general, could appreciate and admire the bravery of his opponents, paid to the defenders of the citadel the well-deserved compliment of allowing them to march out with all the honours of war. Having accomplished this success, the work which came next in the plan of the allied forces was to get possession of Mons, but a great military event was to take place before the accomplishment of this object. This great event was the battle of Malplaquet.

In order to invest Mons it was found to be indispensable that a passage should be made by the Allies through a part of the French lines, and to accomplish this it was necessary to cross a small river. A strong force under the Prince of Hesse was entrusted with the execution of this part of the general plan, and the work was successfully carried out. The Prince of Hesse and his men succeeded in finding a place which was not effectively occupied by the French lines, and they were able to pass the river at some distance above Mons itself, and thus to come between the town and the French. The Prince and his force then invested the town on the southern side. This movement was accomplished without any serious difficulty, and almost without the notice of the French commanders, and it might have been of the most signal advantage to the Allies. A portion of the allied forces was thus established between Mons itself and that part of the country into which the French, if defeated in open battle, would naturally endeavour to make a retreat. Marshal Villars found himself compelled either to abandon Mons or to risk everything on a battle. Marlborough was in favour of undertaking the battle at once. A division of opinion among the Allies took place here—such a division of opinion as had on many a former occasion led to a delay in the onward movement. Marlborough wished above all things to strike a blow at once and give the French forces no opportunity of establishing

themselves in a strong position. The Dutch Commissioners were in favour of delay, because there was
an expectation that some reinforcements would soon
come up from before Tournay and the Dutch did
not believe that the allied army was strong enough,
just at that time, to risk a decisive battle.

All through the campaigns in this region of the
war the Dutch allies had been cautious about general
engagements, and had set themselves, as far as they
could, against any movement which seemed to involve a serious risk and might be delayed with
advantage. The policy of the Dutch had been always
that which is natural to a small population ; a policy
habitually of defence and resistance rather than one
of enterprise. It had been the fate of the Netherlands in their previous history to have to contend
against forces numerically far stronger than any they
could bring into the field. No country in the world
has ever shown a greater capacity for stubborn and
untiring resistance than that of the Netherlands, but
their struggle against the domination of Spain, pro-
longed as it had to be through successive generations
and victorious at last, had trained them above all
things to a policy of defence.

It is therefore not surprising, nor is it to be
reckoned to the discredit of a brave and intelligent people, that the Dutch did not always, under
the new conditions, throw their whole souls into
such daring measures of enterprising attack as
those which the genius of Marlborough was
ever ready to undertake. What seemed to Marl-

borough the course best calculated to ensure success
at a momentous crisis often appeared to the Dutch
commanders a disproportionate risk.   In this particular instance Prince Eugene, who was then as at
all times perfectly ready to fight, was yet quite
willing to listen to the counsels of the Dutch and to
take the chance of waiting for the further reinforcements.   Two days were thus lost to the plans of
Marlborough.   To those who can now calmly look
back on this chapter of history it seems perfectly
clear that if Marlborough had been allowed his own
way, and had been supported with enthusiasm by his
allies, the result would have been a complete victory
obtained without anything like the tremendous loss
and sacrifice which marred the success of Malplaquet.
The French forces were able to obtain by this delay
the one advantage which they most desired to have.
They were enabled to take up a strong position and
to entrench themselves effectively, and thus to make
the victory obtained by the Allies as dearly bought
a triumph as the history of modern warfare records.

The ground around the village of Malplaquet had
at one time been a mere forest, and although much of
it had lately been cleared, cultivated, and made habit-
able, it was still thickly wooded here and there, and
the troops who now occupied it had every opportunity
of making their resistance strong and their defeat
costly.   The battle of Malplaquet was fought on the
11th of September, 1709.   It was a battle of desperate
attack and desperate resistance.   The French troops
fought with splendid courage and with a pertinacity

which at one time must have seemed well nigh indomitable. When once the actual engagement had begun there was little chance for strategic movement or for sudden inspirations of military genius; it was a contest of hand-to-hand fighting on a gigantic scale. The commanders on both sides certainly did not spare themselves. Marshal Villars, the French commander, received a severe wound at an early part of the engagement. He absolutely refused to be carried off the field, and insisted on having a chair brought to him that he might still direct the movements of his men. The gallant marshal, however, was not allowed to carry out his brave purpose. He fainted from loss of blood, and had to be borne insensible from the field of fight. On the side of the Allies, Prince Eugene met with a somewhat similar mishap. A bullet wounded him in the head just behind the ear, but he utterly refused the urgent requests of his officers that he would retire even for a few moments and have his injuries looked to, declaring resolutely that there would be time enough to think of all that if he survived until the end of the battle, and if the wound were mortal there would be no use in wasting moments over it.

Marlborough himself was in a very poor condition of health on the day of the battle, and a report actually spread abroad for a while among the Allies and among the enemy that the great commander had found his death upon the field. Marlborough's time, however, had not yet come. The victory was with him and his allies, but the French were able, when the day had turned decisively against them, to accomplish a retreat in good order. Marshal Villars is said to have declared, when all was over, that one other such defeat to the French would have meant the ruin of the English army. His words may have been meant as an adaptation of a famous classical saying, but he had good practical and present reason for his boast. The victorious allies lost in the battle more than 20,000 men, while the defeated French, who had all the advantage of their strong position, suffered a loss of hardly more than half that number. The battle of Malplaquet was memorable in one especial sense for Marlborough and for history. Malplaquet was Marlborough's last great battle. He was a student of Shakespeare, and if he could have been favoured with a glimpse into the future, he might have said, 'Here burns my candle out, ay, here it dies, which, whiles it lasted,' gave light to England and to England's victories. Under the same conditions he might also have said, again in the words of Shakespeare, 'If 'twere now to die, 'twere now to be most happy.'

Meanwhile the campaign on Spanish soil had been dragging on at a slow and staggering pace. The victory obtained over the allied forces at Almanza had proved even more damaging in its effects than had been expected. So damaging had it been that it might almost be called decisive. It forced the Allies into a complete change of policy, and instead of the brilliant and daring movements which had signalised on their part the earlier progress of the campaign, they appear to have made up their minds only for defensive action—to hold their own as long as they could, and not to expose themselves to any serious risks.   Lord Galway, whose command had failed so signally at Almanza, was recalled from his position, and put at the head of the English troops in Portugal. The Emperor was urged to give the command in Spain to Prince Eugene, who could have made something of it if anybody could, but the Emperor would not remove Eugene from the field on which he was then engaged, and a sort of compromise was effected by the appointment of an English and a German commander.   General Stanhope was the English commander.   'Stanhope,' says Lord Macaulay, 'was a man of respectable abilities both in military and civil affairs, but fitter, we conceive, for a second than for a first place.'   The qualification is perfectly just, but at the same time it is only right to say that Stanhope had some of the best gifts of a commanding officer—that he had a thoroughly soldier-like spirit, and might have rendered great service under a great commander. The German commander was Staremberg, whom Macaulay describes as 'a methodical tactician of the German school.'

It is probable that no commander endowed with less than the genius of Marlborough, or at all events, less than that of Eugene, could have accomplished any great results for the Allies during this period of the Spanish campaign.   The allied armies were badly provisioned, were ill supplied in every way, and had lost heart after the disaster of Almanza. The allied generals, however, although they were not able to do anything worthy of record on the mainland of Spain, were able, by the sheer favour of events, to obtain for their cause the accession of the island of Sardinia, and to effect the capture of Minorca. Sardinia was willing and eager to declare for the Archduke Charles, and when an English fleet was sent within sight of the island, the declaration was at once made, and the island was for the time secured to the cause of the Allies. The capture of Minorca was an actual conquest, and one of great importance. The English fleets had been put to incessant trouble with the recurrence of each winter by the want of some sheltering harbour during the worst part of the year. The lack of such a shelter had compelled the fleets to return time after time to the protection of English seaports, thus giving their enemies opportunities for quietly and safely repairing their strength and their defences during the interval.

It had long been the desire of Marlborough that Port Mahon, the principal harbour of Minorca, and, indeed, one of the very best ports in all that Mediterranean region, should be taken by the Allies. It is a certain historical fact that Marlborough, just at the right moment, strongly urged upon Stanhope the immense importance of making a sudden effort for that purpose. The credit of the manner in which the capture was effected belongs unquestionably to Stanhope, but the original idea of attempting the capture was the inspiration of Marlborough, who, like an accomplished chessplayer, never allowed his mind to lose sight of any part of the board. Stanhope had no easy work to do when he set about prevailing upon the naval commanders to accept his plan for the seizure of Port Mahon. Port Mahon was well known to be strongly defended, and the general belief among the Allies was that those in possession of it would hold out to the very last in its defence. Stanhope had a nature and a spirit which inclined him to favour daring plans, and he seems to have made up his mind that nothing should hinder him from attempting the enterprise he had at heart. He compelled the acceptance of his project by a stroke of happy audacity. When he had explained and discussed his plans long enough, apparently without carrying conviction to the naval men whose help he needed, he withdrew from the futile debate, and went to work on his own account. He had his transport vessels got into immediate preparation, he embarked his troops on board them, and then despatched a message to his naval friends announcing that he was setting out on his way to Port Mahon, and leaving it to them to follow him or remain behind according to their inclination.

It need hardly be told that the result of this message was to bring the fleet promptly to his support. It was not likely that brave naval commanders would hang back at such a time from sustaining him in his daring expedition. The work of landing his men and his artillery on the steep and rocky coast proved the hardest part of the undertaking. It took him nearly a fortnight to accomplish this work, but once he had begun, the end of the struggle was not long

delayed, and within four days Port Mahon was
occupied by the troops of the Allies.   Stanhope was
so thoroughly impressed with the importance of
securing this harbour for England, that he earnestly
recommended the Government at home not to give
up their new possession to the Archduke Charles,
but to retain it as their own, for the present at all
events, and to hold it as a security for the repayment
of the large and liberal advances which England had
made to Charles for the purpose of enabling him to
carry on his part of the campaign.   With this object
in view, Stanhope, of his own motion, filled the place
with English troops only as an occupying force, and
the Archduke had no choice but to put up with the
arrangement.

Minorca, in the course of later history, was
taken from the British and retaken by them, and
was captured and recaptured until it was finally
handed over to Spain at the settlement of Amiens.
It has a melancholy association for English readers
from the fact that in an attempt to relieve Minorca,
then blockaded by a French fleet, the unfortunate
Admiral Byng committed the error of judgment
which led to his being brought home under arrest,
tried, and convicted of neglect of duty, sentenced
to death and executed.

The capture of Minorca appears to have made a
decided impression on some at least of those who
were engaged in maintaining the cause of France.
The Duke of Berwick was no longer in command of
the French forces in Spain.   He had been succeeded

by the Duke of Orleans, whom we have already mentioned in this history, and whose peculiar reputation has little or nothing to do with military enterprise. The Duke of Orleans was a nephew of King Louis, and was destined after the death of that Sovereign to become Regent of France. His private life was one which might fairly be described as infamous, and he is remembered as the patron and the pupil of Cardinal Dubois. The Duke of Orleans endeavoured to enter into negotiations with Stanhope for the purpose of arranging a basis of settlement on which he believed, or professed to believe, a satisfactory peace could be concluded. The proposal made by Orleans was that the two rival candidates for the throne of Spain should be withdrawn—the Allies to withdraw the Archduke Charles and King Louis to withdraw Philip of Anjou. If that part of the proposal could be agreed upon, then Orleans modestly suggested that he himself might probably be regarded by the two principal disputing States as a suitable and acceptable occupant of the Spanish throne. Nothing could be more absurd than such a proposition; but, from what we know of the character of the Duke, it seems quite possible that it might have commended itself to his wayward and fantastic humour as a sort of compromise which would help all the disputants out of a difficulty.

Orleans had in his nature some of the whimsicalities as well as the love for freakish debauchery which we commonly ascribe to the typical Oriental despot. The ingenious arrangement which he suggested might have suited very well for a story after the fashion of the 'Arabian Nights,' or for a comic opera of more modern days. Stanhope, we may be sure, did not take it seriously, but for the time at least he affected to give it some consideration, and while he declared that it would not be possible for the Allies to throw over the candidature of the Archduke Charles, he suggested that means might perhaps be found of constructing, out of the wreck and welter of disputed territories, something like an independent kingdom on the throne of which the genius and the ambition of Orleans might find a fitting place. Unluckily for Orleans, some knowledge of the negotiations he had opened, and was attempting to carry on with General Stanhope, reached the ears of men for whom it was not intended, and was conveyed before long to King Louis himself. The King did not find it possible under these conditions to leave his nephew any longer in command of the French troops in Spain. It was not convenient to make any public scandal about the whole business, but it was clear that the Duke of Orleans was not quite the man to represent, as head of an army, the interests of the King of France. The whole incident has to a modern reader something distinctly farcical about it. It has to be borne in mind, however, that Europe was at that time a field for the working of all sorts of fantastic schemes, for the setting up of new thrones, and even the creation of new States. The Duke of Orleans, himself a member of a royal family, may perhaps be excused for thinking that he

D 2

had as good a right as any other Prince to become a
candidate for a disputed throne.

Stanhope showed himself, through all this part
of the campaign, an energetic commander eager to
carry out a forward policy. Until the capture of
Port Mahon nothing of much importance had been
done by the Allies in Spain since their defeat at
Almanza, and Stanhope was certainly doing all that
lay in his power to put an end to the long period of
comparative inaction. He had succeeded so far as to
obtain from the Government at home such reinforcements as put him in command of a larger army than
any which had yet displayed itself on that field of the
war. He was doing his best to prevail upon Staremberg, his colleague in the control of the allied forces,
to accept his plans for active and unceasing movement. Staremberg, who was a commander of the old
school, was probably of opinion that campaigning
ought to have its regular alternations of activity and
repose, and he does not appear to have appreciated
Stanhope's idea that the enemy ought always to be
kept upon the move. Bishop Burnet, who like many
other very good men, is somewhat given to discern-
ing a sinister motive in the action of public personages
whom he does not thoroughly admire, gives it out that
Staremberg had lately become jealous of Stanhope's
growing reputation, and was not anxious to assist him
to any increase of fame. Burnet is even of opinion
that in some actual movements, where the prompt
co-operation of Staremberg might have secured an
immediate success, the Imperial general deliberately

held himself aloof, and allowed the plan of his colleague to become a failure. Whether this be just to Staremberg or not, it is quite certain that Stanhope had much difficulty in obtaining cordial co-operation for the policy which he desired to carry out.

On one particular purpose Stanhope had especially set his heart. The allied forces in Spain had had their field of operations limited for a long time to the province of Catalonia. Stanhope was most anxious to break bounds, and find some more extended field. There was a generous impatience in his spirit which protested against narrow limitations, and his intellect told him that the Allies could hardly pass themselves off as champions and saviours of the Spanish people if they were never to show their faces outside one single province of Spain. Stanhope made up his mind to cross into Aragon, and after a long effort he succeeded in persuading the Archduke Charles and Staremberg to accept his plan. The crossing of a river which during a part of its course forms a boundary line between Catalonia and Aragon was easily accomplished towards the close of July 1710. The allied forces were not long without encountering an enemy. The enemy was the Spanish army, which under the command of a brave old soldier, Villadarias, who had already distinguished himself at Cadiz, was drawn up in battle array to resist the further progress of those who were not unnaturally regarded as invaders. Stanhope was for an immediate engagement, but his colleague still urged counsels of caution and delay. The Spanish army did not give their opponents much time for calm consideration. The Spanish general sent forward a large force of cavalry in order to begin the engagement at once. A feeling of genuine passion went through Stanhope's ranks at the evidence thus given that the Spanish general actually found it necessary to force them into an engagement. The common thought was in every English mind that such was not the character which English armies had usually won for themselves on foreign battle-fields, and probably no one in Stanhope's ranks was more passionately stirred by this feeling than Stanhope himself. Although the hour of the day was late, and darkness was close at hand, and night battles were not then recognised as necessary events in warlike movements, Stanhope put himself at the head of his cavalry and led a tremendous charge.

No romantic story belonging to the early days of European chivalry has in it any incident more striking and more dramatic, than that which belongs to the first shock of battle between these two opposing hosts. Stanhope himself encountered in hand-to-hand combat the general in command of the Spanish cavalry, and dealt him one sabre-stroke which left him a corpse on the battlefield. The engagement did not last long, and had come to an end even before night had fallen upon the scene. The result was a complete success for the Allies. The Spanish camp was taken, and the disaster to the Spanish force was so sudden and complete that all thought of further resistance was abandoned by the Spaniards without a chance having been given to the infantry of the Allies to take any active part whatever in the engagement. This was the battle of Almenara, a victory for the Allies, which because of its suddenness, its instantaneous and overwhelming success, and its picturesque incidents, has won for itself a peculiar fame among the events of that long and far-divided war.

Another great battle was fought immediately afterwards within sight of Saragossa, the ancient capital of Aragon. After his success at Almenara, Stanhope prevailed upon the Archduke Charles and Staremberg, although not even then without some difficulty, to continue their forward movement as rapidly as possible, and he was able to cross the river Ebro without encountering any active resistance on the part of the Spaniards. The crossing of the Ebro might well have been thought to give the Spaniards a most favourable opportunity for checking the progress of the Allies, but for some reason or other Stanhope and his forces were allowed to cross the stream without opposition. Soon the Allies encountered a Spanish army numbering some 25,000 men or more, and therefore numerically greater than the force under the joint command of Stanhope and Staremberg. The Spanish troops fought bravely on the whole, although there was a lack of discipline and of nerve among some of their later levies; but, on the other hand, the veteran Spanish regiments held out to the last with desperate tenacity. The result was a complete victory for the Allies, and that same night the Archduke Charles occupied Saragossa. The Allies had a short period of rest in the famous city, and Charles was in no particular haste to leave it and go forward. Stanhope, however, would hear of nothing but that the Allies should press on without a day's unnecessary delay and occupy Madrid itself. He had his way, the allied forces continued their forward movement, and for the second time during the war, saw themselves in occupation of the Spanish capital.

If Charles had had any fond hopes that his arrival, even at the head of a victorious army, could have been welcome in the capital of the kingdom over which he claimed to rule, he must have been at once and completely undeceived by the manner of his reception in Madrid. The city was not in a position to resist his entrance, but it took good care to show that the lack of resistance did not come from any inclination towards him or his claims. Everyone who could possibly leave Madrid went out of its streets before the allied forces had fully entered. Only those remained who had not the means of finding or paying for a residence elsewhere, and even these made every effort to prove by silent evidence that they regarded the Archduke and those with him as strangers and enemies. The Castilians remained firm to what they believed to be their national cause, and Stanhope's victories could not conquer the heart of Spain.

Meanwhile events were going on at home which must have filled the minds of English commanders on the fields of war with melancholy misgivings as to the practical value of their best efforts. The

reception given to the Archduke Charles by the capital
of Spain was not in itself more significant than some
of the demonstrations of public opinion which were
engrossing the attention of London and of many
another great English city.

CHAPTER XXIII

THE WAR IN ITS EMBERS

THERE can be no doubt that the new English Ministry came into power with hope and expectation to put an end to the war at once. The time, however, did not seem quite propitious for any sudden announcement of such a policy. It was not that there could be supposed to exist on the part of Louis the Fourteenth any desire for the continuance of hostilities. Nothing could be more clear to the minds of the English statesmen in office than the fact that King Louis had had quite enough of the struggle, and was most anxious to bring it to an end if he could only obtain some concession or compromise which might enable him to get out of the difficulty without any actual surrender of all his claims, and by consequence a sacrifice of his dignity. The two great opponents were at this period of the struggle in very much the same condition of anxiety and embarrassment. Each had now had quite enough of the war, but each had made too definite an assertion of objects and claims, and neither could see a way to any satisfactory settlement. So far as the fortunes of the battlefields were concerned, England had unquestionably been victorious thus far; but the Tory statesmen, who had never from the first had any heart in the strife, were quite content that England should rest upon her laurels if only they could find some plausible reason for proclaiming their willingness to come to terms. France, on the other hand, had now no further hope of gathering laurels from the contest, and her ruler would have been even more glad if some conditions of settlement were suggested which would give him a decent excuse for ' throwing up the sponge.'

While the leading Powers on both sides thus stood anxious for peace and perplexed as to the means of getting creditably out of the war, an event occurred which seemed to give to both a providential opportunity of reconsidering their position. This event was the death of the Emperor Joseph, which put the Emperor's brother, the Archduke Charles, whom England and her allies were striving to create King of Spain, in what may be called direct succession to the Imperial throne. According to the usages of the German States the new Emperor would have to be elected to the Imperial position by the vote of the Electorate at Frankfort, but there seemed little doubt that the voices of the Electoral States would invest him with the Imperial title. ' The electors,' as Bishop Burnet tells us, ' were all resolved to choose King Charles emperor.' Some delays took place ; even at a much more recent date the Germanic Confederation was never inclined to be precipitate in its action ; but after a lapse of nearly six months the due formalities were all accomplished, the Electors of Germany saw their way, and the claimant to the Spanish throne was duly proclaimed German Emperor. Here, then, it would certainly seem that a favourable opportunity was given to both the leading States in the war, to reconsider their pretensions and their objects. England and her allies could hardly entertain any serious desire to make the new German Emperor also the new King of Spain. Louis the Fourteenth, on his part, could not but see that the chances of a peaceful settlement, satisfactory to him, were much advanced by the event which to all intents and purposes must modify most seriously the policy of his allied opponents.

For the time neither disputant seemed inclined to come forward as the first and more eager to suggest a final settlement. The state of affairs at Frankfort itself appeared, for the moment, as if it were destined to bring about a prompt renewal of the war. The idea got abroad among the Allies that the French monarch was planning a military movement to interfere with the election at Frankfort, and orders were despatched from Vienna to Prince Eugene, the purport of which was that he must withdraw all the troops he had in Flanders under the command of Marlborough, and take up a position of defence against the expected invasion of German soil by the French troops. Marlborough, of course, was much weakened by the withdrawal of Prince Eugene and his men, and the knowledge of this fact appears to have inspired the French commander, Marshal Villars, with the unlucky boast that he was now in the position to prevent the great English commander from passing into the territory of France. Marlborough promptly gave proof that his old capacity for accomplishing that which was proclaimed impossible had not yet deserted him. He proved without delay that Marshal Villars had made a signal mistake. He advanced into France and captured the town of Bouchain, in what is now described as the northern department of France.

We may linger for a moment over this achievement, because it was the last success of any importance in Marlborough's military career. The plan to besiege Bouchain was entirely Marlborough's own. Marlborough's idea was that, as soon as his advance on the place came to be understood by the French, it would induce them to make some effort for the definite purpose of preventing the capture, and thus give him, with his comparatively small force, an opportunity of encountering a large part of their army on something like equal terms. On the other hand, he felt convinced that the effect must be most disheartening to the French side if Bouchain could be captured without opposition in the very sight of his enemy's forces. The Dutch Commissioners and some of the general officers were disinclined to adopt Marlborough's plan, believing it impossible, or at least very unlikely, that a well-fortified place provided with an effective garrison, and standing in the midst of a large marshy ground, could be captured within a mile or so of a French force superior in numbers to Marlborough's own.

'All about the duke,' says Bishop Burnet,
'studied to divert him from so dangerous an undertaking ; since a misfortune in his conduct would have
furnished his enemies '—by whom, no doubt, Burnet
means his enemies at home—'with the advantages
that they waited for.' Marlborough, however, saw
his way, and was determined to go on. The siege
lasted twenty days, and Marshal Villars made some
efforts to interfere with Marlborough's movements,
but the efforts proved wholly in vain, and the garrison of Bouchain had to capitulate and to be made
prisoners of war. Burnet declares that 'As this was
reckoned the most extraordinary thing in the whole
history of the war, so the honour of it was acknowleged to belong wholly to the Duke of Marlborough ;
as the blame of a miscarriage in it must have fallen
singly on him.'

Besides Bouchain Marlborough took one or two
other places, as if to make clear to his opponents
that they had better not vaunt themselves too lightly
and too freely as to their power of resistance. These
may be regarded as the last of his military successes,
and such as they were, they gave him no chance of
surrounding himself with a new blaze of glory.
They were but incidents which proved that the fire
within him had not flickered. It remained for his
own Sovereign and his own Government to put the
fire completely out.

Meanwhile, the Government in England had
planned out elaborately, at Bolingbroke's instiga-
tion, an expedition against Quebec, with the object,

apparently, of bringing sudden pressure to bear upon the French from a new field of hostilities. To many observers at the time, it hardly seemed possible that there could be any serious purpose in this enterprise so far as the existing campaign was concerned, and this sceptical mood was not discouraged by the fact that the command of the expedition was entrusted to Colonel Hill, the brother of Mrs. Masham, the Queen's new comrade and adviser. In many minds the belief prevailed, and there were apparently good grounds for its existence, that this new undertaking was intended rather as a demonstration against Marlborough than against King Louis. Just at the time it would have been of immense advantage to the Tory Government if some sudden success could have been obtained in any military expedition without the presence, the help, or even the co-operating counsels of Marlborough. Anything that could have called away, even for a moment, the attention of the public at home from the achievements of Marlborough and the necessity for upholding his command; anything that could have shown the possibility of winning victories without him, would have been of inestimable advantage to the purposes of the Ministry just then. The doom of Marlborough was already fully determined, and, come what might, that doom was to be carried into force; but it would have seemed in some degree less inappropriate and less paradoxical if it could have been put into effect immediately after any manner of success had proved that Marlborough was not indispensable to British victory.

The result of the enterprise was only the most dismal of failures, and it might, under other auspices, have acted as a serviceable warning to the Ministry. The whole expedition was badly arranged and miserably provided. The transport ships were too few, and were left wanting in all necessary supplies. As Burnet says, ' a commissioner of the victualling then told me he could not guess what made them be sent out so ill-furnished; for they had stores lying on their hands for a full supply.' The understanding, according to Burnet, was that the ships had supply enough to carry them on to the shores of New England, but the elements were against their arriving within the necessary time, for they were harassed by continual gales off that coast, and they were badly provided with pilots, as with everything else. The ill-managed fleet met with a violent storm at the mouth of the St. Lawrence; many of the vessels became mere wrecks; and there was nothing for it but that the unlucky fleet should return to England as quickly and with as little further damage as possible. Britannia certainly did not rule the waves on that occasion, and the struggle for the possession of Quebec had to be put off to some more favourable opportunity.

The Quebec expedition was not by any means the most important undertaking which the Ministers were endeavouring to carry out on their own account. Negotiations had already actually been opened by the Tory Government with the ruler of France. These negotiations were begun and conducted for some time in perfect secrecy—at least in such secrecy as could well be kept up between two hostile sets of negotiators, each of whom was alike distrustful of the other and alike willing to commit and betray the other where any stratagem could have that effect. The Tory Ministers were fully determined to come to terms with Louis, whether their allies were willing or unwilling to accept such a policy. They did not trust the Allies, and did the best they could to keep from them all knowledge of the arrangements which were the subject of inter-communication between England and France. For the purpose of the Ministers, it was above all things necessary to get rid of the Duke of Marlborough.

The objects of the Tory Government and those of Marlborough were absolutely irreconcilable. Marlborough was at least perfectly consistent in his policy. Quite apart from the victorious general's ambition to continue the war, which he had thus far carried on so successfully, until he should have made its success complete and final, Marlborough as a statesman was utterly opposed to the idea of giving up the main objects of the struggle just when the struggle seemed on the very eve of accomplishing all the purposes for which it had been undertaken. He was still resolute in pressing on the Government his long-cherished plans for an advance movement which should make the soil of France the closing battlefield of the war, and by means of which he felt convinced that the terms of peace would be dictated by English plenipotentiaries in the French

capital. Of late he had received no encouragement
from home for the carrying out of his policy, and
it had always been difficult for him to inspire his
allied commanders with any enthusiasm for his
projects. Still, it was one thing for the Government
at home to withhold all encouragement from Marlborough's definite and daring plans, and quite
another thing to seek for peace on almost any terms,
while the man who declared that he could compel the
enemy to accept his terms was yet in the command
of the allied armies.

In point of fact, a peace could not have been
made in spite of Marlborough, and over Marlborough's head, while he was yet actually the Commander-in-Chief of England's forces, nor was it
possible for the Ministry to make England believe
that the Queen's civil advisers knew more about war
than Marlborough did, and were better judges than
he as to the value of the plans which he proclaimed
to be sure of success. It had become clear to the
minds of the Tory statesmen that so long as Marlborough remained in command, he would still be the
actual and not the nominal commander. He was in
the way, and means must be found for getting him
out of the way. We shall presently have to give
some account of this most extraordinary chapter of
history. Just now, it is better to describe at once
the few incidents of importance which mark the
closing scenes of the whole war.

The negotiations between England and France for
terms of settlement were not carried on in such

secrecy that the full meaning of them could not come
to the knowledge of Prince Eugene. Marlborough's
brilliant comrade well understood the purport of all
that was going on, and he soon became convinced
that the English Ministers were determined to enter
into arrangements with France whether England's
Allies approved of the terms of settlement or were
utterly opposed to them. Eugene took prompt
and active but ineffectual steps to prevent Queen
Anne's Government from following out the policy on
which they were evidently bent—the policy of bringing the war to a close under whatever conditions, and
obtaining peace on any terms. He hurried over to
England, and there did all he could to press his views
upon the Queen's advisers. He was of course received
with great respect, and even cordiality, he was over-
whelmed with civilities, with marks of royal favour
and of popular homage, and he became, in fact, the
hero of the hour. But his representations were all
in vain, his advice was urged upon ears deaf to any
such suggestions. The question had already been
settled in the minds of the Tory statesmen, and it
had ceased to be with them a matter of argument.
Eugene went back to his place in the campaign, or
rather it should be said to the place where a
campaign had lately been going on. He had now
to co-operate with a new British commander. The
Duke of Ormond had been appointed to hold the
highest position in the army of England. Prince
Eugene received from the States of the United
Provinces the command of their forces, and was

assured that he should have their full support in any
course he thought it needful to adopt. The whole
force of the Allied Powers was now considerably
stronger in numbers than any army the French
King could put into the field. Bishop Burnet comments on the sensation which the news of their
superiority created in England.

Now would have been the time for the forward
movement so often recommended by Marlborough ;
but even if the Duke of Ormond had been a
soldier of Marlborough's capacity, he could have
done nothing to carry out that policy. He was only
a nominal, and not a real, commander. He was
sent out with instructions which amounted in substance to an order that he was to do nothing without
the previous sanction of the authorities at home.
No military commander with any genuine claims
to such a position would have accepted the office of
Commander-in-Chief under conditions which made it
impossible for him to put his capacity to any practical test. 'The present ministry,' Burnet observes,
' had other views ; they designed to set the queen at
liberty from her engagements by these alliances, and
to disengage her from treaties.' Burnet also observes
that the Duke of Ormond was ' well satisfied both
with his instructions and his appointments ; for he
had the same allowances that had been lately voted
criminal in the Duke of Marlborough.' This seems,
perhaps, a little hard upon the Duke of Ormond,
but it is quite certain that he had humiliated himself
by consenting to take, under whatever conditions,

a purely nominal command, and to submit to be,
as he was scoffingly called by many at the time, ' a
general of straw.'

The next incident in the story was the arrangement of an armistice between the English and the
French.   Then the Duke received sudden orders to
separate the English soldiers, and all soldiers who
were receiving English pay, from the forces of the
allied States.   A large number of these soldiers,
who, although receiving English pay according to
the arrangements of the campaign, were not British
subjects or Englishmen, refused positively to obey
any such orders, and to detach themselves for the
purpose of forming a separate army under the Duke
of Ormond.   Their Governments, seeing clearly that
the whole alliance was coming to an end, backed
them up in their refusal.   There was nothing left
for Ormond but to withdraw those English officers
and soldiers who were willing to follow him in this
unexpected reconstruction, and the result was that
he took with him only about 12,000 followers.   The
truth was that England had all along been working
out the campaigns rather with her funds than with
her own native-born soldiers, and that the number of
British subjects enrolled in these forces was small
indeed, when compared with the numbers of mer-
cenary troops from various German States whom
England had hired and paid to do the work of
fighting.

Down to a much later date the forces of England engaged on various foreign battlefields, and

even on battlefields at home—at all events, on battlefields in Ireland—were always made up in a large proportion of Hessians and other Germans who were willing to accept the pay of the English Crown, and do such business of fighting as might be put into their hands.   Nothing, it is said, could exceed the dissatisfaction, and even the indignation, with which the English officers and soldiers received these new orders, and the unwillingness with which they obeyed the command to separate themselves from comrades who had fought side by side with them, who had shared their dangers and privations, and helped them to win their victories on so many fields of hard-fought battle.   The orders, however, had to be obeyed, and they were obeyed, whatever might have been the personal emotions of many of the brave Englishmen who had to carry them out.

When all was done Eugene still remained in command of an army numbering about one hundred thousand men, and Eugene himself saw no reason why the campaign might not even yet be carried on with good hopes of success.   His army was in a strong position, and occupied what was still called the road to Paris, that road which, there can be little reason to doubt, would have been followed despite all resistance if Marlborough could have had his own way and were still at the head of the allied forces.   But it soon became clear that the English troops had been the heart and the moving spirit of the campaign, and that when they were withdrawn from their central place in the armed body there was not much chance left for Eugene

to accomplish anything like a substantial success.
Eugene was then besieging the town of Landrécies,
and if he could succeed in capturing that place,
there seemed nothing, for the time, to stay his further
advance into French territory. Eugene's movements
still excited great alarm in France, or at all events
in the Court of King Louis, although nobody could
have known better than the King that the union of
the great Allies was fast coming to an end.

Louis was in one of his heroic moods, in one of those
moods which he was wont to relieve by the issuing of
some portentous proclamation or the writing of some
grandiloquent letter. He wrote a letter to Marshal
Villars assuring the Marshal that his Sovereign had
perfect trust in him, but declaring that if by some
unexpected misfortune Villars should fail in preventing the enterprise of Prince Eugene, the King himself would rally all his troops around him, would
take the command and would perish on the battlefield at the head of his men, or would die in defence
of his country. This can only be regarded under
all the accompanying conditions as a display of the
mock-heroic. Nobody could have known better than
King Louis how little intention there was on the
part of the most important of the Allies to press the
campaign too closely against the Sovereign with whom
they were already conducting negotiations for a
peaceful settlement. King Louis must also have
known very well that Eugene's lines were so widely
extended as to render a rapid concentration impossible,
and that if a strong attack were made on one part

of Eugene's army, it would be extremely difficult for him to receive prompt succour from another. Nobody would be rash enough or unkind enough to say that Louis if driven to such a desperate resolve would not have carried it out to the end. The whole life and training of great Sovereigns usually prepare them to meet the worst danger with dignity and courage. But it may be taken for granted that King Louis knew perfectly well, as he penned this despatch, that there was not the slightest chance of his being driven to so sublime a resolution.

Villars, however, seems to have become animated with the determination to show that he could do something. He took advantage of the difficulty imposed upon his enemy by the comparative weakness of Eugene's too widely extended lines in many parts. He made what seemed to be an attack on Eugene's camp outside Landrécies, and then, suddenly changing his apparent plan when Eugene had been put somewhat off his guard, he won a decided victory over Eugene's troops at Denain. So sudden was Villars' attack that Eugene himself was taken wholly by surprise, and was not on the battlefield in time to retrieve, if it could be retrieved, the fortune of that fight. He was even compelled to give up the siege of Landrécies, and Villars actually recaptured three of the towns which the Allies had taken, one of them being that very town of Bouchain the capture of which had been the last achievement of Marlborough's military career.

The war had burnt to its last embers. The

defeat of Eugene's troops had naturally the effect of making the Dutch more than ever determined to come to a peaceful settlement with France on the best terms possible for the security of their own country.   It was clear to them, no doubt, that when the English withdrew from the struggle, and when the latest event in it was a defeat for those of the Allies who still lingered on the field, there was little hope for any further continuance of military operations.   The War of the Spanish Succession was over.

Prince Eugene lived to fight other battles, and on other fields. It was still his fortune to inflict defeats upon the Turks, as he had done in his earlier days—to scare many a Turkish encampment, as the German poet Freiligrath puts it, in one of his spirited ballads.   But so far as these volumes are concerned, the brilliant figure of Eugene appears no more.

CHAPTER XXIV

BOLINGBROKE AT HIS ZENITH

BOLINGBROKE had now reached the highest point of his political career. We may assume that the strongest ambition of that mind, which held so many ambitions, was success in the great game of politics. He now divided with Harley the actual business of ruling the State, and it cannot be questioned that he entertained high hopes and occupied himself with secret plans for becoming the one ruling power under the Queen herself. Nature had endowed him with a genius for success in more than one field of conquest. He aspired to be a great writer, and he believed himself to be a great thinker. He had a thirst for social success, and loved to be regarded as a star in the artistic firmament. He delighted in the consciousness that he was looked up to by men, and he was proud of his triumphs over the affections of women. He could not endure the thought of playing a secondary part in any game, and, philosopher as he professed to be, we cannot picture him to ourselves as a contemplative observer of life in any field of action, or as content to study the movements of others in such a field without a passionate desire to show that he could do better than all the rest. It could hardly be said that he loved political life, or philosophy, or literature, or art for its own sake. Each department of men's intellectual power seemed to him, according to the mood he was in, a sphere in which to assert his supremacy.

We are often told by serious writers, and in obedience to their teaching we sometimes try to believe, that modesty is the usual accompaniment of genius. The reading of great biographies, and indeed one's ordinary observation of life, might make us feel well assured that there are many cases in which the highest intellectual faculties are found in companionship with a supreme self-conceit. This companionship is nowhere more strikingly displayed than in the life of Bolingbroke. Had his intellectual powers been even a little less great than they really were, he might never have risen above the level of the brilliant and clever amateur, who loves to amuse his mind in various departments of study and work, who never distinguishes clearly between work and pastime, and who makes essay at too many crafts to become master of any one. Bolingbroke's splendid and genuine gifts saved him from such a fate as this, but great as was the success he achieved as a statesman and as a writer, it is easy to see that a certain lack of sincerity in politics as well as in thought prevented him from rendering at any time full justice to his own intellectual capabilities. As a statesman he seems to have been absolutely without any guiding principle, and his efforts to be a great thinker brought him to no higher place than that of a brilliant but an easy sceptic.

One of Bolingbroke's biographers, Mr. Thomas Macknight, observes that his life 'abounds in vicissitudes; there are great changes of scene and of fortune; he was born with great intellectual endowments, and also with the strongest passions; and it is assuredly a curious and interesting study to observe their effects through the eventful times in which his lot was cast. His character assumes by turns many varying and apparently contradictory phases; and yet, when carefully analysed, it appears peculiarly consistent and uniform as a whole, working towards a definite if not a very satisfactory end.'

The consistency, as it seems to us, is to be found in the fact that Bolingbroke followed through his whole career the light of his own instincts and of his own genius, and seemed to regard the whole course of living history merely as a path for him to tread towards the satisfaction of his own personal ambition. Other consistency than this it would be hardly possible to discern in his strange and varied life. ' Why was it,' Mr. Macknight asks, ' that, in action as well as in speculation, a man so gifted as Bolingbroke was so completely unsuccessful? Why was it that his life was but a series of defeats?' The closing sentence of this able and interesting biography answers very frankly the question proposed in the preface. The life of Bolingbroke, that sentence tells us, ' will not be without a memorable moral, full of warning

to the most brilliant and ambitious, if it show that
even great intellectual endowments, high rank, and
the finest opportunities, are not in themselves sufficient to constitute an enduring political success; but
that all these qualifications, without some earnest
and steadfast faith in a great cause as the representative of a great principle, without something
which can be said to take a man out of his narrow
individual selfishness, and make him zealously up-
hold what he believes to be the best interests of his
country and of mankind, cannot always avert morti-
fication and defeat from their possessor, nor secure
the lasting respect and approbation of the world.'

At the time which we have now reached Bolingbroke may fairly be assumed to have got the conviction satisfactorily into his mind that he had
found his place at last, and that the great work of
his life lay all before him. No man ever enjoyed
more thoroughly or was better fitted by intellectual
qualities to undertake a political and especially a
parliamentary career. The great art of parliamentary debate had only just begun to be recognised as
a leading power in the movements of public life
at the time when Bolingbroke began to prove his
capacity for leadership in the contests of eloquence.
He had now, while still only in the prime of his days,
risen to a position in the State which even in the
case of men with gifts hardly inferior to his own is
commonly the reward of a career drawing towards
its close. He had a marvellous capacity for hard
work, and found a positive delight in the mere

official labour which to so many eloquent debaters
seems a wearisome and exhausting tax upon the
nerves and the physical endurance. Not that
Bolingbroke was in the habit of admitting that he
took any delight in the exceptional work and
responsibility put upon him while Harley was still
recovering from the effects of his wound. He
seemed, in fact, rather inclined to make the very
most of the especial trouble thus imposed upon him,
and sometimes amused his friends, and in particular
those who believed they thoroughly understood him,
by his frequent complaints concerning the work he
had to get through and the official burdens he had
to bear. Swift, for one, felt sure that he could see
the real meaning of these complaints, which were
not characteristic of Bolingbroke, and took it for
granted that an inherent dislike to Harley was the
chief inspiration of the dissatisfaction expressed so
often in Bolingbroke's looks and words.

It is quite certain that up to the time when
Bolingbroke obtained his peerage, and especially
during the considerable interval which followed after
Harley had been removed to the House of Lords, the
whole work of leadership in the House of Commons
became Bolingbroke's duty. Never was any man in
the history of the English Parliament better fitted
for such a position and for such work. Harley had
been a very skilful parliamentary leader. He was
one of the men whom we have read of or observed
in political life who, without conspicuous abilities or
commanding intellect, have a certain art, or perhaps

it should rather be called a certain knack, for the management of parties, and who are able to acquire much influence, and even a certain degree of fame, by personal skill in their ways of getting round all kinds of men, suiting themselves to various tempers and temperaments, smoothing away difficulties, and making things easy all round.

But Bolingbroke was born with a positive genius for parliamentary debate. He was a great orator, and his oratory was especially of that order which suits itself to the atmosphere of the House of Commons. In the boldest and loftiest flights of his eloquence there was always a strain of sustained argument, there was always an appeal to the practical and business-like intelligence and habits of his audience, and even when he became most thrilling and most impassioned his appeal never went wholly over the heads of his listeners, never soared beyond the level of their intellects, their purposes, and their sympathies. This is, of course, an essential condition of all true oratory, of all oratory which has for its purpose to touch the brains and the hearts of men, but it is especially true of that which we recognise as the highest order of parliamentary eloquence. We know that some at least of the greatest orators who ever addressed the House of Commons—let us take Edmund Burke as an example—have acquired their highest fame by the judgment of those outside the House itself, or of those who, belonging to the House, were at the pains of studying the great speeches as recorded works, but that their

best efforts sometimes failed in their immediate effect
upon the assembly which they were intended to
persuade and command.   Bolingbroke did not, like
Byron's Marino Faliero, 'Speak to time and to
eternity—not to man.'   Bolingbroke spoke to man—
to convince him, to captivate him, to master him
—and his characteristic gift was all his own when
he spoke to man in the House of Commons.

Harley had nothing whatever of the orator's
gifts.   He had no imagination; he had no passion;
he had no grace or beauty of style; he possessed
neither wit nor humour.   We all remember what
was said about a once famous English Lord Chancellor—that no man could ever have been so wise
as Thurlow looked.   Something of the same kind
might fairly have been said about Harley, and Harley
had, at all events, a better private reputation than
Thurlow possessed.   But Harley's highest skill lay
in his capacity for passing himself off as a wise and a
profound man, and for contriving to make other men
believe that it would be for their advantage if they
were to listen to his persuasions and to accept his
leadership at his own estimate of its value.   Bolingbroke, on the other hand, had the way of sometimes
making himself appear less genial and also less
earnest than he really was, and it was perhaps owing
to that peculiarity in him that Swift and others
did not believe that he really disliked the hard
work imposed upon him quite as much as he said,
and became convinced that he really enjoyed the
work to the full, and only grumbled at it because it

gave him an opportunity of showing, indirectly, his dissatisfaction with his friend and colleague, Harley.

Bolingbroke has often been compared with Alcibiades, and there is much of aptitude and justice in the comparison. There was a distinct dash of the frivolous and also of the theatric, mingled with the stronger, more earnest, and more commanding qualities of his temperament and genius. When he came to conduct the business affairs of his office nobody could be more careful, more methodical, or more precise. There was no chance while he was at the head of a department that important letters or State papers would be left lying about so that clerks in the office might be free to study their contents or to make copies of them if they felt thus inclined. Many of the important letters and despatches which it came within Bolingbroke's province to issue he actually wrote out with his own hand, in order that he alone among the officials of his department might know what they contained until the proper time should arrive for making them public. As a matter of course it often happened that he desired to obtain an exact copy of one of these important papers, and in such cases he not merely wrote out the document with his own hand, but was also careful to copy it with his own hand.

Bolingbroke wrote and spoke French with fluency and accuracy, an accomplishment not very common among the English statesmen of his time, and in many of his dealings with foreign Ministers he was able to

make use of the language which was then much more
familiar than English in all parts of the Continent.
So earnest was he for a thorough understanding of all
the political affairs with which he had to deal, that
during the diplomatic negotiations concerning the
succession to the Spanish throne, he studied with
intense care the language of Spain, in order that he
might be able to read for himself all State papers,
letters, and other documents written in Spanish.
One cannot help recalling the story told so often
about Harley's urgent advice to a seeker after some
office at the Prime Minister's disposal—the advice to
learn the Spanish language—and of the blank disappointment felt by the office-seeker when, being able
to return to the Minister and announce that he had
made himself well acquainted with Spanish, he was
informed that he had now gained the immense advantage of being able to read 'Don Quixote' in the
original. We may take it for granted, without any
biographical information on the subject, that when
Bolingbroke had made himself acquainted with
Spanish he did not fail to read in the original Spain's
greatest literary masterpiece.

Bolingbroke loved literature of all kinds, and
during his intervals of retirement, short or long, from
official and parliamentary life, he devoted himself
with equal eagerness to the study of books, to the
delight of field sports, and the life of the country.
He was a keen sportsman; he was fond of indulging
himself now and again in the work of gardening; he
loved trees; he loved flowers, and turned with zest

every now and then to a close study of botany.
Perhaps a certain amount of harmless vanity entered
into the zeal with which he gave himself up to all
those various pursuits. It pleased him, when he was
staying at his country seat near Windsor, to think
that the resident gentry admired his bold riding, that
the local gardeners felt a profound respect for his
knowledge of flowers and plants and trees, and that
he was looked up to by the village farmers as a
landlord who knew everything about a farm. The
fact was that at all times his natural inclination was
to make himself the master of any work which he
had to undertake, and of every official department in
which he had to serve. No man of his time, not
even Marlborough himself, made a more attractive
and fascinating figure in society and in life generally
than Bolingbroke. He was singularly handsome and
graceful, picturesque in his appearance and in all his
movements, winning and charming in his manners.
He was all the more attractive as a companion
because, while he had ever the courtesy and the
dignity of what would then have been called a fine
gentleman, there seemed to be nothing artificial or
made-up about him. He was not one of the fine
gentlemen whose urbanity seems to be deliberately
assumed as the bearing proper to his rank, the sort
of studied and formal dignity which keeps all but
intimates at a distance. On the contrary there was
a good deal of impetuosity about his manners; he
was free to show that he had a temper of his own ;
he could enter with heat into a heated argument, and

could sometimes meet opposition of opinion with a very blunt contradiction. All this made him the more captivating, not merely to his intimate friends and companions, but even and perhaps especially to his inferiors in rank. Some of these latter felt it a positive honour when a man of such position treated them so like equals as to condescend to sharp disputes with them, and he won on them by what seemed to be the ingenuous and unrestrained impetuosity of his nature. A great man is never so charming to his inferiors as when he lifts them in that sense to his own level by showing that he wishes them to see him exactly as he is, and conceals his real feelings behind no mask of conventional dignity.

Bolingbroke had two great weaknesses—his love of wine and his love of women. The love of wine he carried to an excess even for those hard-drinking days. He delighted in revels and orgies of all kinds, and it seemed at one time as if no excess in drinking could interfere seriously with his work as a statesman and a political leader. He would slave in his office or in the House of Commons all day, then spend the whole night in carousing with his companions, and present himself at the customary hour next morning to all appearance ready for a full day's work. He delighted to entangle himself in all manner of amours, and although his first wife was a gifted and charming woman, completely devoted to him, he was ready to fall in with every opportunity of illicit intrigue that came in his way, or even to go far out of his way in quest of such an opportunity. He could make love to a fine lady of the Court if the chance offered, and he could with equal zest devote himself for the hour to the captivation of some little milliner or some woman of a still lower order. Swift tells us in one of his letters that he sometimes left Bolingbroke's supper-parties at a rather early hour because he could not permit swearing or blasphemy or indecent talk in his presence, and he did not wish to put too long a restraint upon the light-hearted company.

For a long time Bolingbroke and Swift were close associates and friends, and Swift was constantly to be found at Bolingbroke's residence in town or country. There was, so far as one can judge, a great inherent difference between the natures and the temperaments of the two men. Swift had depths of feeling which did not belong to the brighter and lighter mental constitution of Bolingbroke. Swift was never more profoundly in earnest than when he talked or wrote in a vein of levity or satire. Bolingbroke had a vein of levity running through all his most eager and earnest efforts at the mastery of any subject, or of any set of men coming within the range of his ambition for conquest. Swift was a philosopher even in his jest; Bolingbroke was something of a jester, or at least of a trifler, even in his philosophy. But the two men were close companions about the time which we are now describing, and those may well be envied who had frequent opportunity of listening to the unrestrained interchange of ideas between Bolingbroke and Swift.

Bolingbroke was still in the early prime of life

when he had thus reached what may be called the
zenith of his career. His most devoted admirers
might well deny that this highest reach of his political
career is to be regarded as the highest measure of his
fame. The works on which his reputation as a man
of letters and a thinker must mainly rest were not
accomplished by him until a much later period of
his life, when his work in active politics was done;
but at the time when he had become one of the two
leading men in the Government of Queen Anne, and
was proposing to himself to become the one leading
man in that Government, he was still comparatively
young. He was born, of a good old family, in
1678, at Battersea—that low-lying region south of
the Thames where his grave was afterwards to be
made, and where there are still many memories and
even some enduring memorials of his life and fame.
He was educated at Eton and travelled a good deal
on the Continent in his youth. In those days it
was a natural event in the life of a young man who
came of an influential family and had powerful
friends that he should find a seat in the House of
Commons. Bolingbroke entered Parliament in 1701,
as a member of the Tory party, and he soon made it
evident that he was a born master of the art of
parliamentary eloquence. It is not too much to say
that Bolingbroke was one of England's greatest
parliamentary orators, that his name deserves to be
classed with the names of the two Pitts, of Fox,
Canning, and Gladstone. He became prominent in
political life at a time when the principles of Whig

and Tory were getting to be somewhat undefined in their character, or at all events in their application to the practical business of a statesman's career.

Bolingbroke was not by any means a man to regulate his life too strictly by the tenets of a creed which was already getting to be somewhat out of fashion. The Queen on her throne saw herself compelled by the duties of her constitutional position to put up, from time to time, not only with Whig Ministers but even with Whig doctrines. It is not surprising that a man of Bolingbroke's personal ambition, energy, and capacity for onward movement should find himself often compelled, for the sake of his own career, to make his devotion to the principle of Toryism a sort of private worship, and in the active business of life to make use whenever he could of Whig men and even of Whig measures. In this, indeed, he was not different from Marlborough; but Marlborough, if he had been so inclined, could always have pleaded that he was a soldier, that his work in life was the business of war, and that he had only to do his duty as a commander whatever might be the Ministry or the policy which had sent him into the field.

Bolingbroke and Marlborough were close friends for a long time, and there must have been something peculiarly attractive to each man in the leading personal qualities of the other. Of Bolingbroke it may justly be said that even to those who study his life and his works at this comparatively remote distance of time, he always seems most attractive not

as a statesman, not as an orator, not as a writer, but
as an individual, as a personality. When we think
of many or most other great men, we think of them
chiefly for what they actually did, but when Bolingbroke comes to mind we are apt to think first of all
of the man himself, of his individual character, of
the personal force which he became in the world of
his day. We can easily trace this influence animat-
ing some of the writers who have devoted themselves
to what they believe to be his complete vindication.
Some of them, however acute and impartial in their
judgment on other subjects, are evidently carried
away by the fascination of the man. They cease to
be critics and become devotees. They are not satisfied with claiming the fullest allowance for the
political errors, inconsistencies, and wrong-doings
of their hero, but set themselves to make out that
he was always consistent and always right; that he
was consistent when at one moment he acted on
a principle which he had denounced a short time
before; that he was right when he avowed one
doctrine and acted on a doctrine which was distinctly
its antagonist; that in every step he took and in
every measure he pressed forward he was actuated
solely by the most unselfish purpose and never was
swayed by the impulses of his personal ambition.
It is not necessary to Bolingbroke's fame or to our
recognition of his noblest qualities that we should
thus endeavour to set him up as that which he
never claimed to be—a perfect model of political
straightforwardness, sincerity, and virtue.

A man ' gifted with such rare gifts and tried by such strong temptations,' as Macaulay said of Byron, may well be excused, as human nature goes, if he sometimes strays from the direct path and sometimes mistakes the promptings of his own ambition for the dictates of patriotic inspiration. We shall see that Bolingbroke at the time which we have now reached was already well inclined to make small account of his friendship with Marlborough. Bolingbroke had undoubtedly sound and statesmanlike reasons for desiring that the war should come to an end, and that peace should be obtained on the best terms available for England under all the conditions. He saw, however, that Marlborough, as the soldier in command of England's forces, was not likely to regard the best means of bringing the war to an end from the same point of view as that which a Tory statesman of somewhat light principles and a sceptical turn of mind might adopt.

Marlborough, as we have shown already, was, like many another great soldier, no lover of war for war's own sake. But Marlborough could not help believing that the honour and even the safety of England must depend to a great extent on her capacity to dictate the terms of peace. He was convinced that it only needed a bold and spirited forward movement to make it clear to France that England was in this position, and that France must take the terms she offered or accept still more humiliating conditions within the fortresses of Paris.

Bolingbroke, therefore, made up his mind that Marlborough would be an impediment in the way of the negotiations for peace which were just then coming into action, and that these negotiations must be conducted without any knowledge of them coming to the ears of Marlborough, until Marlborough could no longer have any chance of interfering with their progress.

Bolingbroke had long seen that the feeling of Queen Anne was turning entirely against Marlborough. It may be questioned whether at any time the Queen felt personally drawn into cordial liking for her greatest soldier. At the opening of her reign she had always regarded Marlborough as a Tory, and for this reason was inclined to accept him with a certain degree of sympathy and confidence. But it soon became clear to her that Marlborough was quite ready to put his Tory principles aside when they appeared likely to affect his dealings with Whigs, whom it was important to conciliate for the purpose of carrying on the special work which was under his direction. Anne herself had to put up with the Whigs while they were strong enough to make it necessary for her to consult them in the administration of State policy, but she did not on that account make any greater allowance for the political flexibility of Marlborough. Probably she had intellectual acuteness enough to see that Marlborough had really no deep-founded political principles, and she would have preferred a man who could sometimes put aside sincere principles for

present expediency to a man who had no principles
at all.

As time went on it became more and more
evident to those around her that the Queen was
growing colder and colder in her bearing towards
Marlborough, and this could be seen plainly enough
even before the events came about which put
an end to the rule of Marlborough's wife. Bolingbroke was not a man who could fail to observe the
Queen's growing dislike to Marlborough, and he was
not a man likely in the least to allow any feelings of
former friendship to interfere with the promotion of
his own career. The coming events were already
casting their shadows before, and Bolingbroke soon
saw that nothing was to be gained for him by
adherence to Marlborough's side or by any regard
for Marlborough's feelings. At the time, therefore,
when definite negotiations for peace began to be in
preparation, he did not feel the slightest hesitation or
scruple in playing out his own part without taking
Marlborough into counsel—in acting as if Marlborough were not in existence. There is not the
slightest reason to believe that he really harboured
any feeling of dislike to Marlborough, as he did
towards Harley, but Marlborough seemed just then
the man of all others most likely to stand in the way
of the projects which Bolingbroke had at heart, and
there was nothing for it but to put Marlborough out
of consideration.

Bolingbroke was not a man to cherish deep
dislikes. Somewhat too much has been made by

many writers of what is supposed to have been his implacable hatred for Harley. There is ample evidence, and evidence beyond dispute, that Bolingbroke felt deeply hurt by the priority of promotion given to Harley, and that he never concealed his feelings on the subject when among his intimate friends.

In such companionship Bolingbroke was never done with disparaging Harley, satirising him, and making merry over his many oddities and weaknesses. There can be no doubt whatever that Bolingbroke's mind was set upon obtaining for himself the highest position in the Queen's confidence and in the administration of State affairs. The desire to be the first in every path of success was a passion ingrained in Bolingbroke's nature, and he may be fairly excused if he failed to see in Harley a man really qualified to be his rival in a struggle for political supremacy. Even if the two men had never been brought into rivalry, there was much in Harley which could not but have excited the ridicule and contempt of such a man as Bolingbroke. Harley's ponderous pedantries, his solemn affectation of profundity and wisdom, his narrow-mindedness, his transparent egotism, and his utter incapacity for following out any great purpose, must have been in any case intolerable to a temper and an intellect like those of Bolingbroke. But there seems no reason to accuse Bolingbroke of any deep-seated dislike to Harley, or indeed of any feeling towards him beyond the idea that he was a pretentious and absurd sort of person who just then stood in the way and ought to be got out of the way by some process or other as soon as possible.

Bolingbroke was capable of strong likings and even of lasting friendships where the accomplishment of his own work and the success of his own career did not seem to be endangered in any way by such sentiments and such associations, and he was not one of those whom Dr. Johnson could have commended as good haters. Charles James Fox once said of himself that he never could be much of a hater, and in the better part of Bolingbroke's character as well as in his parliamentary gifts there was much which seems to have a certain kinship with the nature and the genius of Fox.

At the present moment the two men who stood most in Bolingbroke's way were Harley and Marlborough, and the degree of liking or disliking he may have felt towards either would not have materially affected the course which he was ready to pursue. In the political history of Queen Anne's reign the two greatest names by far are those of Marlborough and Bolingbroke. Each man was without a rival in his own field. There was no soldier like Marlborough; there was no parliamentary orator like Bolingbroke. Each man alike was wanting in that steadfast consistency of purpose which is only to be found in alliance with the most unselfish and exalted nature, and with profound conscientiousness. But there was an underlying levity in the temperament of Bolingbroke which had no

place in the character of Marlborough. Bolingbroke
gives one the impression of a man of genius who
found delight in the contemplation of himself during
his performance of some great artistic part, in considering how this or that accomplishment or achievement became him, and in congratulating himself on
his success in winning the world's admiration for
each particular performance. When Marlborough,
on the other hand, had a great part to play, he felt
nothing but the determination to play it to the very
best of his ability, and never seems to have asked
himself whether the world was likely to admire
him more on this day and on this field than
on any day or field which had seen his success
before.

Although he had come to be one of the two
leaders of the Government, Bolingbroke soon began
to find that he was not growing much in the favour
of the Queen. To Bolingbroke, who was content
with nothing but complete success in every attempt,
the comparatively distant terms at which he was
kept by the Queen proved very hard to bear. He
became possessed with the opinion, and had probably good reason for entertaining it, that the Queen
believed him to be in too close and friendly an
alliance with Marlborough, whom she had now
come to regard with distrust and dislike. Then
there came the utter failure of the Quebec expedition, a project which had had its origin in Bolingbroke's own active and adventurous brain. His idea
had been nothing less than a scheme which was to

accomplish the clearing out of the French altogether
from the North American continent, and the securing
to England undisputed possession of the whole
American territory. One of his ambitions was to
distinguish himself as a great and triumphant war
Minister, and some of those around him had reason
to believe that he felt confident not only in the
success of the scheme, but convinced that it would
give him a fame in history surpassing anything that
had been achieved by the victories of Marlborough
on the European continent. Thus there came up
in his mind a sentiment of rivalry between himself
and Marlborough, and it probably seemed to him
that the success of his enterprise would make him
the most important man in the State, and give him
the first place in the regard and confidence of the
Queen.

Even the very arrangements for the expedition he
appears to have thought of turning to account, with
the view of ingratiating himself in the royal favour
by the process of conciliating the royal favourite.
He put all the land forces destined for the expedition
under the command of Brigadier Hill, Mrs. Masham's
brother, and he wrote a letter to Brigadier Hill urging
him in fervent words to make the most of the great
opportunity given him, and 'to pursue with vigour
an undertaking wherein the honour of our Mistress
and the most durable advantages to our country are
concerned.'

The expedition, as we have told already, proved an
absolute failure. Much as the failure must have dis-

couraged and disheartened Bolingbroke at first, it
only, after a while, served to turn his thoughts to the
necessity of some other enterprise which might prove
beyond doubt his capacity for conducting the affairs
of State.   This time his thoughts turned rather in
the direction of an accomplished peace than of a
successful war.   His great object was to come to some
terms with France, whether with or without the full
approval of the Allies, which should put an end to the
whole struggle, and open a new field for the genius
of a great statesman at home.   Under these conditions the preliminary arrangements for peace were
begun without any knowledge on the part of Marlborough.   The great soldier was still conducting his
active campaigning work on the Continent, and, for
a time, knew nothing whatever of the arrangements
that were going on to bring the whole struggle to a
sudden close.   Up to this time Marlborough had been
not only the soldier in command of the Queen's forces,
the general who was authorised to conduct the whole
of the military operations which belonged to the work
of the Allies, but also the statesman, diplomatist, and
envoy who was endowed with chief control of all
negotiations and all arrangements.   Now on a sudden
Marlborough found himself quietly left out of the
whole business, put aside and reduced to a power-
less condition, while arrangements, of which he
had never been allowed to know anything, were being
carried on by the administrators or the administrator
at home.   The temptation had proved too much for
Bolingbroke, and Marlborough soon understood but

too well that he was sacrificed to the ambition of
the man who had hitherto professed the most sincere
admiration and loyal friendship for him.   Bolingbroke and Marlborough had now to go their different
ways.

CHAPTER XXV

'GONE TO SWEAR A PEACE'

SOME of the words spoken by Constance in Shakespeare's 'King John' might well be quoted as an illustration of the feeling which prevailed with many in England, and probably with Marlborough among the rest, when it became known for certain that the preliminaries of peace were already undergoing the process of negotiation in France. 'Gone to swear a peace !' cries the indignant Constance.

False blood to false blood joined ! Gone to be friends !

Even the name of Louis and the indignant question about the provinces which Louis was expected to acquire make the application all the more distinct and appropriate. 'France friend with England !' is her impassioned exclamation of wonder and incredulous horror. Those who felt as Constance in the great drama did, must have found it hard to believe, when the news came in Queen Anne's day, that the English Sovereign and her advisers were actually preparing to make peace with France under almost any conditions. France was still regarded by a large proportion of English men and women as the hereditary and natural enemy of England. The war had been provoked, and had in truth been made popular among the majority of the English people, by the unfortunate policy of King Louis, when he refused to recognise the principles of the English Revolution, and actually treated the exiled Stuart as if he were the reigning King of England. But, although that ill-omened act gave the immediate impulse to the war, there could be no doubt that the aggressive and grasping policy of the French Sovereign had been the main cause of the long struggle. Englishmen had been told by some of the most impressive and influential among their leaders that if France ventured to make Spain part of her dominion she would become a power which must be an intolerable menace to the liberties of Continental Europe, and must before long be a dangerous rival to the influence of England abroad, and even to her security and peace at home. No one could tell at what moment France, thus encouraged to aggression, might not actually make the cause of the Stuarts her own, and endeavour by armed force to restore the Pretender to the throne of England.

During the whole course of the war there had been occasional alarms about French expeditions to Scotland to effect a landing there, and assist the Highland clans to begin a revolutionary movement in favour of the exiled family. Nothing that had occurred during the war—not even the most brilliant victories of Marlborough—had made so great a change in the conditions of the French power as to afford any guarantee to England that such a policy might not yet be put into execution by King Louis or one of his immediate descendants.   Little was known in England, at the time, of the degree to which the resources of France had been exhausted by the long war, while there was full and disheartening knowledge of the extent to which the struggle had drained the treasure and lavished the blood of England. Even the preliminary conditions of the peace, so far as these were yet known to the great bulk of Englishmen, did not seem to promise any security against an early extension of France's actual dominion.   Suppose that the grandson of the French Sovereign were not formally and actually placed upon the throne of Spain by an agreement between France and the Allied Powers, who was to say how soon some new arrangement might not be devised which would make the Spanish monarchy a tributary to the House of Bourbon?   Solemn pledges had been broken by Sovereigns during very recent days, and secret engagements had been made, the meaning of which was only avowed and proclaimed when it became too late to frustrate them by any force but that of conquering arms.

So far as the general public in England were able or were allowed to understand the full bearings of the whole controversy, it did not appear that the terms proposed to be secured by the peace were worth anything like the vast sacrifices which had been made for the undertaking and the maintenance of the war. Of what avail were the victories of Marlborough, of Peterborough, and of Eugene, and the capture of

Gibraltar, if the French monarch were now to be
allowed to obtain such terms of peace as he might
easily have obtained had he been so inclined at the
very opening of the war ?   In what sense could the
expansion of French dominion be said to undergo any
abiding check from the conditions which the Allies,
after all their victories, were now willing to accept at
his hands ?   Such were the questions which men at
home in England, and Englishmen even on Continental
battlefields, were asking themselves when it became
known beyond question that those who acted on behalf
of Queen Anne were already entering into actual
arrangements for a peace with France.

The minds of Queen Anne and her confidential
advisers were, however, clearly made up.   The
Government of Harley and Bolingbroke were determined to come to terms of peace, either with or without the consent of the Allies.   It is only just to say
that the Allies, for their own part, were most eager to
come to an immediate understanding with France,
even without the co-operation of England, if such an
arrangement could possibly be accomplished.   There
was no feeling of enthusiasm whatever among the
English people either for their German or their Dutch
allies.   The Dutch had for a long time been regarded
chiefly as inconvenient competitors in the business of
commerce and navigation, and the people of England,
notwithstanding the Act of Succession which provided
them with a Hanoverian family to rule over them, had
never felt or professed any particular sympathy with
the German States.   Harley and Bolingbroke were

both well acquainted with the common feelings of
their countrymen on these subjects, and did not
believe that serious difficulties would be put in the
way of their negotiations by any consideration on
the part of the English public for Dutch or German
interests.

The reader of history will find as he studies the
origin, the progress, and the conclusion of this great
war, that it involves two quite distinct questions with
which the judgment of the world has to deal. The
first question to be considered is whether the English
Government were justified in undertaking such a
war for such a cause; and the second is, assuming
or admitting that the war ought to have been undertaken, was it justifiable to bring it to a close on
such terms? It may be taken for granted that, in
the England of the present day, no set of statesmen could venture on proposing that a struggle of
terrible moment, involving tremendous risks and
sacrifices to the people of these countries, should be
undertaken for the sake of preventing the people of
Spain from accepting a particular Prince as their new
Sovereign, even though that Prince should happen to
be a member of a family already reigning in another
Continental country. English public opinion would
now regard the question as one altogether for the
settlement of Spain and the Spanish people, and if the
Spaniards could put up with the Sovereign offered
for their acceptance, England would assuredly never
think of interfering with the course of Spanish
succession by force of arms. But it must be owned

that the existence of such a public opinion in England is of very recent growth. Even living men can remember a time when the majority of Englishmen might still possibly have thought it a duty to undertake an armed intervention in order that a member of some reigning royal family on the European Continent might not be imposed or accepted as a ruling Sovereign in some other continental country where the regular succession to the throne had become suddenly vacant. It may be taken for granted that, if just before the time of the Crimean War the Czar of Russia had prevailed upon the ruling classes in Constantinople to accept a Russian Prince as a successor to the vacant throne of an Ottoman Sultan, the majority of Englishmen would then have been fervently in favour of an armed intervention to resist that project, even though there had been no diplomatic treaties whatever in existence which seemed to give England a more or less direct title to intervention. At that time, and under those conditions, the one idea would have been that, if a Russian Prince were allowed to become the ruler of Turkey, that arrangement would make Russia supreme master over all the nearer East and would deal an intolerable blow to the just influence of England.

The feelings which governed the minds of many Englishmen in the days of Queen Anne were not in this sense less reasonable than the feelings which might have governed most of the English statesmen and parties in the earlier years of Queen Victoria's

reign. We must not therefore find fault with the
political leaders and parties during the reign of
Queen Anne if they did not regard the increase of
French influence and the expansion of Bourbon
dominion over Continental Europe with the calculat-
ing composure of a political economist, or study its
possible effects from the exalted observatory of a
moral philosopher. It has also to be borne in mind
that the men and the party who at the opening of
Queen Anne's reign were mainly opposed to the war
with France, were opposed to it, not because of the
vast sacrifice of English life and English treasure for
a question which had nothing to do with England's
domestic and vital interest, but because it was a
project of war against the Sovereign and the State
friendly to the interests of the exiled Stuarts. If we
judge Queen Anne and her leading advisers by the
standard merely of practical politics in their days,
and not by that of the higher morality, or the more
exalted human feeling, we shall not find it easy to
condemn them out of hand because they ventured
on such a task for the purpose of resisting the
ambition and limiting the dominion of France.
There is probably on the whole a better justification to be made for the policy of Queen Anne—
which indeed can hardly be said to be Queen Anne's
own policy—in preventing France from acquiring
dominion over Spain, than there was for the policy
of the Ministers of George the Third in preventing
France under Napoleon from spreading her power
over other Continental States.

But then comes up for our consideration, the second question to which we have already directed attention—the question whether, if we sanction the policy which began the war, we can also sanction the policy which brought it so suddenly and on such conditions to a peaceful settlement. This was the question Queen Anne's Ministers knew that they must soon have to face. So far as Queen Anne herself was concerned it is not likely that she was troubled with doubts or scruples of conscience on the subject. Her heart had never been in the war from the first. To do her justice she was, according to her lights, a conscientious and humane woman. She had no sympathy with the war spirit; she was not touched by the glories of conquest; and she had a sincere wish for the quiet, the prosperity, and the happiness of her people. This particular war brought antagonism to some of her dearest feelings because her inmost sympathies naturally went ever with the exiled Stuarts. But she believed that she thoroughly understood her position as a constitutional Sovereign, and she did not see how she could set herself in opposition to the counsels and the pressure of her constitutional advisers. She, therefore, consented reluctantly to authorise the policy which began the war, and she doubtless told her conscience that no possible alternative was left to her at such a time and under all the surrounding conditions. But when the second and quite distinct question began to come up for consideration—the question whether the war ought to be carried any further if a peaceful

settlement of whatever kind could be obtained—it
is hardly to be supposed that her conscience and her
heart gave her any trouble whatever in coming to a
decision.   Every impulse which she had to control
and subdue when she was called upon to begin the
war, was free to help in guiding and controlling her
when the opportunity presented itself of bringing the
war to a close.

While the opening of the session of Parliament
was drawing near, every effort was made by the
Ministers to bring all those over whom they had
any influence into a frame of mind proper for the
part which the Government had determined to carry
out.   All who were in any way acquainted with
public affairs were well satisfied that some proposals
for peace were under consideration, and the vast
majority of the outer public, who knew little or
nothing of what was going on, would have been only
too glad to hear that the war was coming to an end
almost on any terms.   Harley and Bolingbroke were
nevertheless exceedingly anxious that they should
have a strong body of supporters in both Houses of
Parliament, ready to champion with uncompromising
loyalty whatever course might be recommended
by the advisers of the Queen.   The Duke of Marlborough came from the Continent to take part in
the sittings of the House of Lords, and Burnet tells
us that he 'spoke very plainly to the Queen against
the steps that were already made ; but he found her
so possessed, that what he said made no impression,
so he desired to be excused from coming to council,

since he must oppose every step that was made in that affair.'

Then Bishop Burnet, as is his wont, gives some account of his own personal experiences during this moment of crisis. 'Among others,' Burnet narrates, 'the Queen spoke to myself; she said, she hoped bishops would not be against peace; I said, a good peace was what we daily prayed for, but the preliminaries offered by France gave no hopes of such an one; and the trusting to the King of France's faith, after all that had passed, would seem a strange thing. She said, we were not to regard the preliminaries; we should have a peace upon such a bottom, that we should not at all rely on the King of France's word; but we ought to suspend our opinions, till she acquainted us with the whole matter. I asked leave to speak my mind plainly; which she granted. I said, any treaty by which Spain and the West Indies were left to King Philip, must in a little while deliver up all Europe into the hands of France; and, if any such peace should be made, she was betrayed, and we were all ruined; in less than three years' time she would be murdered, and the fires would be again raised in Smithfield.'

Bishop Burnet's talk must seem rather extravagant to the mind of a modern reader, but it is only fair to say that a good many of Bishop Burnet's contemporaries were quite ready to believe that any increase to the power of France might mean the restoration of the Stuart dynasty, the rekindling of the fires in Smithfield, and the murder of the

Queen herself either by the executioner or by the assassin. Most of Bishop Burnet's familiar acquaintances had probably come by this time to associate the fires in Smithfield entirely with the reign of Queen Mary, and had forgotten that Smithfield was also illuminated by the fires of religious persecution during the reign of Queen Elizabeth. We may certainly take Bishop Burnet as a fair representative of the class and the political order to which he belonged, and we cannot doubt that the views he expressed to the Queen were the views entertained by a large proportion of Englishmen. Such as his views were they did not seem to make much impression on Queen Anne. He tells us that he continued to urge on her his ideas of the dangers to which she might be subjected ' till I saw she grew uneasy; so I withdrew.' It is perhaps just possible to suppose that the Queen may have become not so much uneasy as to the consequences which Burnet was thus earnestly forecasting, as weary of the length of the Bishop's futile exhortation. Whatever may have been the cause of her uneasiness or her weariness, it may safely be taken for granted that the interview with Bishop Burnet did not convert her from her inclination towards a peaceful settlement of the long dispute.

The English statesmen who had set their minds on the accomplishment of peace were in a position to know by this time that their French opponents were not more anxious than they for any prolongation or renewal of the war. We read in the memoirs of De

Torcy, the French Minister for Foreign Affairs, that an
envoy who arrived in Paris from London during this
crisis began his discourse by asking the French statesman whether he wished for peace, adding that if so
the means of obtaining it were within his reach.   The
words in which De Torcy records his feelings are that
asking him such a question was like asking a dying
man whether he wished to be restored to health and
strength.   The task which had to be accomplished by
Queen Anne and her advisers might, therefore, have
seemed to be little more than the pronouncement of
a mere formula so far as the great enemy of England was concerned.   But we have already seen from
Burnet's words, and many other evidences, that there
was still a certain proportion of Englishmen who
believed that the whole war must be condemned as a
shameless waste of treasure and of life if no results
were now to be obtained from it which would give to
England some solid pledge of security for the future.
Harley and Bolingbroke, more than all other men,
believed that Marlborough would bring his influence
to bear against the adoption of terms which seemed
to render his military triumphs futile and give back
to the enemy all that he had won.   Yet it was not
possible to keep on private negotiations from day
to day if the results were not to be definite and immediate.   Anything might happen if needless delay
were allowed.

Meanwhile the negotiations were going rapidly on.
A conference had already been held at The Hague,
and another at the small town of Gertruydenburg in

North Brabant, but nothing came of these conferences, for England and the Allies were still maintaining their hard conditions. Of late, however, the prospects of peace began to be more clear. The reason for this change soon became obvious to all who had any intimate knowledge of what was going on. In January 1711, the proposals for a peaceful arrangement began to come from the side of England, and it was arranged that a congress should be held at Utrecht for the purpose of establishing a basis of negotiations. There was some difficulty for a while in prevailing upon the allies of England to take part in these new negotiations, but the difficulties were at last overcome mainly by unmistakable evidence of the fact that England was determined to enter on a discussion of terms with France whether her allies went with her or held back. In fact, it appears quite certain that the representatives of the English Government had signed the preliminaries to the final discussion before any decisive step had been taken at home to remove out of the way the one great obstacle to any further negotiation—the authority and influence of the Duke of Marlborough.

The King of France was now put in quite a different position from that which he had occupied during preceding negotiations. The one harsh and humiliating condition which his enemies had then endeavoured to force upon him, the condition that he must himself unite with the Allies in the expulsion of his grandson from Spain, had been withdrawn, and there was not the slightest intention on the part of

England to put forward such a stipulation again. On the former occasions, too, when peace was talked of, the King of France had been put in the position of a suppliant, and the Allies made it plain that they considered the appeal to come entirely from him, and not to have been suggested by any anxiety on their part to bring the war to a close. Now the state of affairs was entirely changed, and from the very opening of this new chapter of negotiations King Louis had been given to understand that England, at all events, was willing and anxious to renew the discussion on a basis which he would be likely to accept. The King of France could not fail to appreciate the significance of this sudden change of front. Nothing had happened during the more recent stages of the war to suggest the idea that England was feeling discouraged by the later events of the campaign. Nobody knew better than King Louis how much the cause of France owed to the slowness and slackness of England's allies, or understood more fully that any want of success which had lately been attending the movements of his enemies was due to the difficulties placed in the way of the English commander by the States which were associated in his enterprise. King Louis understood, as well as Marlborough himself could have done, that if the English commander had been allowed his own full way France would have to accept in the end any terms which might be imposed upon her.

There was continual secret communication going on between the French Court and some of the friends of the Stuart cause who still remained in England. There were leading members of the English Tory party who still maintained a close correspondence with the exiled Stuarts and their friends in France, and thus kept the French Court very well informed as to the results of the recent changes in English political parties. King Louis therefore was quite in a position to understand that he had now at last an auspicious opportunity for making the best terms which he could possibly hope to obtain as a settlement of the whole international question. He knew that his opponents were now prepared to give him all he could possibly ask for or expect, and that they were as anxious as he could be to bring the whole dispute to a conclusion. In truth, the mere opening of the new negotiations was warrant enough that these negotiations were destined to end in peace.

The Conference was opened at Utrecht on January 29, 1712. Before it had gone far in its deliberations an important State paper was presented to the Queen by the House of Commons, the report of a committee on the results of the war thus far, and the sacrifices it had imposed on England. This report set forth that the expenses of the war had gone on multiplying at an alarmingly increasing rate during its later periods, so that while the successes of the earlier years were obtained at a comparatively cheap cost, the more dragging and less decisive movements of its later stages had involved the English people in expense out of all proportion to the former amount.

It must be said that the whole cost of the war thus far would not appear to a modern reader a very enormous sum for the country to have to bear. About twelve millions was the cost in which, according to the report, the English people had been involved by the whole of the campaigns. The art of war has become a much more costly business in our own days, owing in great measure to the expensive inventions with which the developments of modern science have intensified the powers of destruction. But then it has to be remembered that the England of Queen Anne's reign was a poor and thinly populated country when compared with the England of Queen Victoria and of King Edward the Seventh. An amount of outlay, therefore, which would seem but of trivial importance now, even if occasioned by some comparatively insignificant frontier war, naturally seemed a portentous burden to be imposed upon the taxation of the English people when Harley and Bolingbroke were the leading Ministers of State.

The report contained a great deal of information as to the relative proportions of the forces put into the field by the several States in the alliance, and there could be little doubt as to the significant bearing of these passages on the policy of the statesmen who were anxious that England should come to terms of peaceful settlement on her own account, even if she could not secure the co-operation of her allies. The terms of the agreement originally entered into among the Allies were that the German

States should keep ninety thousand men in the field,
England forty thousand, and the Dutch Provinces
one hundred and twenty thousand. The great
disproportion in numbers which was thus imposed
upon the Dutch Provinces admitted of easy explanation. Queen Anne and the Emperor had each to
send their troops out of their own country and to
keep them employed on foreign battlefields, while
still, of course, under the necessity of raising and
always maintaining forces strong enough for the
defence and security of their own soil. The territories of the United Provinces were, on the other
hand, to a great extent the actual battlefield of the
war, and Holland, while resisting the common enemy,
was at the same time defending her own ground.
In point of fact the arrangement was that forty-two
thousand of the Netherland forces were to be employed in manning and defending the Dutch garrisons
at home, and the Low Countries were only under
agreement to keep sixty thousand men on the actual
battlefield.

The report pointed out that, so far as the military movements in Spain were concerned, Holland
had made hardly any contribution either in men or
in money. The King of Portugal, who was one of
the Sovereigns engaged with the alliance, had never
sent into the field anything like the number of
soldiers which he had engaged to contribute and
for the maintenance of which he had actually been
receiving subsidies. Representations having a similar bearing were made in the report with regard to

the manner in which the naval forces of Great Britain had been drawn upon, and of the utterly disproportionate efforts which she had had to make, by her war vessels and her transports, for carrying on operations around the shores of Spain and Portugal. The report did not take much account of the fact that England, by the use of her navy around the coasts of Spain and Portugal, had gained some substantial and enduring advantages which she did not feel herself called upon, and was not expected, to share with her Allies. There was, however, unquestionable justice in the statement that 'the more the wealth of this nation hath been exhausted, and the more your Majesty's arms have been attended with success, the heavier has been the burden laden upon us.' It is beyond all reasonable dispute that after every signal victory gained by Marlborough and the English forces, the demands of the Allies became more exacting for fresh subsidies to enable them to carry on the war.

Another passage of the report is well worthy of quotation. 'At the first entrance into this war,' so runs the passage, 'the Commons were induced to exert themselves in the extraordinary manner they did, and to grant such large supplies as had been unknown to former ages, in hopes thereby to prevent the mischief of a lingering war, and to bring that in which they were necessarily engaged to a speedy conclusion; but they have been very unhappy in the event, while they have so much reason to suspect that what was intended to shorten the war hath

proved the very cause of its long continuance ; for
those to whom the profits of it have accrued have
not been disposed easily to forego them; and your
Majesty will from thence discern the true reason
why so many have delighted in a war which brought
in so rich a harvest yearly from Great Britain.' The
report then went on to make more distinct representations with regard to the policy pursued by
England's allies. It pointed out that the German
Empire had already been a territorial gainer by some
of the conquests during the war, and yet was drawing
from England the fullest proportions of supplies that
could have been demanded even if the Empire had
been a loser and not a gainer by the developments
of the struggle. It also insisted that the United
Provinces had already secured positive advantages
for themselves against any possible encroachments
by France in the future, and significantly suggested
that these very advantages might be turned to
account against England herself in the event of
any hostility arising between Great Britain and
Holland.

The main purpose of the whole report was, in fact,
to fill the mind of the Sovereign and the country at
large with the idea that the less England took into
consideration the interest and the inclinations of the
Allies in the arrangements for peace, the more would
she be doing justice to her own rightful claims and to
the interests of her own people. One of the closing
sentences in the report contains some words which
must have been well understood by Queen Anne and

her most confidential advisers. These words expressed
the hope and the belief that 'your Majesty, in your
great goodness to your people, will rescue them from
those evils which the private councils of ill-designing
men have exposed them to.' It was impossible not to
understand that the allusion to the evils brought about
by the private counsels of ill-designing men referred to
the part which, according to the judgment of those
now in power, had been performed by the great commander whose ruin was already pre-arranged. This
was the only passage in the report which laid itself
distinctly open to such an interpretation. The main
and consistent object of the report was to assure the
Queen that the less regard she paid to the counsels
and the interests of her allies the more cordial
and complete would be the support which she might
expect from her faithful Commons.

The report is an important historical study
because it illumines so completely the condition of
mind which prevailed among the majority in the new
House of Commons, and among her Majesty's advisers
who were maintained in power by the strength of
that majority. Swift, in one of his letters to Stella,
speaks of the report and says, 'I believe it will be a
pepperer.' In another letter Swift tells that he was
urged by Sir Thomas Hanmer, the chairman of the
committee, to help him in drawing up the report and
had consented to do so, but adds, 'I do not know
whether I shall succeed, for it is a little out of my way.'
Burton seems to have good reason for the opinion
which he expresses that the unmistakable hand of

Swift is not to be traced in the report, 'though it is printed in collected editions of his works.'

The chief interest which the report now has for us is found in the fact that it enables us to understand the mood of mind which was governing English statesmen when they offered to enter on the new negotiations. The result might have been foreseen from the very outset. The King of France must have been the most stolid or the most visionary of men if he did not see that his happiest chance had actually sought him out. He had only to ask and to have, so long as he did not put forward any demand of fantastic extravagance. Louis the Fourteenth was quite shrewd enough to see that an opportunity had come which he did not create and might never be able to restore. His favouring chance had been gained for him not on the battlefields of the Low Countries, or Germany, or France, or Spain, but in the political, social, and ecclesiastical combinations and antagonisms of England herself.

The men in power around Queen Anne had something yet to do before they could feel quite comfortable and secure in the carrying on of the Utrecht negotiations. We shall therefore have to turn back a little in the tracing of our history in order to show how they accomplished their purpose and made the way clear for convenient arrangements with the King of France.

Bishop Burnet, when telling the story of the negotiations, records a fact which is well worth mentioning because of the personal interest attach-

ing to it and becomes still more worth mentioning
because of the peculiar fashion in which Burnet sets it
down. 'One Prior,' he says, 'who had been Jersey's
secretary, upon his death '—on Lord Jersey's death,
that is to say—'was employed to prosecute that
which the other did not live to finish. Prior had been
taken a boy out of a tavern, by the Earl of Dorset,
who accidentally found him reading Horace; and
he, being very generous, gave him an education in
literature; he was sent to the Court of France in
September, to try on what terms we might expect a
peace; his journey was carried on secretly; but
upon his return, he was stopped at Dover; and a
packet, that he brought, was kept, till an order came
from Court to set him free; and by this accident the
secret broke out.' This 'one Prior' so contemptuously mentioned by Bishop Burnet was the celebrated poet Matthew Prior, who was employed in
many important diplomatic missions and seemed well
qualified for his work. Prior, like many another
poet of his time, was born of humble parentage and
was helped through those early struggles into literature, which otherwise might have been weary and
painful, by the generosity of an appreciative patron.
It seems a little strange that a man like Bishop
Burnet, who mixed so much in the circles from
which patrons and patronage came, should not have
heard anything from his Court friends about the
career of the rising poet and diplomatist, and should
have found no other way of describing him than by
setting him down simply as 'one Prior.'

CHAPTER XXVI

'I FALL UNDER THIS PLOT

WHEN Macbeth is contrasting his own condition as a living man with that of him whom he has done to death, he numbers among the troubles which wait upon his own life 'malice domestic, foreign levies.' If Marlborough had been studying in advance the causes of his own downfall, he would have had no occasion to include foreign levies among them, and might have fairly ascribed them all to malice domestic—at least to the malice of his enemies at home. It is not too much to say that the whole conditions of Europe might have been altered for a time if the victor of Blenheim could still have retained his position of ascendency over the movements of Queen Anne's Government. Whether we approve or disapprove of the policy which brought the long war to an end, we can hardly have any doubt that the result of the war and the terms of its final settlement would have been entirely different if Marlborough had been allowed to carry on his forward movement into the heart of France. By no set of men at home or abroad was Marlborough's strength more completely recognised than by those of his own countrymen, who now found

themselves compelled to choose between renouncing
their cherished policy and forcing Marlborough out
of their way. The Queen's advisers were confident
of the strength they had acquired in the new Parliament, and were well resolved to increase that strength
by whatever means the utmost straining of constitutional authority could place within their power.

It may be mentioned as significant evidence of
the control which the Ministers had obtained over
the new Parliament that they were able to get the
measure against Occasional Conformity passed into
law on March 12, 1712. This measure, it will be remembered, had been introduced again and again, and
was carried in the House of Commons more than once,
but was lost in the House of Lords. The title of the
measure began: 'An Act for Preserving the Protestant Religion by better securing the Church of
England as by law established,' and the title further
described it as intended to continue the toleration
granted to Protestant dissenters by former legislation.
The purpose of the measure was to declare that anyone, whether he had occasionally conformed or not,
who held a government or corporation office, was to
be disqualified by the act if he afterwards attended
the meeting of a conventicle. Nor was this unlucky
person left in any doubt as to the precise nature of his
offence. A conventicle was defined to be a meeting
of ten persons or more, occupied in religious ceremonial or worship other than that authorised by the
English Prayer-book, and, even though the conventicle should be held in a private dwelling for the

purpose of concealment, the law declared the meeting
equally penal if there were ten persons present
besides the members of the family who occupied the
home.   Even if the liturgy of the Church of England
were ostensibly used on such occasions, the penalty
was still to be enforced if prayer for the Princess
Sophia (whose name stood next in succession to that
of Queen Anne) were omitted from the disloyal ceremonial.   Each offender under such conditions would
be liable to a fine of forty pounds, and would be
incapable of holding any office under Government or
under a corporate body.   The object of this Act was
not merely to discourage Dissent, but also to prohibit
any manifestation, either by omission or commission,
of sympathy with the cause of the exiled Stuarts.
We can easily understand that the mind and heart of
Bolingbroke were not any more than the mind and
heart of Queen Anne herself profoundly concerned
in the passing of such a measure, but the time
seemed to require it, and both the Queen and Bolingbroke felt constrained to go with the time.   The
first opportunity was seized for satisfying the passion
of religious intolerance throughout the community,
and the measure at last was thus carried into law.

The men in power began to feel that the time
had come when a decisive blow must be struck
for the accomplishment of the purpose they had
at heart.   They felt, too, that the decisive blow
must be directed against Marlborough.   The day of
coups d'état had not yet passed from the course of
English history.   Men of the time had seen what may

be called the conquest of England by William the Third. They had seen the old dynasty of the Stuarts deposed and its hereditary representatives driven into exile. They had seen a Stuart Princess called to the throne under conditions which made her the Sovereign of a constitutional monarchy—a Stuart Princess who was herself a devoted member of the Church of England. They had seen the hereditary succession transferred by Act of Parliament to a foreign family living in Germany. Such a generation could not yet have grown into anything like a genuine recognition of the true principles of constitutional government, and could hardly feel surprised when the practices of constitutional government itself were made available for the purpose of accomplishing something very like an act of despotic power. The result of the recent elections had made it clear to those now at the head of the State that they had a force behind them strong enough to maintain them in the carrying of measures to accomplish their immediate purpose, even though a part of that purpose might be the overthrow of the great soldier who had borne the flag of England in triumph over so many foreign battlefields. The House of Commons might be safely counted on to maintain Harley and Bolingbroke in the projects which they were determined to carry out, but it was anticipated that there would be some difficulty with the House of Lords.

Now, the House of Lords has at all times, since parliamentary government came to be established in

England, been regarded as the chief obstacle to the accomplishment of great measures tending towards political progress and the principle of civic equality and popular freedom. Of late years we have come to regard it as no longer a power to prevent the ultimate passing of such measures, but only as a power to obstruct and delay them for a time, until the loudly and resolutely expressed determination of the majority outside shall have convinced the obstructive Peers that the time has come for them either to give in or to run the risk of destroying their own institution. It has, however, happened every now and then at all times since the revolution of 1688, that the House of Lords shows, in particular instances, a creditable and honourable desire to resist some act of despotic force on the part of the majority in the House of Commons. The leaders of the State, at that period of Queen Anne's reign which we have now reached, felt well satisfied that the overthrow of Marlborough was not to be accomplished without a strong opposition on the part of the hereditary assembly, and they knew that the constitution itself had provided them with an easy way of getting over the difficulty.

On December 7, 1711, Parliament was opened as usual by Queen Anne in person. The speech from the throne contained an announcement which could have left no doubt among all who heard and all who afterwards read it, that the mind of the Government was made up to bring the war to a close under whatever conditions. 'I am glad,' the Royal Speech

declared, 'that I can now tell you that, notwithstanding the arts of those who delight in war, both
place and time are appointed for opening the treaty
of a general peace.' There could be no doubt in the
mind of anyone that the allusion to those who
delight in war proclaimed the doom of Marlborough.
Not only was a peace to be made, but an example
was also to be made of the great commander but for
whose genius in war peace at any price might long
ago have been enforced on England. One of the peers
on whom the Government especially relied, and who
had travelled a long journey in order that he might
be able to take a part in the debate, made a speech
which showed more plainly still the intentions of
the statesmen in power. This peer was the Earl of
Anglesey. He emphatically declared in his speech
that it ought to be left to her Majesty herself to conclude a peace when she thought it convenient for the
good of her subjects, and he added that 'we might
have enjoyed that blessing soon after the battle of
Ramillies, if the same had not been put off by some
persons whose interest it was to prolong the war.'
The Queen had left the throne according to the usual
form soon after the delivery of the Royal Speech,
but she had not left the House itself. She merely
retired to the royal enclosure or pavilion which was
always prepared for her, and where she remained
sometimes in order that she might listen to the
debate.

The occasion was assuredly one of great moment,
and of something like dramatic interest in the story

of the crisis. The Duke of Marlborough was in the House, and his rising at once to take part in the debate showed how thoroughly he understood the entire significance of the words which had been delivered from the throne, and of those which had been spoken by the peer who had further illustrated their meaning. Marlborough was no more of an orator than Napoleon Bonaparte or the Duke of Wellington. The gift of eloquence is not often bestowed on great military commanders, and Julius Cæsar remains in history one of the few examples of a great warrior who was also a great orator. Marlborough seldom took part in parliamentary debate, and was not fond of speech-making at any time or under any conditions, but his speech on this occasion showed that quiet and complete self-control which never seemed to desert him at the most trying moments of his career, whether on the battlefield or in the council-chamber, and it wanted nothing of the dignity which ought to belong to the utterance of such a man at such a moment.

Marlborough told the House of Lords that he could appeal with perfect confidence to the Queen herself to say whether, during the time that he had served her as general and as plenipotentiary, he had ever failed to inform her and her council of all proposals of peace that had been made, and had not constantly applied to her that she would give him instructions as to the course which he ought to pursue under the conditions which he had brought to her knowledge. Then he went on to declare in tones of the deepest earnestness that he had ever been desirous of a safe, honourable, and lasting peace, and that nothing had ever been farther from his purpose than any thought of prolonging the war for his own private advantage, as his enemies had most falsely insinuated against him. He assured the House that if there were nothing else to inspire him with a desire for a lasting peace, his own advancing years and the long fatigues and troubles he had undergone made him earnestly wish, above all things, for retirement and repose in order that the remainder of his life might be given up to preparation for eternity. He called upon the House to take account of the fact that he could no longer have the slightest motive to desire a continuance of the war, seeing that he had already been most generously rewarded, and had had honours and wealth heaped upon him far beyond his desert and his expectation both by her Majesty and her Parliaments; but he took the opportunity of declaring that he was of the same opinion as the rest of the Allies that the safety and liberties of Europe would be left in imminent danger if Spain and the West Indies were surrendered to the House of Bourbon.

There can be no doubt that the Duke of Marlborough's words made a deep impression on a large number of those to whom they were addressed. The opinion of such listeners was in all probability only a forecast of the judgment which history has since adopted and maintained. Whatever the public and private errors and faults of Marlborough, there

seems no just reason to believe that in his great
career as a soldier he was inspired and governed
mainly, as so many other famous soldiers have been,
by a love of war for its own excitements and its own
successes, by a love of conquest, and a passion for
military renown and for personal aggrandisement.
Given the policy of the war against France, there is
no reason to accuse Marlborough of any ambition
other than the ambition to conduct that war to a
complete and a lasting success. The fault to be
found with the policy of the war must be traced
back to a period of history before the time when
Marlborough could be justly accredited with any
power to direct the statesmanship of England.
Those who were satisfied that the safety of England
and the stability of the revolution accomplished by
William the Third depended on a stern resistance to
the expansion of French dominion over Spain and
other parts of the European Continent, could have no
fault to find with Marlborough for the manner in
which he endeavoured to conduct this policy to
success. There was, therefore, direct and immediate
significance in the words which he used when he
insisted that the liberties of Europe would still be
left in danger if security were not obtained against
the extension of Bourbon dominion over Spain and
the West Indies.

At this distance of time it is easy enough to
contend that the dearest interests of England were
involved in maintaining the internal prosperity
of the English people and the populations under

English rule, and that it mattered little to these populations whether one Sovereign or another reigned over the Spanish people. But at the time when Marlborough was thus addressing the House of Lords no idea of this order had come up as an element in British statesmanship. Indeed, the thought of a policy which merely concerned itself with the welfare of the populations under English rule, and disclaimed the principle of intervention in the affairs of foreign countries, would have been as strange and intolerable to the statesmanship of England just after the French Revolution as it was to the statesmanship of England under Queen Anne. It must have been clear to every mind, at the time when this debate was taking place in the House of Lords, that the words of the Royal Speech were intended to convey a censure not upon the policy of the war but upon Marlborough himself. An amendment to the address was moved by the Earl of Nottingham which, if it did not actually express this sentiment, yet went at least so far as to adopt and to vindicate the warning conveyed by Marlborough at the close of his speech. The amendment called for the insertion of a special clause in the Address declaring that, in the opinion of the House, 'no peace could be safe or honourable to Great Britain or Europe if Spain and the West Indies were allotted to any branch of the House of Bourbon.' This was of course an amendment hostile to the Ministry and it was carried on a division by a majority of sixty-two against fifty-four.

The Government, however, did not think it judicious to treat the amendment as one of hostile intention. This was merely a question of parliamentary tactics, and as the Government were not by any means prepared to declare that further annexations by the House of Bourbon would not be fraught with danger to the liberties of Great Britain and of Europe in general, there seemed no unavoidable necessity for the advisers of the Queen to treat the amendment as anything other than a reasonable, or at all events harmless, addition to the text of the Address. The clause was therefore inserted without any further division, and the trouble was over, for the time, in the House of Lords.

The Queen's Ministers were strong and safe in the House of Commons. There, too, an amendment was moved declaring that no peace could be lasting which allowed Spain and the West Indies to become part of the dominion of the House of Bourbon. The amendment proposed in the Commons was made additionally emphatic by words which declared that a peace established on such terms 'might endanger the safety of her Majesty's person and Government, the Protestant Succession in the House of Hanover, and the liberty of Europe.' This amendment, when pressed to a division, was rejected by a majority of 232 against 106. The Government made up their minds to secure their position in the House of Lords by a bold and unusual step—the creation of twelve new peers. Such a course is unquestionably within the power of the Crown. In more recent times the threat that the power would, if necessary, be called into actual exercise, has on more than one memorable occasion been found enough to overcome the intended resistance of the House of Lords, and to compel the Peers to submit to the will of the Sovereign and the majority, without subjecting themselves to the intrusion at one moment of several new and unwelcome members.

The advisers of Queen Anne carried out their purpose without waiting to give to the Lords any choice of action. Twelve new peers were at once added to the numbers of the hereditary chamber. So open and obvious was the purpose of this creation, that three or four of the new peers were the eldest sons of noblemen who themselves sat in the House of Lords, and the sons would in the ordinary course of events succeed to the seats occupied by their fathers. It need hardly be said that the new men thus introduced were the heirs of peers who were known to be devoted followers of the Government. A certain feeling of astonishment, and even a sensation of scandal, was aroused when it was announced that one of the new peers was Sir Samuel Masham, the husband of the Queen's latest favourite. Two of the new men were distinguished lawyers who might in any case have been regarded as likely to obtain the reward of a peerage, and several others were fairly well entitled to such an elevation. But of course the obvious meaning of the whole arrangement was to bring at once into the House of Lords a number of steady Tories, who could be relied upon to follow the Ministers faithfully in whatever course it was their pleasure to take. An amusing story which has found its way into accepted record tells that when the new peers took their seats in the House of Lords for the first time, a Whig nobleman scornfully put the question whether the twelve who had thus been simultaneously summoned to attend were prepared to vote separately or through the mouth of their foreman. The whole event has a certain historical value, if only because it shows that the Queen's advisers were determined to have their way, and cared little whether such independent opinion as might then be in existence approved or disapproved of the peremptory action by which they had secured the power to carry out their policy. It was always a relief to the Queen's mind to find herself under strong and resolute guidance, and this time, at least, her own inclinations were entirely on the side of those who could make it clear to her that she was now following her own wishes and theirs without any actual infringement of the authority which was given to her by the constitution.

The crushing blow soon came. The Queen wrote a letter to Marlborough with her own hand, in which she announced to him his dismissal from all his public appointments. She informed him that accusations had been made against him to the effect that he had actually taken perquisites himself from a Jewish contractor who had entered into an engagement to supply the army with bread, and that the moneys received by Marlborough in this manner had

amounted, during the past few years, to a sum of
more than sixty thousand pounds. The Queen also
told him that he had been charged with deducting
two and a half per cent. from the pay which the
Sovereign allowed to her foreign soldiers, and that
this latter acquisition amounted during the same
time to a sum not far short of two hundred thousand
pounds. Marlborough sent to the Queen a reply
which certainly bore in it a complete vindication of
his conduct according to the recognised principles of
his position and his office at the time. He declared
that he had received the moneys in accordance with
all the precedents and practices accepted by other
men who held command like his, and that in any
case the money had never been employed for his
private use, but had been expended for the purpose
of obtaining secret intelligence about the movements
of the enemy, and for other objects which were
recognised as part of the regular and permissible
business of warfare.   Nothing could be more positive
than his declaration that no part of the sums thus
received had gone into his own purse, or had been
expended in any manner directly or indirectly for his
own personal interest.

The charges which the Queen embodied in her
letter to Marlborough were founded on the report of
a commission appointed to inquire into and report
upon the state of the public accounts. This report
was published in January 1712. Marlborough was
then at The Hague and he despatched at once to the
commissioners a formal statement of his case—of his

defence, as it may well be called.   His letter contains
the frank admission that certain sums were received
by the Commander-in-Chief, but he declared that it
had been the recognised privilege of the British generals commanding in the Low Countries, both before
the Revolution and since, to accept such allowances,
and he assured the commissioners at the same time in
the most earnest manner ' that whatever sums I have
received on that account have constantly been
applied to the service of the public, in keeping secret
correspondence and getting intelligence of the enemy's
notions and designs.'   So far as we can now judge
of impartial public opinion at that time, it would
certainly seem that such impartial public opinion
as there was gave a cordial acceptance to Marlborough's explanation.   Marlborough had followed
precedents which we must now all regard as decidedly
objectionable, but he had only followed precedents,
and had devised no evil practices of his own.

That a man holding the position of Commander-
in-Chief should receive any allowances or perquisites
whatever from the contractors who supplied his army
with stores, or should be allowed to make any deduc-
tions from the rate of payment authorised by the
Sovereign for the maintenance of foreign mercenaries,
appears to us now an utterly unjustifiable and mon-
strous practice.   But when Marlborough asserted that
such had been the recognised practice for men in
his position, both before and since the Revolution,
there does not appear to have been any indignant
denial on the part of those who must have been well

qualified to speak as to the accuracy of his assertions. The word of the great soldier may fairly be believed when he declared that the money which had thus come into his hands had been applied by him for purposes which he considered to be advantageous to the national cause, and had not been pocketed by him as bribes, and spent for his own personal advantage. Marlborough had undoubtedly acquired a reputation for avarice and love of gain, and his wife was generally believed to have always kept a steady eye on any chances of personal acquisition. Such suspicions as these, however, were prevalent and common when Marlborough was at the height of his favour with Sovereign and public, but they had never before taken the shape of direct and odious charges amounting to personal corruption and peculation of State money. Marlborough's enemies had now no thought of considering calmly the charges made against him. His ruin was determined on, and the chief anxiety of those who were leagued against him was lest the Queen might be induced to delay her action, and in the meantime some revulsion of feeling in the public mind, as the whole story became known, might come to the help of the great soldier, and insist that he must at least have a fair and open trial. The charges made against him by the report of the commission were welcomed by the men in power, because they gave what seemed to be a reasonable excuse for a decision which had already been determined on. The doom was then proclaimed.

Thus the great career of Marlborough came to an end. He withdrew from public life altogether, and remained but for a short time in England. The death of his old friend and companion Godolphin, the statesman who had managed with skill and success the financial arrangements necessary for the opening campaigns of the great war, occurred a few months after Marlborough's fall. Godolphin died at Marlborough's own house, near St. Albans, on September 15, 1712. This melancholy event, this passing away of the colleague who had worked with him in the spring-time of his fame, must no doubt have made life in England more and more distasteful to Marlborough, and it would have been trying enough in any case to such a man, who never professed to be of a philosophic turn, to endure an existence of inactivity and something like obscurity at home. He went abroad, and did not return to England until the accession of George the First opened for him a welcome and a restoration of the honours and dignities which had been so suddenly taken from him.

At this time of day when we can survey the whole career of the man with minds free from political partiality we may safely come to the conclusion that he was not guilty of the worst and most ignoble charges urged against him by his political enemies. He may be freely acquitted of the charges of peculation and embezzlement which were put forward as the cause of his disgrace. Some of the financial arrangements which were imputed as crimes to him would hardly be regarded in our days as justifiable transactions on the part of an English Commander-in-Chief, but it must be remembered that many acts which were not considered irregularities in those days would be set down as irregular and intolerable in a time like the present. This fact of course would not justify or excuse some of the acts which Marlborough was accused of having committed, for if they had been matters of common occurrence in the business of a Commander-in-Chief, they could not possibly have been turned, at a moment's notice, into actual crimes even by the most audacious and unscrupulous of political enemies. Some of the acts charged against Marlborough were undoubtedly offences against the civil and moral code of that time as well as against the civil and moral code of our own day. But these are the charges of which Marlborough declared himself to be absolutely innocent, with regard to which he gave substantial proofs of his innocence, and about which even at the time his enemies were unable to discredit his testimony. The worst allegations that were made against him seem to have been made but as an afterthought and in the hope of finding justification for a step which those who had had too much of him were already, and in any case, determined to take.

The judgment of history must be that, whatever Marlborough's faults, he was treated by his country with ingratitude. He had served England on the battlefield as she has seldom been served before or since, and his name must ever rank with the names of the greatest commanders in history. When we think of his want of political principle we must always bear in mind that the political principles of that time were in a curiously fluid and unsettled state; that the Queen on her throne saw herself sometimes compelled to act as the agent of systems and opinions with which in her heart she had no sympathy; that the cause of the Stuarts found embattled advocates on British soil more than once after Queen Anne had passed away. Marlborough was only like some other men high in office and in power when he was found in confidential communication, now and then, with the representatives of that which was not even yet believed to be a cause wholly lost and a dynasty dethroned for ever. He was an ambitious man, in many ways a selfish man, and he never proclaimed any exalted standard of public or private morality. But there is no reason whatever to doubt that while he was engaged in the work for which his genius so splendidly qualified him, he had in his mind and at his heart, above all other objects, the success of the State and of the cause which he represented on the field of battle.

Whatever judgment may be formed as to the value of the peace which was brought about by Marlborough's political enemies, there can be no question that he was absolutely sincere in his conviction that such a peace would not prove to be worth the price which his country would have to pay for it. Were he entirely in the wrong and they entirely in the right on this question, the judgment of history on Marlborough's personal integrity of purpose must remain absolutely unaltered. It is easy to understand that a constitutional Sovereign might have seen some danger to the Crown and to the State in the popularity of such a man, and in the possibility of his becoming a sort of military dictator. But no consideration of this kind can affect the verdict of history as to the course which was taken to bring about the ruin of Marlborough, and the policy which was adopted in order to give that course a semblance of justification. The story of Marlborough's fall forms the darkest chapter in the record of Queen Anne's reign.

CHAPTER XXVII

EUROPE RECONSTRUCTED—ON PAPER

THE conferences to arrange the terms of peace opened at Utrecht on January 29, 1712. There was much difficulty found by the English Government in prevailing on their allies to enter into the conferences, and the new German Emperor held obstinately out for a long time against any proposals for a peaceful settlement. Charles, the new Emperor, on behalf of whom as claimant of the Spanish throne the Allies had begun the war, was for holding out to the bitter end, and fighting the French as long as the fight could be kept up. Since his accession to the Imperial throne he had ceased to be a candidate for the crown of Spain, but he seems to have thought that he was badly treated by his allies when they began to enter into negotiations without him, and in point of fact he did endeavour for a while to maintain the war on his own account, and out of his own resources. He soon found, however, that the task was beyond his strength, and the fact that those who had been his allies were already coming to terms with France made his efforts seem hopeless even to himself. Charles made a peace of his own with the King of France, but the whole story may now be told as one historical narrative, and the event which the world remembers is the settlement come to at Utrecht, and not the separate, or as it might be called collateral, arrangement agreed to between the King of France and the German Emperor.

The conferences at Utrecht went to work composedly and complacently to reconstruct the scheme of the European Continent. In those days a conference of diplomatists, representing sovereign States, assembled to consider the terms of peace after a long war, was not likely to trouble itself much with the interests and sentiments of the various populations concerned in the arrangement. The business with which diplomatists had to occupy themselves was only the adjustment of some terms of compromise which the Sovereigns who were represented in the council chamber could be prevailed upon to accept. It was to be a give-and-take work altogether so far as these Sovereigns were concerned, and if they could see their way to an agreement, it did not enter into the minds of diplomatists that anybody else could have right, or inclination, or opportunity to interfere. The modern doctrine of nationalities had not yet come to be a recognised force in political affairs. Much of the history of Europe since the Middle Ages is recorded distinctly enough in the annals of these various conferences, congresses, and other such settlements. It is not to be understood that the congresses and conferences really settled anything in a true and lasting sense. As diplomacy then conducted its business there was no genuine basis sought for such a settlement, nor did the diplomatists even suspect that such a basis could be found. The story of the successive congresses and conferences becomes a record of European history because it shows how, step by step, or blunder after blunder, the statesmen of Europe came nearer and nearer to the only true and real conditions by virtue of which a lasting peace could be obtained.

The conferences at Utrecht had to deal with the affairs of England, France, Germany, Holland, Spain, and Portugal, and many other States, directly and immediately; and indirectly with the affairs of other States which were not represented in the diplomatic council chamber. But there does not seem the slightest reason to suppose that the diplomatists at Utrecht ever thought of asking themselves whether this or that proposed arrangement would be likely to obtain any hold over the populations of the States to which it was to apply. There was, for instance, no other idea with regard to Italy than the idea that it was a country to be divided up amongst various native or foreign rulers, a part given to reward this one and a part given to buy over or to buy off that other. It was no more thought likely that the populations of these various allotments might raise any objection to the new arrangements than it would be thought likely now that the cattle and sheep on a farm about to be sold would have any reason or any inclination to object to the occupancy of the new purchaser. The family compacts, the private arrangements between certain reigning families on the European Continent which followed, and in a certain sense came out of the Utrecht settlement, were not in themselves more thoroughly narrow-minded and worthless than the arrangements seriously discussed and solemnly ratified by the negotiators who came to represent England, France, Germany, and the other States concerned in those councils which gave another attribute of celebrity to the old Dutch city.

The Congress of Vienna seems to us now a very antiquated and ineffective piece of machinery. But an entirely new stage of political development had been accomplished in Europe between its time and that of the Utrecht conferences. At the Congress of Vienna evidence had been given that at least there were statesmen who saw that the interests and the wishes of populations would have to be considered thenceforward, as well as the inclinations and the interests of sovereign rulers. No such idea had made its way into the mind of European diplomacy at the time of the Utrecht sittings. The French Revolution intervened between the two eras of diplomacy, and although the Congress of Vienna was called together to reconstruct Europe after what seemed to be the collapse of the Revolution, yet the main principles which that Revolution had asserted found at least some recognition in the minds of diplomatists whose business it was to take part in the work of reconstitution. The conferences at Utrecht had no occasion to trouble themselves about the sovereignty of peoples, or the right of nations to choose their own rulers, or the difficulties of founding any lasting system of government in a country which had never been allowed an opportunity of taking any part in the choice or in the working of its constitution.

The conferences dragged on for a long time. Much of the delay was caused by the difficulty of inducing some of the Allies to enter cordially into any plan of settlement, and even in the case of those who did enter into such a plan the difficulty of prevailing upon them to recognise any but their own interests. The general result was that what may be described as a series of separate arrangements was entered into between France on the one side and the States of the late Alliance on the other. The Treaty was finally signed at the Congress on April 11, 1713, by the representatives of Great Britain and of her allies, except the Emperor, and by the representatives of the King of France. Perhaps the most conspicuous feature of the treaty was that part of it which established the grandson of King Louis on the throne of Spain with the title of Philip the Fifth. The war had been undertaken by Great Britain and her allies to prevent a Prince of the House of Bourbon from becoming King of Spain, and now the Treaty of Utrecht declared that the Prince of the House of Bourbon was to be King of Spain. Thus far the victory distinctly remained with France and Louis the Fourteenth. England, however, had her compensating advantages. France fully acknowledged the order of English sovereignty established by the Act of Succession. This article of the Treaty dis-

tinctly proclaimed the acknowledgment by France
of the succession 'of the most Serene Princess Sophia
and her heirs in the Protestant line of Hanover.'
The words of the Treaty were explicit and almost
effusive on this point. His Most Christian Majesty
'recognised sincerely and solemnly the said succession to the Kingdom of Great Britain and pledged
to this recognition his faith and his word as a king,
as well for himself as for his heirs and successors.'

But King Louis had to go still farther in his
accommodation with England. He promised for
himself and his heirs and successors that every care
should be taken to prevent the person who during
the lifetime of King James the Second had taken the
title of Prince of Wales, and on the death of King
James had taken the title of King of Great Britain,
and who had more lately gone 'voluntarily' out of
France to live elsewhere, from ever returning into
any of the provinces of that kingdom at any
possible time or under any possible pretext. King
Louis must have felt that there was some humiliation
in all this part of the agreement to set off against the
triumph accorded to him by that other part which
acknowledged his grandson as King of Spain. The
delicate diplomatic phraseology which described the
Stuart claimant as having voluntarily taken himself
out of France could not have much power to deceive
even Frenchmen as to the pressure which had been
brought to bear upon their Sovereign to hasten his
honoured guest's departure. King Louis had recognised the descendant of the Stuarts as King of England

in the most solemn and ostentatious form; he had
allowed the exiled Prince to keep up a royal court
in France; and it was only after years of warfare,
and when Marlborough's forward movements seemed
destined to threaten Paris itself, that King Louis
found it necessary to suggest to the exiled Stuart the
expediency of his voluntarily seeking a home out of
France.

The treaty contained a stipulation that the
sovereignty of France and of Spain should never
be united in the same person. Such a stipulation
must have seemed even to Harley and Bolingbroke
absolutely necessary in order to make the treaty
acceptable to the people of England, who had made
such sacrifices for the proclaimed purpose of preventing France from annexing Spain to her dominions.
But this clause in the treaty had very little substantial value in itself. A Bourbon Prince was now set
upon the throne of Spain, and it is quite easy to
understand that before many generations had passed
a descendant of that Prince might, in the natural
order of things, succeed to the inheritance of the
throne of France. If the French people and the
Spanish people were satisfied, it does not seem very
likely that a new generation of Englishmen or of
Austrians or of Dutchmen, would have combined to
undertake another tremendous war for the settlement
or unsettlement of a foreign succession. Some such
condition had to be made in order to satisfy political and diplomatic exigencies, and Louis probably
found little difficulty in accepting an agreement

which was not likely to interfere with the European conditions of his time.

The territories which bore the name of Hudson's Bay and had been occupied by the French were to be restored to England, with the stipulation that all French subjects who had settled there were to be permitted to leave the territory and take with them whatever property they desired to remove. Nova Scotia, St. Christopher, and the neighbouring regions outside the border of Canada were yielded to England, and by this means the Sovereign of Great Britain obtained undisputed right over a vast extent of territory. The treaty also contained a stipulation that the French occupants of Canada should not interfere with or endeavour to expel or molest in any way those tribes of Indians known as 'The Five Nations,' who were understood to have attached themselves to the friendly protection of England, or any other tribes that should in future seek shelter under the strength of an alliance with their English neighbours. The French reserved the right to fish within certain limits along the shores of the Hudson's Bay and Nova Scotia territory. France agreed to demolish the fortifications and to fill up the harbour of Dunkirk, which the English Government at that time appear to have looked upon as a standing menace to British trading interests. This particular stipulation was not carried out, and the English statesmen would seem before long to have forgotten all about it. England was to retain possession of Gibraltar and Minorca, and Minorca was fought for, taken, and retaken several times in succeeding years, and was finally given up to Spain at the Peace of Amiens in 1802.   Gibraltar, it need hardly be said, is still under the flag of England, and although during a later reign there was a certain inclination on the part of the English Sovereign to restore the Rock and the Fortress to Spain, that inclination soon passed away, and nothing seems farther from the mind of English statesmanship and the English people to-day than any thought of handing back to Spain that Mediterranean stronghold which was so suddenly and surprisingly won for Queen Anne during the War of the Spanish Succession.   Spain can hardly be said to have gained anything by the Treaty of Utrecht, while she lost all her possessions in Italy and in the Netherlands.   Prussia gained by the treaty the formal acknowledgment of her position as a kingdom, and from that time she may be said to have set up as a rival to Austria for ascendency over the Germanic States.

Italy was parcelled out to satisfy the claims and purchase the compromise of princes who had taken a part in the war.   Milan and the kingdom of Naples were given to Austria, and Sicily was handed over to the Duke of Savoy.   The King of Sicily found means some five years after to exchange his island with Spain for Sardinia—exchanges of territory were also made in those days without much inquiry as to the inclinations of the inhabitants. The Sovereign who had been Duke of Savoy before the Treaty of Utrecht, thus became King of Sardinia,

and his successors maintained that kingdom down
to the days, within the recollection of living men,
when the Kings of Sardinia developed into Kings of
Italy. The Elector of Bavaria, who had taken sides
with France, was restored to his dominions, and the
Elector of Hanover was recognised in his rights as a
ruling prince. The region known as the territory of
Orange passed over by process of peaceful exchange
into the ownership of France. On the death of
William the Third the territory of Orange went by
inheritance to the childless King's sister, who had
married the Prince now recognised as the first King
of Prussia. This little territory was entirely surrounded by France, and it seemed much more convenient to the great States concerned in the Treaty of
Utrecht that it should be formally consigned to the
sovereignty of King Louis.

There is something curiously interesting in the
history of this principality, so completely a part of
France, and now so completely identified with France
in the minds of the numberless travellers from all
parts of the world who visit the picturesque regions
in the neighbourhood of Avignon. The principality
had come by inheritance to one of the Nassau family,
and through him gave a title to the successive heirs of
that line. Then, by the chance which we have mentioned, the principality passed over to a Prussian
owner. The exchange which was made by the Treaty
of Utrecht was the most advantageous for all the
States concerned in the engagement, and it now remains only one of the curiosities of history that an

internal part of French territory should at one time have been owned by the princes of Nassau, have given a descriptive name to William the Third of England, and have afterwards become the inheritance of a king of Prussia.

One of the arrangements which belonged to the Treaty of Utrecht has a peculiar significance for English readers, and recalls some entirely painful and humiliating recollections. Nothing could set off in more startling contrast the difference between some of the conditions of civilisation at the time of Queen Anne's rule and those which prevail in England and almost everywhere else in our own days, than the agreement which was entered into at Utrecht between Great Britain and Spain, the agreement which bore as its title the Spanish word Assiento. History has kept up the name of this memorable and disreputable agreement to the present hour. The Assiento was simply an agreement or assent between England and Spain that England should have the privilege or the monopoly of supplying negro slaves to the Spanish colonies on the western side of the Atlantic. This was regarded at the time by English statesmen as a privilege England was well entitled to ask and to receive, and concerning which there could be no possible question of honour, decency, or morality. It was regarded as the most natural thing in the world that a country like England which had large merchant fleets should secure for herself a good trade in the capture and sale of negro slaves, and a monopoly in the traffic with any State which had need of such cargoes and was not so well provided with the means of obtaining the desired live stock. The Spanish colonists on American soil were greatly in need of cheap labour to carry on their work for them, and the cheapest and best labour, according to the views of the time, was to be found in negroes captured on African soil and carried off to the country where their daily toil could be made most useful to their owners. That a negro should be captured and sold into perpetual slavery, a slavery for himself and his children, seemed to the civilised world in the days of Queen Anne, and down to a much later time, about as natural and as unobjectionable a proceeding as the capture and the sale of wild cattle. Some of the most enlightened statesmen of England and France at the time when the Treaty of Utrecht was made must have been as humane, according to their own code of humanity and standard of education, as any of those who in a later age applauded the thrilling words of Brougham when he denounced 'the wild and guilty phantasy' that man can have property in man. But even among professed teachers of religion in the days of Queen Anne the doctrines of Christianity had not yet struck their roots so deeply down in the human heart as to make the recognition of man's right to an inheritance of freedom a commonly accepted principle of conscience.

The conditions of the Assiento were at first embodied in a treaty which had been in operation between France and Spain, but at the Peace of

Utrecht it was arranged that England should have the benefit of the agreement. England was to have by this stipulation the privilege of importing 4,800 negro slaves into the Spanish colonies of America within thirty years. The terms of the contract, which were the same as those embodied in the agreement between France and Spain, set forth precisely the kind of negro slave to be imported into the Spanish colonies, prescribed that slaves of both sexes were to be imported, defined the limits of age within which the living property was to be captured and sold, and in every possible way made the terms of the bargain quite clear. The Assiento gave a new and vigorous impulse to the slave trade, and it has bequeathed to England the melancholy fame of having been the principal instrument in setting up the system of slavery throughout the North American colonies. It may be added that this ill-omened contract had, as one of its indirect consequences, the effect of helping to create and float that South Sea Company, or rather that strange development of the company which was known as the South Sea Bubble, and was the cause of a tremendous commercial convulsion in the succeeding reign.

The Dutch obtained, as the result of the part they had taken in the war, a certain rectification of their frontier lines, and the possession of some towns and fortresses the ownership of which appeared to confer on them a guarantee against French encroachment in the future. This was not perhaps very much of a

gain to Holland after all the risks she had undergone
and the sacrifices she had been compelled to make.
It does not even seem quite clear that the new
arrangement would have been much of a security
to Holland if, in the course of time, any of her
powerful neighbours had thought it advisable to
undertake an invasion of her territory. But there
was nothing else to be done when the negotiations
for peace were on the way to settlement, for it was
certain that England would not undertake further
risks and make fresh sacrifices for the sake of satisfying her Dutch ally. The Dutch had to be content
with what they could get, and the result of their
alliance with two of the great European Powers
had probably, although indirectly, some influence
in the promotion of Holland's subsequent prosperity.
The Dutch seem to have learned the lesson by the
war that a small State is not likely to gain much
benefit from a military alliance with great neighbours,
and had therefore better keep as far as possible
out of all kind of warlike adventure. Since the
Peace of Utrecht, Holland has for the most part
confined herself to looking after her own interests,
and has become a peaceful educated and prosperous
state. Perhaps, too, it may well be asserted that
the fighting capacity which the Dutch had shown,
as well in the War of the Succession as in their
own great struggle for independence, would be
likely to discourage even very powerful neighbours
from a policy of adventurous invasion, and would
prove a better security for the small State than the

possession of the fortress towns or the rectification of the frontier.

English statesmanship underwent severe and just reproach for one part of its policy in the settlement of the treaty. This was the part which is commonly and very fairly described as the abandonment of the Catalans. The Catalans, the population inhabiting certain regions of Catalonia, had cordially adopted the cause represented by the Archduke Charles. They were, indeed, the only Spanish population who had actively demonstrated their sympathy with that cause, and had sacrificed brave lives in its support. While the negotiations for peace were still going on the Catalans were in arms on the battlefield, and were naturally counting on the support of the Allies who had set up the Archduke Charles as the Sovereign of Spain. It might well have been assumed that when the arrangements for peace began to take definite shape the English statesmen would insist on enforcing some stipulation for the immunity and protection of the brave Spaniards who had fought side by side with them, and who without their help must now be left to the mercy of Spain's Bourbon Sovereign. There was still a British force in Spain while the arrangements for peace were drawing towards a close, and the Catalans must have expected that some measures would be taken by England to secure them against being treated as mere rebels by the incoming ruler of Spain. The English statesmen, however, did nothing of the kind, but left the Catalans without any pledge or guarantee whatever

to the mercy of their new ruler. We may anticipate
the progress of history for a little in order to say
that, after the Treaty of Utrecht had become an
accomplished fact, the desertion of the Catalans
was made a subject of discussion in the House
of Lords. Lord Wharton and Lord Sunderland
raised the question there, and contended that
' the Crown of Great Britain, having drawn in the
Catalans to declare for the House of Austria, and
engaged to support them, those engagements ought
to have been made good' by some arrangement
in the treaty securing the Catalans against any
harm.

The defence of the Government was undertaken
by Bolingbroke, who assured the House that the
Queen had used all her endeavours to secure for
the Catalans the enjoyment of their ancient liberties
and privileges. But he contended that the engagements into which the Queen had entered could
hold for no longer a time than while the Archduke
Charles was still in Spain, and that as the Archduke,
who had since risen to the imperial dignity, had
himself taken no steps to maintain the rights of
the Catalans, the Queen was not in a position to do
anything more than make use of her good offices on
their behalf. Such a defence as this could hardly
have imposed upon anyone who took the slightest
interest in the safety of the Catalans, or who had
any just perception of the degree to which the honour
of England was involved in their defence. The
House of Lords presented an address to the Queen

on the subject, and the Queen assured them in reply that, ' at the time she concluded her peace with Spain, she resolved to continue her interpositions, upon every occasion for obtaining these liberties, and to prevent, if possible, the misfortunes to which that people were exposed by the conduct of those more nearly concerned to help them.'

The further interpositions, if any such ever were made, do not seem to have been pressed forward in a manner likely to bring about the results which the Queen declared she had in mind. The Catalans, in fact, were left to their fate, and it is recorded in history that the Queen's promise of protection was hung on the high altar of the Cathedral in Barcelona, as a solemn protest against the worthlessness of the engagement into which England had professed to enter on behalf of the Catalan population. When the new King of Spain assumed his throne the Catalans were regarded by him as rebels in arms against his authority. They were called upon to surrender, but they utterly refused to yield, and made up their minds to resist so long as resistance should be possible. They defended Barcelona with splendid bravery, and might have defended it effectively if the new King had had none but his own forces with which to subdue his rebels. The King, however, was able to obtain the help of French troops under the command of Marshal Berwick, and although the Catalans held out for a long time, yet the city was stormed and taken in the end, and no interposition on England's part took

place to prevent this grim and tragic settlement of
the Catalan question.   We are now anticipating by a
little the course of history, for the resistance of the
Catalans outlasted the reign of Queen Anne, but it is
as well to complete at once this melancholy chapter
in the records of the war.

The peace negotiations included an arrangement
made for a commercial treaty between England
and France.   The whole of the Utrecht negotiations
were, to a great extent, the work of Bolingbroke's
inspiration, and the commercial treaty with France
was almost exclusively his project.   The fame of
Bolingbroke is not usually associated with the
business of commerce, and it does not appear that
at any previous part of his life the great orator,
writer, and man of pleasure had given any particular
attention to the study of commercial questions or
of political economy.   But he suddenly became filled
with a desire to establish an improved system of
international relations between England and France
in their commercial dealings, and he undoubtedly anticipated that policy of Free Trade which no English
Government ever thoroughly adopted until Sir Robert
Peel had become a great Prime Minister and a convert to Free-Trade principles.   The main purpose of
Bolingbroke's treaty was to declare that for the
future the trade and commerce of England and
France were to be placed on a footing of equality as
regarded customs and tariffs, and that each nation
was to be dealt with by the other on the same terms
as those accorded by each to the foreign State up to

that time most highly favoured.   In other words, the lowest duty which the financial administration of either country found it necessary to impose on imports coming from any foreign State was to be applied to English goods entering France and French goods entering England.

Bolingbroke's ideas on the subject of Free Trade were entirely in advance of the economic doctrines and the views on trade interest which prevailed at his time, and the announcement that such a commercial treaty had been made at Utrecht and ratified by the Queen's Government created positive consternation among the commercial and trading classes in England. An outcry was raised that the very existence of English manufacture was threatened by the adoption of a policy which would throw this kingdom open to the competition of all its manufacturing rivals in France.   Bishop Burnet describes the sensation which was created among the trading classes by the provisions in the treaty for removing the prohibitions and high duties imposed at that time on the productions of France.   'The traders in the city of London and those in all the other parts of England were alarmed,' he tells us, 'with the great prejudice this would bring on the whole nation.   The Turkey Company, those that traded to Portugal and Italy, and all who were concerned in the woollen and silk manufactures, appeared before both Houses and set forth the great mischief, that a commerce with France, on the foot of the treaty, would bring upon the nation; while none appeared on the other side, to answer their arguments, or to set forth the advantage of such a commerce.'

Burnet regards it as evident that none of the trading bodies had ever been consulted on the subject, while he adds that the Commissioners for Trade and Plantations had had the project laid before them by the orders of the Government and they were invited to make their remarks on it. Then Bishop Burnet proceeds to discourse on what was one of the minor political scandals of the day—the manner in which the project had been brought under the notice of Bolingbroke and adopted by him as his own. Burnet's version of the story is that 'Arthur Moor, who had risen up, from being a footman without any education, to be a great dealer in trade, and was the person of that board in whom the lord treasurer confided most, moved that they might first read it everyone apart, and then debate it; and he desired to have the first perusal; so he took it away, and never brought it back to them, but gave it to the Lord Bolingbroke, who carried it to Paris, and there it was settled.' Arthur Moor was a man whose position and dealings created much talk at that time, and who was commonly accredited with having been the instructor of Bolingbroke in all that he knew about questions of trade and commerce. It is quite true, as Bishop Burnet tells us, that Arthur Moor—whose name is spelt by some writers as Moore—was originally a footman, and had little or no education to start with. But he appears to have been a man of great ability and a special capacity for making use of

any opportunities of acquiring knowledge or exerting
influence which might come in his way. The very
fact that he was able to become the teacher and the
guide of Bolingbroke, even on one great question of
public policy, is proof enough that he must have
had intelligence and force of character quite out of
the common order. There appears to be a general
agreement among writers who have commented on
the character of Arthur Moor that he was sordid and
grasping by nature, and that he would have recoiled
from no undertaking which promised to bring him
pecuniary advantage. On subjects of trade and commerce he became for a time Bolingbroke's constant
adviser.

Mr. Macknight, in his Life of Bolingbroke, says
it was under Moor's 'great encouragement that
Bolingbroke sent out the expedition to Canada ; and
it was Moore who received the order on the Treasury
for the twenty-six thousand pounds, of which twenty
thousand mysteriously disappeared into the pockets
of Lady Masham.' Moor was certainly a better
authority on questions of international trade than on
Canadian expeditions, and the fact that he succeeded
in impressing Bolingbroke with a faith in his advanced views as to political economy is certainly not
to Bolingbroke's discredit. Under Moor's influence
Bolingbroke put the treaty of commerce with France
into shape, and made it a part of the conditions
settled by the Treaty of Utrecht. The commercial
treaty had, however, to obtain the sanction of Parliament in England. Queen Anne retained the sovereign

authority, as it was then understood, to enter into a treaty of peace of her own accord, but she did not claim any such arbitrary power over the arrangements for a treaty of commerce. The Government succeeded so far that the House of Commons was induced by a large majority to pass the vote giving leave for the bringing in of the Bill which embodied the articles of the treaty. But after this the opposition of all the trading interests concerned became too strong for the supporters of the measure. The Whig party was then supposed to be farther advanced in ideas of commercial freedom than the slow and steady Tory party, but most of the Whigs nevertheless opposed the Bill and probably would have been ready to do so in any case, if only because it was an important ministerial measure.

Had Bolingbroke been still in the House of Commons he might have done something by his persuasive eloquence, his gift of argument, and his political tact to obtain new supporters for his Bill, but since his elevation to the House of Lords there was no one in the representative chamber who could do the work which he might have done. Members of the House of Commons knew that a general election was near at hand, and few of them would have liked to face such an ordeal if their votes in the existing Parliament had turned all the manufacturing and trading classes against them. At one important stage in the progress of the measure the Government were defeated by 194 votes against 185. The

majority was small, but it was convincing. Since the
first reading of the Bill the feeling of the House had
been growing steadily against the measure, and it
was felt by the Government that the longer the debate
went on the greater would be the strength of the
opposition. The Bill was therefore abandoned, and
there was an end of the commercial treaty. Harley
was understood to have had no great interest in the
measure, and most assuredly he was not the man to
appreciate advanced ideas on questions of international trade and commerce. The outcry of the
trading interests was that such a treaty would simply
impoverish the Englishman in order to enrich the
Frenchman, and probably such a description of
Bolingbroke's policy would have harmonised well
enough with Harley's views on the general subject of
international trade. Bolingbroke took the loss of his
measure deeply to heart. In his letters to Prior
and others of his friends he deplored the action of
the House of Commons, and through the whole remainder of his career he seems never to have lost his
keen sense of disappointment. The familiar French
proverb which describes the man as unhappy who is
in advance of his age might, in this instance at least,
have applied to Bolingbroke.

Except for this one part of the arrangements, the
Treaty of Utrecht may be said to have passed into
realisation in all its important propositions. It was
signed on the 11th of April, 1713, by the diplomatic
representatives of England and France and of all the
other allies except the German Emperor. There is

not on the whole much serious difference of opinion in history as to the practical wisdom of the part which was played by English statesmanship in the making of the treaty. The motives of the English statesmen who carried the measure to success may well be questioned, and the whole policy which set the war going may easily be assailed and condemned by those who regard, above all things, the interests of the British populations. But when we ask ourselves directly and simply whether, after so many years of war, the English statesmen could do anything better than accept a peace even on such terms, we shall find ourselves compelled to admit that nothing could have been gained for British interests by a further prolongation of the struggle. The true interests of the people of these countries had never been concerned in the war, and every year of the war's continuance only involved them in new and unmeaning sacrifices.

The Treaty of Utrecht brings with it no glory to the English statesmen by whom it was arranged and concluded, but the verdict of history must be that any reasonable terms of peace were better than the further prolongation of such a war. The illustrious composer Handel, who was then settled in England, was invited by Queen Anne to compose a Te Deum and a Jubilate in celebration of the peace, and he complied with the request and received from the Queen a liberal pension as his reward. To most Englishmen the music of Handel

set to such a theme must have seemed a fitting and
noble glorification, but there must have been some
Englishmen, too, in whose ears it sounded like a dirge.
The one great fact was that the War of the Spanish
Succession had come to an end.

CHAPTER XXVIII

THE HUGUENOT REFUGEES

THE continued persecutions by means of which the Sovereign of France hoped to free his country from that which he regarded as religious heresy had a distinct and marked effect upon the history of England's commerce, manufacturing industry, and intellectual development. The Revocation of the Edict of Nantes made life in France all but intolerable to the Huguenots and to others who, like them, had set their hearts on maintaining their own convictions as to religion and religious worship. The study of this period of history gives us another illustration of the evil effects which come from the attempt made by the rulers of any country to suppress by legal penalties individual freedom of faith and thought. France is not the only country which provides us with such examples and illustrations. The history of England herself teaches us many lessons to the same wholesome effect. Religious bigotry, exercised by the ruling powers, has again and again created sectarian and local hatreds which have brought about in their time something like civil war. Now the Protestants, and now the Roman Catholics, are the victims of such intolerance, and are driven by it to the alternative of becoming either refugees or rebels. But we have perhaps in the conditions which came from the Revocation of the Edict of Nantes the most remarkable and the most effective picture in little of the calamities which such a policy of persecution inflicts at last on the country whose rulers have made persecution their policy.

We have seen already in the course of this narrative how the severities practised against the populations of the Cevennes created a new and unexpected danger for France at the time when she most needed national unity to maintain her against her enemies in war. But the uprising of the Camisards was little more than a passing incident in the events of the long struggle between France and the States arrayed in arms against her. The religious persecution her Sovereign carried on was the immediate cause of an emigration which deprived her of the intellectual and industrial services of whole masses of her citizens who could have contributed beyond measure to her national prosperity if only they had been allowed to live at home in peace, and worship their Creator according to the dictates of their own consciences. By a stroke of fate which might have seemed like a dramatic proclamation of censure on such a persecuting policy, the intellect, the industry, and the technical skill which would otherwise have been at the service of France became the means of nourishing and strengthening the power of France's greatest rival,

England.   A perfect flood of emigration set out from
the Huguenot districts of France, and the refugees
found for the most part their new home on English
soil.   The trade, the industry, and the industrial
science of England received new and lasting benefit
from the intelligence, perseverance, and orderly
lives of the new settlers, whom unjust and cruel
legislation had driven from their own homes to find
a settlement and a welcome in English cities and
towns.   The literature of England was improved and
enriched from generation to generation by many of
those who sought on English soil for a relief from
religious persecution.   Even the military service of
England was a gainer in many splendid instances by
the policy which had banished capable and brave
soldiers of French birth from the land of their forefathers.

So far as Louis the Fourteenth was concerned
there was no moral palliation to be found for his
adoption of such a policy.   We can all understand,
even if we cannot excuse, the conduct of the en-
throned fanatic and bigot who firmly believes that
his own form of religion is the only one which
can open the way for man to the higher life here-
after.   A distinguished free-thinking writer of
modern days has declared that he could quite
understand and even sympathise with the policy of
the Inquisition when he regarded that policy from
the Inquisition's own point of view.   The doctrine
of the Inquisition was that man's eternal salvation
depended upon his acceptance of the one true Faith,

and the writer to whom we refer declared that from that point of view any degree of persecution, any number of burnings at the stake, any infliction whatever of temporal sufferings would be warranted by the hope of thus coercing the majority of men into an acceptance of the religious principles which alone could secure their eternal welfare. Many a fanatical ruler who made religious persecution a part of his duty was unquestionably and sincerely animated by that conviction, and for a potentate of that order our free-thinking author would have had some consideration. But even our free-thinking author himself could have found no such excuse for the policy of Louis the Fourteenth. Few men of his time could have had less feeling of religious devotion, less sentiment of any kind which had to do with religious belief, than the Sovereign who revoked the Edict of Nantes. King Louis was a thoroughly unprincipled, selfish, and frivolous profligate who cared only for his own ambition, his own pleasures, his own likings, his own hatreds, and nothing that we read in the records of his life suggests that he was ever inspired by any feeling of genuine religious fanaticism.

The emigration from France went on increasing day after day, and before long an entire population of French refugees had settled in England. Many fugitives from France for the same cause found their way into other countries, and wherever they made a new home for themselves they won an honourable reputation for energy, intelligence, good conduct,

and success.   Up to the present day, we can see
that in the various parts of the world where the
French refugees sought a settlement they have proved
to be meritorious and valuable members of the community.   England, however, was for the most part
the chosen home of the refugees, and their coming
may be said to have opened a new and distinct
chapter in the industrial and intellectual progress of
the country.   Schomberg, one of William the Third's
famous generals, belonged to a family of Germans
who had come under the dominion of the French
Crown when the Alsatian provinces were made by
annexation a part of France.   When the Edict of
Nantes was revoked, the Schombergs became refugees
and found a home in England.   The head of the
family, Frederick Schomberg, took service under
King William, was by him created a duke in the
English peerage and rewarded for his services by
liberal grants of money.   Schomberg was killed in
Ireland at the battle of the Boyne.

John Hill Burton, in his History of the Reign of
Queen Anne, points with especial attention to the
service rendered to English literature and to the
story of England's progress by Rapin de Thoyras,
who is known to fame as the historian Rapin.   'He
belonged'—we quote the words of Burton—'to a
family of the original Huguenot stock ; and he was
twenty-eight years old when the Revolution of 1688
brought him to the conclusion that the sure place
of refuge and comfort for one of his nature and
opinions was Britain.   He served under his country-

man De Rouvigny, whom we know better as Lord
Galway, and was wounded in the Irish war. Conscious of the freedom enjoyed in the country of his
adoption, he studied its laws and constitution, and it
dawned and gradually strengthened on him that he
should trace to its origin the national progress that
had developed itself in the English constitution. He
was a close observer of the existing working of the
constitution, and gave a signal rebuke to the common
opinion that no foreigner can understand it, in a
thoroughly instructive commentary on the political
divisions such as he found them during his abode in
Britain.'

This first study of Rapin's was 'A Dissertation of the rise, progress, views, strength, interests,
and characters of the two Parties of the Whigs and
Tories.' Rapin had greater work in his mind than
any mere essay on political parties, however keenly
studied and carefully explained. Burton observes
that 'With the singleness of purpose necessary to
the accomplishment of great discoveries or other intellectual triumphs, he resolved to devote his life to
the task of bringing into light the hidden treasures,
of which he had discovered the external traces
as a geologist believes that iron or coal or copper
will be found in the rocks distributed under his feet.
For such a design the resources of life must in the first
place be secured; these would not come as the immediate fruit of his labour, for that was not available until he had spent seventeen years on his task.
He had some little remnant of the patrimony of an

old respectable family.   Bentinck, Duke of Portland,
King William's favoured minister, countenanced him,
and he managed so to live as to be able to pursue
his great project in freedom.   But one item in his
arrangements showed that he was not endowed with
much more than the bare necessaries of life.   He
found that he could not afford to live in England
until his work was completed.   Hence, having made
collections of such materials as he could only find in
England, he settled himself in Rhenish Prussia for
the completion of his work and his life.'

The English reader is not likely to be free from
a feeling of regret that no means could be found to
enable Rapin to continue his work and his life in the
country which he had hoped to make his home, and
where he had won some distinction in battle before
he had sought renown in books.   When the Edict of
Nantes was revoked, Rapin went in the first instance
to seek refuge in Holland, where he enlisted in a corps
of Huguenot volunteers; made the acquaintance of
William of Nassau; became devoted to him and to
his cause; followed William, then only Prince of
Orange, to England in 1688, and distinguished himself as a soldier at the Boyne and the siege of
Limerick.   The natural course of things would have
been that Rapin should settle down for the remainder
of his life in the country which he had freely chosen
as his home, and should not have been compelled by
the mere necessity of cheap living to complete his
work and his existence in another country.   The
English reader is perhaps inclined to feel a little

ashamed that some means was not found in England
for the historian to conclude his English History
among the people whose national growth and development it was the main work of his life to describe.

Much has been said in later days about the
degrading effect of the patronage system in literature,
and Thackeray made it a proud boast that in modern
days no Englishman of letters would condescend to
accept the bounty of a patron. It is indeed a better
time for literature when the patrons of literary men
are the publishers and the public, but it cannot be
denied that in former days many a work which we
now regard as a perennial treasure of English letters
could never have been completed—could probably
never have been undertaken—but for the help given
by some rich man who had an appreciation of
literary promise. Goethe in one of his writings
records the fact that, if he had been an indigent
young author, he might have had, for the mere sake
of earning a living, to seek popularity by producing
some dramatic piece in the style of Schiller's
'Robbers,' which was then the rage in Germany—
a style which Schiller himself entirely abandoned
when he had created a public willing to welcome
his nobler dramatic efforts. No author now in any
country could desire or could tolerate a revival of
the patronage system if such a restoration were
possible or were needed. But the readers of books
must nevertheless feel some regret that at a time
when the patronage system did exist and flourish in
England, some patron was not found who could have

enabled Rapin to complete his history in an English home.

Rapin made a complete study of such materials as he could get hold of in chronicles and libraries. Foremost among his studies were the works of Holinshed and the Chronicles of Scotland and of Ireland. Of course the works of Holinshed and the various other chronicles from which Rapin had to draw his materials were to a considerable extent made up of fable and romance. Holinshed was, as Burton says, 'essentially the standard historian of the three kingdoms, and his works were popular in England in editions profusely adorned with picturesque woodcuts.' Burton rightfully defends such authors as Holinshed and Boece from the charge that they 'must either have been afflicted with intellectual imperfections or guilty of telling gross falsehoods,' when they reproduced as serious history narratives which clearly belonged to the realms of oral tradition, romance, and fable. But at the same time he does, we think, less than justice to the chroniclers in his anxiety to do full justice to the conscientiousness, the judgment, and the in- tellectual skill of Rapin in extracting the genuine reality from the surrounding mass of legend and fable which the chroniclers gathered together. No praise can be too high for Rapin's penetrating and methodical labour in distinguishing between authentic history and mere legend in the books which alone were to furnish the material for his monumental work. Burton, however, goes on to say—'It may surely be at last pronounced as an established opinion, that absolute fact is the foundation of all history, and that it must come clearly to the surface, and be seen uncorrupted by any element of dubiety, as the foundation whereon any decorative elements, rhetoric or philosophical, may, if they are desirable, be raised.'

Then Burton declares that 'The great merit of Rapin was in his striving to complete a history subject to this condition; and it is almost as touching as the old image of the good man wrestling with the storms of fate, to follow him in the struggles of his task.' Not a word too much can be said in praise of Rapin's purpose and of its result, but we find it hard to believe that Rapin could have worked at his history without any regard for the legends and the fables preserved by the old chroniclers, or could have accepted as his guiding principle that there can be no foundation for history but in matters of ascertained fact. There can hardly be a surer guide to the early history of any people than may be found in the legends and traditions of their ancestors which, in the days before scientific research, were accepted as truthful narratives. The mere fact that such stories were accepted at one period of semi-darkness as an actual account of what had happened in days more distant and yet more dark, supplies the historian with most valuable material for the formation of a judgment as to the earliest growth and development of the race whom he has set himself to describe. We may reject, if we will, the whole

Homeric story as mere legend and fable, but we have none the less to acknowledge that a history of the Hellenic race constructed without any reference to the traditions and beliefs which these poems illustrate would leave us very imperfectly informed as to the growth and character of the people for whom the Parthenon was built and the plays of Sophocles were written. We may feel quite certain that a really capable student of history like Rapin did not fail to take the fullest account of all the traditions and legends preserved by the old chroniclers when he was preparing his History of England. A record of ascertained facts and dates must be indispensable to history but it cannot be history itself.

Burton rightly observes ' It was not until he reached the period of the Saxon Chronicle and the History by the Venerable Bede, that the historian of the British Isles at that time could find his feet on any firm ground.' Burton gives a very interesting account of the chronicles, manuscripts, and libraries which Rapin was able to study in order to make a safe beginning of his great work and bring it to a satisfactory completion. Nearly thirty years of his life were occupied in his task—a life-work indeed in every sense. Rapin brought his book, which he called ' L'Histoire d'Angleterre,' down to the Execution of Charles the First. A continuation, compiled for the most part from notes and unfinished passages left by Rapin, was published by David Durand, which carried the reader on to the death of William the Third. The whole work of course was written in

French, but an English translation was afterwards
brought out by Nicholas Tindal, and Tindal himself
carried on the historical theme until he had brought
it down to the close of George the First's reign.

Rapin's work at once found numerous students
and earnest admirers. It won for itself the high
encomium of Voltaire, to whom we must at least
accord the merit of understanding, as not many other
men have done, the art of writing history. Voltaire's
admiration, we may take it for granted, was not the
less readily given because the author of the book
had been driven into exile to escape from religious
persecution. Perhaps we shall think all the more
highly of Voltaire's appreciation when we remember
that the two historians did not in the least resemble
each other in narrative style. Voltaire wrote history
with a peculiarly light and brilliant touch which
could lend the charm of romance to the driest and
most exact record of mere facts, while Rapin's main
idea was to put his readers in full possession of all
that could be relied upon as authentic record of
England's growth and development. Rapin's work
may certainly be regarded as the first History of
England complete up to its own time, and the
foundation of all the histories following and yet to
follow it which tell to the world the story of the
English people.

It would hardly be possible to overrate the
advantages which the skilled labour of the British
Islands derived from the settlement here of Huguenot
refugees. In those days skilled labour of the better

order was not very common among English mechanics. Such of the Huguenots as were compelled to find a means of living by handiwork of any kind were, for the most part, gifted with a skill and an intelligence which peculiarly adapted them for the crafts that required manual dexterity, a certain refinement of taste, and something like scientific precision. The craft of clockmaking and watchmaking, the construction of ornamental wares, the production of tasteful fabrics—these and similar branches of industry soon began to be recognised as the special occupation of the exiles who were crowding into the poorer and busier quarters of London and other important cities and towns. It began to be observed at the time that however poor and hard-worked these foreign refugees might be, they usually showed a taste and refinement in the decoration of their humble homes which could rarely be seen in the tenements occupied by English mechanics.

The public of England was benefited at the expense of some of the great manufacturing communities in France. Lyons, for instance, which was growing to be the great centre of industry for the production of fabrics made out of silk, was a heavy sufferer from the ill-omened policy which revoked the Edict of Nantes, and saw some of the best of her silk weavers compelled to give up their homes and seek for shelter and for customers in English communities. 'If silk was wrought in England,' Burton says, 'before the refugees came over, it was of a

coarse fabric and trifling in extent, generally for the
casual decoration of other textile fabrics.'   But with
the immigration of the French refugees all manner of
figured silks and satins, silk velvets and brocades,
became familiar to the English purchasers. 'The phe-
nomenon was seen'—we quote from Burton again
—' of the French silkworm's cocoon imported into
England to be worked into a fabric by French
workmen and then exported to France or elsewhere
abroad.'   The refugees also took a leading part in
the invention and adaptation of machinery to do
the work which up to that time had been accomplished altogether by hand.   It need hardly be
said that the mechanism of those comparatively
distant days has long since been superseded by
machinery of an entirely superior and different order,
worked by forces the use and application of which
had not been discovered at the time when the
Huguenot refugees were settling down as occupants
of workshops in England.   But it is quite certain
that in many of our industrial departments, even of
those which have come to be regarded in later days
as distinctively English, the first application of
mechanism to productions formerly wrought by the
human hand is to the credit of the skilled artificers
who were driven from their native country and found
a home in the British Islands.

Many of the refugees, or at least of the descendants of the refugees, who had become accustomed to
English life and English ways, and saw no prospect
or had no longer any wish to separate themselves

from the fortunes of the country which had sheltered them, began to change their French names and adapt themselves to their new home by the substitution of Anglicised translations for their French patronymics. A writer, whom Burton describes as 'a close observer and student of the old and recent history of the French working refugees in London,' tells us that 'the Lemaîtres called themselves Masters; the Le Roys, King; the Tonnelliers, Cooper; the Lejeunes, Young; the Leblancs, White; the Lenoirs, Black; the Loiseaus, Bird.' Not all refugees, however, followed this practice, for we are assured by the same authority that there were many of the Huguenot exiles, and even of the poorest among them, who still held firmly and faithfully to their family names, and that at one time there might be found in London slums and garrets men depending for their daily bread on the least remunerative of handicrafts who still bore names which had once held high distinction in the history of France. Indeed, if we come down to a much later period we may find in literature, in science, in art, in law, in commerce, in politics, in the army and navy, the names of men who have won distinction for themselves, and whose names, still carefully preserved and not transformed by any Anglicising process, proclaim that their bearers belong to some of the Huguenot families whom religious persecution had driven from France. But whether the names remained unchanged and were French to the last, or grew slightly modified in the course of generations, or became translated for popular convenience into genuine English, the descendants of the expatriated Huguenots were always known in England as intelligent, valuable, and, in some cases, most distinguished citizens of the country in which they had found a home and a welcome.

In later days some of the most eminent men who devoted their lives and their abilities to the cause of advancement and progress in every department of English life—philanthropists, reformers, leaders in every movement for the welfare of humanity—were the descendants of the Huguenot exiles. To mention only one instance out of many that could be given, we may refer to Sir Samuel Romilly, a man who rendered inestimable service to the mitigation and the reform of the criminal code, to the abolition of slavery, and to every great educational work for the benefit of the poor and the lowly, the son or grandson of a Huguenot watchmaker whose ancestor had settled as a skilled workman in London. In literature and thought it is only necessary to give the name of Harriet Martineau and of her brother James Martineau. The policy of Louis the Fourteenth had conferred almost as much benefit on the country of his most powerful enemy as it had brought injury upon his own.

We must not, however, seem to give countenance to any idea that France was the only offender in those days, or ever since, against the great moral principle of liberty of conscience. Every other country in Europe had sinned, or was sinning, or was about to sin against the same principle. The policy of rulers and States in those days, and even in later times, was too often inspired by the idea that the first duty of men in power was to enforce their own religious doctrines by penalty or disqualification of some kind.   Even those who had themselves suffered most severely from religious persecution were only too apt, when the opportunity came in their way, to enforce in their turn the same principle of religious persecution.   The reader of this book will have seen already in its pages that many an exile from France fought in the ranks of the English army against England's French enemies.   But he will also have seen how at the same time Irishmen, driven by persecution from their own country, were fighting under French generals against the forces of England on many a Continental battle-field.   The Puritans from Britain who went out to found a free home for themselves in the New England on the other side of the Atlantic were for a long time as keen in the repression of any faith or worship not in conformity with their own opinions, as if they had never themselves known what it was to feel the injustice of religious persecution. In truth, the doctrine which maintains the right of every man to follow the dictates of his own conscience in all that belongs to religion and its forms of worship is but a modern idea in the development of civilisation.   The more broadly that idea is expanded, and the more faithfully it is illustrated in the policy of government, the closer civilisation will approach to what we may hope to be its destined consummation in this world.

CHAPTER XXIX

'THE SPECTATOR'

ON Thursday, March 1, 1711, an event took place
which was destined to make an abiding impression
on the history of English literature. This event was
the first appearance of 'The Spectator,' a periodical
which made as distinct an impression upon English
journalism of that time as was produced, although
in a very different way, by the publication of
'Punch' during the early part of Queen Victoria's
reign. 'The Spectator' was not by any means the
first of the journals composed altogether of bright
literary essays, humorous and satirical for the most
part, on living men and manners, nor was 'Punch'
by any means the first of English comic newspapers.
But 'The Spectator' and 'Punch' alike made a
distinct fame, and each is always regarded as the
highest illustration of that order of literature which
it professed to illustrate. The first issue of 'The
Spectator' opens with some lines which may ap-
propriately be quoted here as an excuse for a brief
story of the origin of the journal and the men
who created its fame. 'I have observed,' says this
opening essay, 'that a reader seldom peruses a book
with pleasure till he knows whether the writer of it

be a black or a fair man, of a mild or choleric disposition, married or a bachelor, with other particulars of the like nature that conduce very much to the right understanding of an author.'

Probably the writer of the essay would not have been prepared gravely to defend the opinion that men and women seldom enjoy the reading of a book unless they know a good deal about the private history of the man who wrote it; but the writer of the essay found it convenient to start this ingenious proposition in order to get an opportunity for a delightful imaginary narrative concerning the promoters of ' The Spectator.' In this narrative there come to life some of the most fascinating figures known to English literature. For the moment, however, we shall follow the impulse given by the opening sentence of ' The Spectator ' with the object only of describing in veracious record the men who were mainly concerned in the production and the maintenance of this famous journal. The name of Joseph Addison has been already mentioned more than once in this history, and is indeed brought into immortal association with the reign of Queen Anne.

Addison was born in 1672, was the son of a rector in Wiltshire, was educated at various schools, Charterhouse among them, and at Queen's College and Magdalen College, Oxford. He took to literature at an early age, and was fortunate enough to obtain the powerful patronage which was then almost absolutely necessary to anything like a prosperous

career for a young beginner.   He was able to spend
four years in travel through the Continent, chiefly
in France, Italy, the Netherlands, and the German-
speaking States, and thus obtained inexhaustible
stores of observation to stimulate and feed his brilliant and genial, ever kindly, albeit satirical, humour.
His natural tastes were such as to lead him into a
variety of fields, and he seemed for a while to feel
equal delight in them all.   He cultivated the muses,
as the phrase would have gone in his day.   He loved
to write poems; he was fond of music, and actually
produced an opera, as at a later period he produced
a comedy and a tragedy.   He enjoyed describing his
travels in Italy; he developed a taste for historical
narrative; he revelled in essay writing, and he was
drawn into political and parliamentary life, in which
afterwards he came to hold more than one high
official place.   Now, the man who attempts success
in so many fields is likely in most cases to prove
nothing more than that he has been endowed by
malign destiny with the fatal gift of the amateur—in
other words, that he is ever trying new fields of
labour and never finds any which seems especially
his own.   Joseph Addison was saved from such a
fate by the fact that he possessed that distinctly
creative gift which we call genius, the gift that
always finds, sooner or later, its own special work
to do.   The world now regards, and we venture to
think will ever regard, Joseph Addison as the chief
writer in 'The Spectator,' and not as the author of
'The Campaign' or of 'Cato'; not as the member

of Parliament; and not as the Secretary of State.
No literary essays in any language have ever surpassed, or are ever likely to surpass, some of those
which Addison contributed to the pages of 'The
Spectator.'

His principal colleague in the work was Richard
Steele, afterwards Sir Richard Steele, one of the most
brilliant figures in the life and the literature of his
time. Steele was an Irishman by birth. He was
born in Dublin, where his father practised as an
attorney, in the early part of the year 1672, only a
few weeks before the birth of Addison. His father
and mother both died while he was yet a child,
and he came into the care of an uncle who was
secretary to the Duke of Ormond. The Duke took
an interest in the boy, and sent him to Charterhouse School, where he came for the first time into
the companionship of Addison. Then he was sent
to pursue his studies at Oxford, and under the
sudden impulse for a military life he enlisted in
the Horse Guards during 1694.

Steele was lucky in finding patronage from the
very first. Some of the verses which he published
on the funeral of Queen Mary attracted the attention
of a noble lord who appointed him his private
secretary and afterwards obtained for him an ensigncy
in the Coldstream Guards. His love of literary
work still held possession of him, and he tried his
hand at writing plays. In the meantime he had fought
a duel, severely wounding his man; and this
exploit appears to have brought him into a penitent

mood from which came his production 'The Christian Hero.' Then he varied the monotony of the devotional mood by writing a play, gave up for a time his military pursuits and wrote another and yet another play. His dramatic works were successful enough to encourage him to further efforts in the same direction, but once again he found it convenient to diversify his existence by becoming captain in a regiment of foot, and further by engaging in the then somewhat popular researches and experiments for the discovery of the philosopher's stone. He did not discover the philosopher's stone, but he married a widow who had large estates in Barbadoes, and it may be that in this way he did succeed in turning something into gold. Soon afterwards he was made Gentleman-in-waiting to Queen Anne's husband, Prince George of Denmark. His wife lived but for a short time after their marriage, and Steele did not devote himself for long to the disconsolate state of a widower, but contracted a love match with a beautiful young woman, to whom he was tenderly attached.

Steele, still a comparatively young man, had by this time seen a good deal of life, had studied humanity from various points of view, and ought to have been peculiarly qualified for the kind of literary work which concerns itself especially with men and manners. He attracted the attention of Harley, who gave him the post of gazetteer, with a salary of three hundred a year, and at a later period he was appointed Commissioner of Stamps. He it was who originated 'The Tatler' newspaper, and in its production he had the helping hand of Joseph Addison. 'The Tatler' was in a certain sense the precursor of 'The Spectator'; but, as we shall see presently, 'The Spectator' started on a distinct and original plan of its own which had not been fore-shadowed by any previous project of newspaper essay writing. There is much difference of opinion as to the original author of the plan. There are contemporary chroniclers who distinctly maintain that the original idea came up in the mind of Addison, and that he communicated and explained it to Steele, who was taken with it instantly, and was delighted to render it all the service in his power. On the other hand, there are writers of the same time who insist with emphasis, and with assurance of precise information, that Steele first conceived the idea, and that Addison cordially adopted it and lent it all his help. It does not much matter now whether this friend or the other was the author of the original idea, but considering the initiative taken by Steele as founder of 'The Tatler,' it seems not unreasonable to suppose that it was he also who became possessed with the happy inspiration which led to the starting of 'The Spectator.' It is quite certain that the names of both friends must remain alike and inseparably associated with 'The Spectator' in literary history. Addison and Steele were the Gemini, the Heavenly Twins, to adopt a more modern literary phrase, whose light illumined that generation and many later generations through the medium of the brilliant and successful journal.

'The Spectator' had a very peculiar plan of its own. The natural and ordinary form for such a newspaper to take would have been to devote itself merely to a series of essays on the doings and manners, the fashions and follies, the public and private life of the days to which the essayists belonged. But 'The Spectator' was not content to issue its daily essays in this disconnected and, so far as the public were concerned, anonymous form. 'The Spectator' called into being a whole set of figures, the *dramatis personæ* of its performance, the men who were to lecture and instruct the town as to its whims, its follies, and its errors, and each of whom was to maintain his own point of view from which to direct his preachings. The idea was to create a 'Spectator' Club, and to make the ways and the characteristics of its leading members perfectly well known to the town, as if these members had been living creatures who might be met in St. James's Street or in the Temple Gardens, or at some country seat on any day of the year. These chosen personages were to favour the world with their own peculiar opinions concerning everything going on in the regions of society, and their expositions were intended to draw forth expressions of approval or opposition, counter criticisms or congenial disquisitions, from society in general. Much in the constructive scheme of 'The Spectator' might have suggested the development of the society novel which made its most lasting manifestation at a later day by the issue of 'Vanity Fair.'

Addison and Steele worked together in the closest literary companionship and with perfect harmony for the daily production of their unique 'Spectator.' The essay which one had written was commonly touched and retouched by the other, and it is not always easy to be quite sure whether any was the exclusive work of either of the gifted writers. Some critics are found to differ even as to the original creation of certain of the figures who had principal parts in this marvellous drama of talk without action. There has been interesting and animated discussion as to the original parentage of Sir Roger de Coverley, and of Will Honeycomb, some claiming the creation absolutely for Addison, and some absolutely for Steele. The controversy now seems to have scarcely a more practical interest, even for literary mankind, than a dispute as to the individual part taken by Beaumont and by Fletcher in the dramas which bear the associated names of these two authors.

Many men of literary mark whose names are still remembered by the reading public were frequent contributors to 'The Spectator.' One man who ranks among the immortals of the reign, Alexander Pope, was actually a contributor; but he cannot be reckoned amongst those who illumined its pages by frequent flashes of light. He published his famous 'Messiah' in one of the numbers of 'The Spectator,' and for another number he wrote a short article which contained a few verses. Some critics have maintained that they could identify other articles as coming from his pen, but we believe that these assertions belong to the field of conjecture only, or are founded merely on what is called intrinsic evidence, an evidence very little to be relied on when a great author has made his style an object of enthusiastic imitation.

Dr. Thomas Parnell is known to have contributed two somewhat allegorical and fanciful essays to the pages of the favoured periodical. Parnell was the author of a poem called 'The Hermit,' which was much admired in his day and is but faintly remembered in ours. Indeed, it would be hardly quite unfair to his literary fame to say that in our day his name is chiefly remembered because of the conspicuous position taken in public life by more lately-born members of his family. Thomas Parnell was born in Dublin, studied in Trinity College and entered into Holy Orders. He was, however, Irish only by birth, and belonged to an old Cheshire family. Sir John Parnell, a member of the same family, played a distinguished part in the Irish Parliament of Grattan's day; Sir Henry Parnell took a prominent part in an English Parliament of a later day; and the name of another member of the family, Charles Stewart Parnell, is likely to be long remembered in political history.

Besides all these writers, who may be regarded as professional literary men, the outer public itself furnished many contributors to the columns of 'The Spectator.' The conductors of the paper freely invited and cordially encouraged such contributions. The object was to obtain expressions of opinion from all classes and orders on any subject of interest which was then engaging attention. Every letter sent in was carefully read, and if it was found to have in it anything worth printing it was published at the earliest possible moment. All such contributions were gone over by Addison or by Steele—more often by Steele—and any letter that appeared deserving of a place in the paper was touched up and put into better shape if it were found to require such remodelling. In rare cases the letters were given to the public exactly as their writers had penned them, nor was this always a tribute to the excellence of their literary style. It happened now and then that some contributor, sadly wanting in literary education, put forth ideas of sound common sense with an emphasis and a bluntness which became all the more telling from the homely phraseology in which they were clothed; and sometimes, too, they were so exquisitely absurd that to publish them exactly as they were written was the most effective way of showing up the absurdity which they strove to defend. Steele took especial delight in going over these contributions from the outer world, and it was said of him by one of his colleagues that he had often by a few happy touches converted a commonplace little epistolary homily into an essay sparkling with humorous illustration.

The fame of 'The Spectator' began to spread abroad everywhere. The paper became the fashion, and it was the right sort of thing that everybody who claimed to be anybody in what was considered the best society should be able to talk about 'The Spectator,' to quote from its essays, and to argue about its arguments. Fine ladies were delighted to show their familiarity with its contents, and some went so far as to send contributions to it, and were so fortunate as to be able to show their contributions in print to their acquaintances. Over twenty thousand copies of the paper were sometimes sold in a single day, and to those who bear in mind the limited extent of the reading population just then, this fact alone will seem a wonderful tribute to the success of a journal which did not even profess to be a newspaper, and chiefly gave out humorous sketches, satirical essays, and week-day sermons. Into the remotest parts of Great Britain and Ireland 'The Spectator' found its way, and it was largely read and discussed by men and women of education in France and in other parts of the European Continent. It certainly is not too much to say that the story of 'The Spectator' forms one of the most delightful and most important chapters in English literature.

Each volume of 'The Spectator' as it came out had prefixed to it the name of some eminent person to whom the more or less editor of the work professed to feel himself under particular obligations. The first volume was thus dedicated 'To John, Lord Somers.' 'None,' says this first dedication, 'but a person of a finished character can be a proper patron of a work which endeavours to cultivate and polish human life, by promoting virtue and knowledge, and by recommending whatsoever may be either useful or ornamental to society.' Then the writer goes on to say, ' I know that the homage I now pay you, is offering a kind of violence to one who is as solicitous to shun applause, as he is assiduous to deserve it. But, my lord, this is perhaps the only particular in which your prudence will be always disappointed. While justice, candour, equanimity, a zeal for the good of your country, and the most persuasive eloquence in bringing over others to it, are valuable distinctions; you are not to expect that the public will so far comply with your inclinations, as to forbear celebrating such extraordinary qualities.'

The second volume is addressed to ' Charles, Lord Halifax,' the third to the ' Right Hon. Henry Boyle,' and the fourth to the ' Duke of Marlborough.' This last dedication begins with an ingeniously graceful fashion of compliment. ' As it is natural to have a fondness for what has cost us much time and attention to produce, I hope your Grace will forgive my endeavour to preserve this work from oblivion, by affixing to it your memorable name.' There are dedications to the Earl of Wharton, the Earl of Sunderland, and Mr. Methuen (the author of the famous treaty with Portugal), and there is a dedication to one purely imaginary person, ' William Honeycomb, Esq.,' who began life in the pages of ' The Spectator' and has not yet ceased to live n the memories of all with whom the reading of delightful literature is a pleasure beyond price. This dedication is in itself a most charming little essay, full of humour and frolicsome fancy; it is made up of affection, admiration and genial, kindly banter, and the object of the dedication, if he were really a living man and capable of appreciating the happy union of *badinage* and compliment, might be pleased to see a life-like picture of himself with all his good qualities and all his personal weaknesses blending into a very harmonious and yet a very realistic whole.

We may now say something about the story of 'The Spectator' itself, for it is, in fact, a story with a purpose. The first number begins with a personal description by the supposed author's own hand of 'The Spectator' himself. 'I design this paper,' he says, 'and my next, as prefatory discourses to my following writings, and shall give some account in them of the several persons that are engaged in this work. As the chief trouble of compiling, digesting, and correcting will fall to my share, I must do myself the justice to open the work with my own history.' Then he goes on at once to tell us that he was born to a small hereditary estate 'which according to the tradition of the village where it lies was bounded by the same hedges and ditches in William the Conqueror's time that it is at present, and has been delivered down from father to son, whole and entire, without the loss or acquisition of a single field or meadow during the space of six hundred years.' The writer informs us that he was born a very grave and

solemn child—so grave, indeed, that, as his mother
had often told him, he threw away his rattle before
he was two months old, and would not make use of
his coral until they had taken away the bells from it.
The gravity and stillness of his youth appear to have
been equally remarkable, and at the university he
distinguished himself habitually by a most profound
silence. 'Whilst I was in this learned body, I
applied myself with so much diligence to my studies,
that there are very few celebrated books, either in
the learned or the modern tongues, which I am not
acquainted with.' On the death of his father this
prodigy of thoughtful silence made up his mind to
travel into foreign countries, and therefore left the
university 'with the character of an odd unaccount-
able fellow, that had a great deal of learning, if I
would but show it.'

An insatiable thirst after knowledge carried the
youth, we are told, into all the countries of Europe
where there was anything new or strange to be seen.
We are even further informed 'to such a degree
was my curiosity raised, that having read the
controversies of some great men concerning the
antiquities of Egypt, I made a voyage to Grand
Cairo, on purpose to take the measure of a Pyramid :
and as soon as I had set myself right in that
particular, returned to my native country with great
satisfaction.' This latter illustration of a traveller's
tale was understood to be a touch at a then living
author who had published a book bearing the sesqui-
pedalian title of 'Pyramidagraphia.' The European

travels might well be understood to illustrate the tastes and the experiences of Addison himself.

'The Spectator' then tells us how he settled down to life in London, ' where I am frequently seen in most public places, though there are not above half a dozen of my select friends that know me ; of whom my next paper shall give a more particular account.' We are told that there was no place of general resort in which he did not make his frequent appearance; ' sometimes I am seen thrusting my head into a round of politicians at Will's, and listening with great attention to the narratives that are made in those little circular audiences.' At other times he enjoyed smoking a pipe at Child's coffee-house, a place of much attraction, to which the clergy in especial were apt to resort as it stood conveniently for them in the immediate neighbourhood of St. Paul's Cathedral. There, he is careful to tell us, he seldom talked to anyone, but contrived to overhear the conversation at every table in the room. 'I appear on Sunday nights at St. James's coffee-house, and sometimes join the little committee of politics in the inner room, as one who comes there to hear and improve.' His face, he tells us, is very well known likewise at other coffee-houses and in the theatres of Drury Lane and the Haymarket. Apparently his especial gift was that of a spectator and of a listener, not a talker, and so little was his motive for frequenting public assemblies understood by those with whom he sometimes silently mingled that ' I have been taken for a merchant upon the Exchange for above these ten

years, and sometimes pass for a Jew in the assembly
of stock-jobbers at Jonathan's. In short, wherever
I see a cluster of people I always mix with them,
though I never open my lips but in my own
club.' 'Thus I live in the world rather as a spectator of mankind, than as one of the species, by
which means I have made myself a speculative
statesman, soldier, merchant, and artizan, without
ever meddling with any practical part in life. I am
very well versed in the theory of a husband, or a
father, and can discern the errors in the economy,
business, and diversion of others, better than those
who are engaged in them; as standers-by discover
blots which are apt to escape those who are in the
game.'

So much of his personal character and history,
'The Spectator' tells us, he has felt bound to
communicate to his readers in order to let them see
that he was not without some qualification for the
business he had undertaken. He explains that of
late he had begun to blame his own taciturnity 'and
since I have neither time nor inclination to communicate the fulness of my heart in speech, I am
resolved to do it in writing, and to print myself out,
if possible, before I die.' For this reason, he tells
his readers, it is his intention to 'publish a sheet-full
of thoughts every morning, for the benefit of my
contemporaries; and if I can anyway contribute to
the diversion or improvement of the country in
which I live, I shall leave it when I am summoned
out of it, with the secret satisfaction of thinking that

I have not lived in vain.'   But he declares there are
limits to the confidential revelations which he is
willing to make to his readers.   He positively
declines to tell his name, his age, and his lodgings.
Such revelations, he explains, 'would indeed draw me
out of that obscurity which I have enjoyed for many
years, and expose me in public places to several
salutes and civilities, which have been always very
disagreeable to me; for the greatest pain I can
suffer, is the being talked to, and being stared at.'
Then this first essay comes to an end with the intimation that the work of 'The Spectator' is carried
on in a club with a number of friends who are
afterwards to be described; that the club meets
only on Tuesdays and Thursdays, but that it has
appointed a committee to sit every night for the
inspection of all such papers as may contribute to
the advancement of the public weal, and he invites
all among the outer public who have a mind to
correspond with him to direct their letters ' to " The
Spectator," at Mr. Buckley's in Little Britain.'

This is, in point of fact, the plot of ' The Spectator.'
Any reader who has gone thus far, and only thus far,
can easily foresee the blending of the real and the
imaginary which makes so much of the charm that
belongs to it.   ' The Spectator,' as he is described by
himself in this opening essay, represents and embodies
the principal experiences and characteristics of Joseph
Addison.   An almost unconquerable shyness re-
stricted the ways and movements of Addison in
general society, and still more especially in political

and public life.   Addison during his career occupied
more than once a commanding position in administrative and parliamentary affairs; but his shy taciturnity rendered it utterly impossible that he could
achieve any personal distinction in such fields.   One
of his only faults—and it was not accounted a fault
in those deep-drinking days—consisted in what
writers of that time would have described as his devotion to the wine-cup.   Macaulay makes this excuse
for him which has charity as well as justice to support it, that wine unlocked the spell under which his
fine intellect lay, and gave him some chance of freely
expressing his thoughts in the companionship of his
fellow-men.   Posterity is not likely to censure with
too much harshness this one weakness in a nature
otherwise so pure and so exalted, seeing that his love
of wine, however it may have helped him to fluency
of speech, did not lead him to mar the beauty and
accuracy of his unsurpassed literary style.

The second number of 'The Spectator' begins to
describe the other leading members of this observant
club.   'The first of our society,' we are told, 'is a
gentleman of Worcestershire, of an ancient descent,
a baronet, his name Sir Roger de Coverley.'   That
name, it is hardly necessary to say, has passed into
literary history with the names of Dr. Primrose,
Uncle Toby, and Colonel Newcome.   His biographer
records of him that 'his great grandfather was
inventor of that famous country dance which is called
after him.'   The Sir Roger de Coverley of 'The
Spectator' Club is described as 'a gentleman that is

very singular in his behaviour, but his singularities proceed from his good sense, and are contradictions to the manners of the world, only as he thinks the world is in the wrong.' This humour, however, ' creates him no enemies, for he does nothing with sourness or obstinacy; and his being unconfined to modes and forms, makes him but the readier and more capable to please and oblige all who know him.' The more modern reader may be a little surprised to hear that the London home of this well-born country gentleman is in Soho Square. The editor of the edition published in 1823 thought it necessary even then to explain by a marginal note that at the time of Sir Roger de Coverley's existence Soho Square was 'the genteelest part of the town.'

The essay gives us some further insight into the life and character of Sir Roger by telling us that it was said ' he keeps himself a bachelor by reason he was crossed in love by a perverse, beautiful widow of the next county to him.' 'Before this disappoint-ment, Sir Roger was what you call a fine gentleman, had often supped with my Lord Rochester and Sir George Etherege, fought a duel upon his first coming to town, and kicked bully Dawson in a public coffee-house for calling him youngster.' Another note in the same edition informs the world, or at least that part of it which came later than Sir Roger's time, that bully Dawson 'was a noted sharper, swaggerer, and debauchee about town; he was well known in Blackfriars and its then infamous purlieus '

Sir Roger took his hard treatment at the hands of his perverse widow so much to heart that he became very serious for about a year and a half, and although his naturally jovial temper got the better of him after a while, he always remained careless of his personal appearance and never troubled himself to dress according to the prevailing fashion. 'He continues to wear a coat and doublet of the same cut that was in fashion at the time of his repulse, which, in his merry humours, he tells us, has been in and out twelve times since he first wore it.' At the time when we make his acquaintance he is 'in his fifty-sixth year, cheerful, gay, and hearty; keeps a good house both in town and country; a great lover of mankind; but there is such a mirthful cast in his behaviour that he is rather beloved than esteemed.' 'His tenants grow rich, his servants look satisfied, all the young women profess love to him, and the young men are glad of his company.' Oddly enough Sir Roger appears to have some of the peculiarities which Thackeray, in his Irish sketches, describes as having impressed him in the manners of Father Mathew, the famous apostle of temperance. 'When he comes into a house he calls the servants by their names, and talks all the way upstairs to a visit.' He is a Justice of the Peace, 'fills the chair at quarter sessions with great abilities, and three months ago gained universal applause by explaining a passage in the Game Act.' Thus we are introduced to the principal figure in 'The Spectator' Club, and the reader has even from this brief description a very clear idea as to the

peculiarities and the general character of Sir Roger
de Coverley.

Some other members of the club are then
described over whose likenesses, however interesting
in themselves, we do not need to linger here, and
then we come to one whose name, like that of Sir
Roger de Coverley, has become classic in our literature. The author of the essay is anxious that the
members of the society 'may not appear a set of
humorists, unacquainted with the gallantries and
pleasures of the age.' He therefore thinks it right
to tell us that 'we have amongst us the gallant Will
Honeycomb, a gentleman who, according to his
years, should be in the decline of life, but, having
ever been very careful of his person, and always had
a very easy fortune, time has made but very little
impression, either by wrinkles on his forehead or
traces on his brain. His person is well turned, and
of a good height. He is very ready at that sort of
discourse with which men usually entertain women.
He has all his life dressed very well, and remembers
habits as others do men. He can smile when one
speaks to him, and laughs easily. He knows the
history of every mode, and can inform you from
which of the French King's wenches our wives and
daughters had this manner of curling their hair, that
way of placing their hoods; whose frailty was
covered by such a sort of petticoat, and whose
vanity to show her foot made that part of the dress
so short in such a year.' 'As other men of his age
will notice to you what such a minister said upon

such and such an occasion, he will tell you, when the Duke of Monmouth danced at court, such a woman was then smitten, another was taken with him at the head of his troop in the Park. In all these important relations he has ever about the same time received a kind glance, or a blow of a fan from some celebrated beauty, mother of the present Lord Such-a-one.'

In this easy and lively way we are introduced to the leading members of 'The Spectator' Club. The reader will meet them again and again as he follows the continuance of the essays. These are the observers who make it their agreeable duty to study the manners and customs of society in town and country, and to record, each after his own fashion, his judgment as to the improvement or the deterioration of the men and women, the orders and classes, who pass under his eyes and provoke his criticism. Each of these students of human nature and human life criticises from his own point of view, and it need hardly be said that Sir Roger de Coverley and Will Honeycomb do not form a judgment according to the same ethical standard. Each member of the club invites contributions from those with whom he is best acquainted, and as everyone from the outer world who is fortunate enough to obtain a place for his contribution is certain to make known the proud fact to all his acquaintances, the result is that each succeeding week there are more and more men and women who aspire to give to the world through the same medium their ideas as to the behaviour of their neighbours in general. Learned divines and even bishops, eminent lawyers, country squires, court ladies, were thus led on to co-operate with the poets and moralists who chiefly conducted the work of the paper. There were many contributions, too, which professed to come from members of various classes having nothing to do with the world of education or of fashion—from shop-assistants, apprentice lads, working girls, rural labourers, a representation of English life as nearly complete as possible being the great object which 'The Spectator' Club was endeavouring to accomplish.

Some at least of the contributions thus professing to come from the outer fringes of life were obviously not genuine, and bore visible marks of being ingeniously constructed to serve the occasion. The fashion then still prevailed in literature of giving humorous names to every fictitious character, which left the reader at no trouble to understand the part played in life by that particular personage. A poacher who writes to 'The Spectator' signs himself Isaac Hedgeditch. A worthy serving man signs himself Thomas Trusty. A dressy young lady signs herself Alice Bluegarter, and so on through an infinite variety of self-revealing appellations. We have completely outgrown this species of humour in our time, and literature has not lost much by the change; but the habit seems much more tolerable in the pages of 'The Spectator' than in those given to the world by writers of a later date, who adopted the mannerism or the trick out of sheer imitation. 'The Spectator'

was but a small paper, containing its literary matter
on two of its pages and some scraps of news on the
other, and each number cost one penny. Many of
the essays were noble specimens of the higher
criticism; many were week-day sermons of which
any pulpit might well be proud; many were short,
pathetic, or humorous stories. Whatever men and
women were doing furnished matter of observation
and comment to the watchful 'Spectator.' But a
consistent purpose animated and inspired the whole
literary work and made it read more like a discursive
story than like a series of disconnected essays. The
principal figures of 'The Spectator' Club were presenting themselves again and again in the narrative,
now describing their own experiences, and now re-
counting the adventures or discussing the humours
of their friends, and each acting in turn the part of
showman to that particular scene in the life-drama
which it was his part to introduce.

'The Spectator' came to an end, not because its
leading conductors might not have carried it on as
long as their lives lasted, but for the reason that its
work was done, its story was told. It came to an
end, in fact, very much as the story of the Pickwick
Club came to an end in a later generation, and as in
the case of the Pickwick Club so in the case of 'The
Spectator,' there was a short resumption of its existence before it was allowed to pass wholly into
retrospect and into fame. Most readers will think
that after the death of Sir Roger de Coverley there
could not be much life left in the story of 'The

Spectator' Club. Most of those who worked in the
project had bright careers still before them and were
to win new honours as they went along. But it may
fairly be said for the two or three leading men in the
immortal literary enterprise that they never won
higher fame than that which the world has given
to them for their work in 'The Spectator.'

During the existence of 'The Spectator' came
into force the Act of Parliament which imposed a
stamp-tax on all printed newspapers. There had already been a duty on paper, vellum, and parchment,
and on certain legal documents. The Act which imposed these duties belonged to the reign of Charles
the Second, but in the days of Queen Anne such a
tax was made for the first time upon newspaper
publications. Lord Bolingbroke, as Secretary of
State, was understood to have been chiefly responsible for the imposition of this tax, and one of the
reasons given for imposing it was said to be the
necessity of endeavouring to put some restriction on
the licence displayed by newspaper writers in their
criticisms on public men. In February 1712, the
Queen sent a message to Parliament in which she
directed attention to ' the false and scandalous libels
such as are a reproach to any government ' which
were then in constant circulation, and she asked her
faithful Parliament to find ' a remedy equal to the
mischief.' A measure was introduced in the session
of that year, the object of which was to impose duties
on silks, calicoes, linen, and other articles of ordinary
use ; and into this measure was put a clause declaring

that ' all newspapers or papers containing public news, intelligence, or occurrences ' were to pay a tax at the rate of a halfpenny each if printed on half a sheet of paper, or a penny if on a whole sheet and not more, and of two shillings a sheet if any audacious publisher were to venture upon starting a newspaper of what would then have been considered an extraordinary size. A tax of a shilling was inflicted by the same measure on every advertisement appearing in any manner of publication which could be liable to the impost already mentioned.

This Act was passed on June 10, 1712. The Act was to come into force on August 1, and Addison, writing in 'The Spectator' on the day before, described that date as 'the day on which many eminent authors will probably publish their last words.' ' I am afraid,' he goes on to say, ' that few of our weekly historians, who are men above all others who delight in war, will be able to subsist under the weight of a stamp and an approaching peace. A sheet of blank paper that must have this new imprimatur clapped upon it before it is qualified to communicate anything to the public will make its way in the world but very heavily. In short the necessity of carrying a stamp and the improbability of notifying a bloody battle will I am afraid both concur to the sinking of those thin folios which have every other day retailed to us the history of Europe for several years last passed. A facetious friend of mine who loves a pun called this present mortality among authors " the fall of the leaf." ' But Addison also announced that he and his companions in literary work were by no means disposed to give up the field because of the new difficulties put in their way; on the contrary, he declared that he and his colleagues intended to continue the issue of their paper, and would meet the tax in the best way they could by charging an additional penny for each number. 'No,' he says, with a light tone of satire in his voice, 'I shall glory in contributing my utmost to the public weal, and if my country receives five or six pounds a day by my labours I shall be very well pleased to find myself so useful a member.'

'The Spectator,' then, did not die with the stamp duty, but survived it, and only came to an end, as we have said already, when its story was told. But the stamp duty on newspapers long survived the days of 'The Spectator,' and continued to interfere with the issue of cheap newspapers for popular circulation down to the time, well within the memory of living men, when Gladstone carried his famous measure for the abolition of that tax upon knowledge, as it was so justly described by the enlightened men who had led the way to his work and lent him their cordial help in its accomplishment.

CHAPTER XXX

IRELAND UNDER QUEEN ANNE

WE have described the relations which existed between England and Scotland before the accomplishment of the Act of Union, and the conditions which rendered that Act satisfactory and propitious to the inclinations and welfare of the one country and the other. Nothing could be more unlike the relations between England and Scotland, up to the time of the Union and after, than those which existed between England and Ireland. England and Scotland, even when parts of the same kingdom, and governed under one crown, were to a great extent independent States, equal partners in one imperial system. They were rivals in trade, commerce, and navigation, and each had her own system of laws and her own national institutions. Scotland had won her great victory of Bannockburn, and when, at a later period of history, the two countries came to be ruled by the same Sovereign it was Scotland which gave a King and a succession to England and not England to Scotland. Ireland, on the other hand, since her conquest by England had always been treated as a conquered country. The great object of England seemed to be the suppression or eradication of

Ireland's national customs, sentiments, and tendencies. There was little or nothing in common between the traditions of England and of Ireland and England seemed ever anxious to emphasise the fact that no such community should be allowed to grow up, so far as she could prevent it.

When England accepted the Reformation, Ireland held fast to the faith of Rome, and her English rulers strove in vain, during many generations, to crush the religious worship of the Irish people by the most widespread and at the same time most minute persecution. Ireland had had but little opportunity for success in manufactures, in commerce, and in trade, and her English rulers did all they could to put a stop to every attempt at rivalry in those directions. Ireland was mainly an agricultural country, and each succeeding struggle against her conqueror had ended alike in the expatriation of the old Irish families and the planting of stranger landlords with English ways— successful soldiers for the most part—in the place of the expelled Irish owners of the soil. Even when England was still ruled by Catholic Sovereigns the treatment of the Irish Catholic population had been just as severe and oppressive as in the days after the Reformation.

Ireland remained faithful to the cause of the Stuarts, not that she had any particular love or devotion for the Stuarts, or any reason for such love or devotion, but because the Stuarts represented that religion to which Ireland clung through all pains and troubles, the religion which England was then persistently persecuting on Irish soil. Ireland had also a strong sympathy with France, partly because France was believed or supposed to have had friendly feelings towards the Irish people, and partly, too, no doubt because France was the avowed enemy of England. There had been at one time a Spanish settlement in parts of the West and South of Ireland, and some of the old towns in these places still kept up the evidences of their Spanish origin, and, indeed, evidences to the same effect are even yet to be seen among the southern and western peasantry. Cromwell had done his best to plant a whole population of English masters in Ireland, and James the Second had made the island a battle-field during his later struggles to maintain the Crown of England against the invasion of William of Orange. Down to a much later day few English statesmen seem to have thought it worth their while to consider whether the Irish people might not be won over to a real companionship with England by a policy of justice, of mercy, and of brotherhood. The one prevailing idea appears to have been that for the welfare of England and for the security of England's rule it was absolutely necessary to suppress the Catholic worship by any process, and to convert the Irish tiller of the soil into a mere serf and vassal depending for his very life upon the will of his master.

There were, at the time with which we are at present dealing, no United States across the Atlantic where the Irish peasant might find a home and the means of prospering, and there were no great self-governing English colonies which could hold out to him any fair prospect of religious equality and personal independence.   When the Irishman of those days had the means to seek a new career outside the power of the English Crown he was ready to devote his services to some foreign State, all the more ready if that foreign State happened to be an avowed enemy of England.   We have seen already in this history that the representatives of many famous Irish houses gave themselves up thus to the service of some foreign State and died on Continental battle-fields fighting against the armies of England.   The visitor to Rome may see at this day, in one of the great churches there, the tombs of two illustrious exiles who had striven in vain to maintain on Irish soil the struggle against the English conquerors.   Even amongst Irish Protestants, although many of them were naturally drawn by religious affinity to accept the English supremacy with welcome and devotion, there were some in each generation who threw in their lot to the last with the losing national cause.   It is a somewhat curious fact, well worthy of grave consideration, that down to days very near our own every effort at armed rebellion in Ireland and for Ireland has had Protestant leaders at its front.   This fact cannot be too earnestly impressed upon the minds of readers who might be apt to think that the whole question between England's rule and Ireland's resistance was merely a conflict of religious sects. Statesmanship in England had not yet risen to the idea that the killing of rebels is not the best way of extinguishing rebellion.

Ireland had a Parliament of her own in the days of Queen Anne, but it was not by any means an independent Parliament like the Estates of Scotland, and it was of no value whatever as a representative of national opinions and interests. Long before the fall of the Stuart dynasty a measure had been carried into law which rendered the Irish Parliament a mere dependent on the Parliament of England, or, in other words, on the English Government. This measure, which has become famous in history as Poyning's Act or Poyning's Law, was passed during the rule of Sir Edward Poyning, then Lord Deputy or, as we should now say, Lord Lieutenant of Ireland, at the close of the fifteenth century. It made all measures passed by the English Parliament absolute law in Ireland, and it further prevented the Irish Parliament from passing any measures applying to Ireland alone which did not receive in advance the approval of the Sovereign and the Council of England. Thus the legislation for Ireland was made wholly dependent even for its initiation on the will of the English Sovereign, and whatever that Sovereign and the English Parliament chose to enact became law for Ireland. It has also to be remembered that the Irish Parliament was in no sense whatever a representative institution, and that during the greater part of its existence all those who belonged to the national faith, or could be supposed to represent the national opinions, were excluded by law from any share in its deliberations. Poyning's Act was not repealed until April, 1782, when the peaceful but very ominous agitation of Henry Grattan and the Irish volunteers compelled the English Sovereign and his Parliament to give, for the time, to the Irish representative assembly the right to make laws applying to Ireland.

In Queen Anne's days, as in all other days, the Lord Deputy was generally some English nobleman who stood high in the favour of the political party then prevailing in England. Many enactments had been passed under these conditions, which dealt invidiously with whatever trading and commercial enterprises might be undertaken in Ireland, and made the interests of the smaller island entirely subservient to those of Great Britain. No one professing the national faith in Ireland could hold any public office in Parliament or out of it. Even in the comparatively enlightened days of Queen Anne measures were introduced again and again with the object of abolishing, or at all events restricting, the sort of toleration which was allowed to Catholics in Ireland during the reign of Charles the Second. When the Duke of Ormond, who had played a part not particularly distinguished in the great campaign, was sent over to Ireland to manage affairs in that country as Lord Deputy, the Irish House of Commons, constituted under the conditions we have just described, presented for his approval a list of new measures intended 'to prevent the further growth of Popery' Bishop Burnet tell us that the House

'pressed the Duke with more than usual vehemence
to intercede so effectually that it'—the first of the
proposed measures—'might be returned back under
the Great Seal of England.' This was, of course, a
necessary condition for any further proceeding with
the measure, and the Duke of Ormond, entering
warmly into the spirit of the whole business, gave his
gracious promise 'that he would recommend it in the
most effectual manner and do everything in his power
to prevent the growth of Popery.'

The modern reader may be well excused if he
finds something broadly farcical in all this process of
legislation. The country to which it was to be
applied had a population the vast majority of whom
were then, as now, devoted adherents to the Church of
Rome. The Irish Parliament, to whom was entrusted
the right at least of asking leave to introduce measures
for the government of the Irish people, was a body
from which all persons professing the religion of
the Catholic Church were rigorously excluded. This
curiously constructed representative Irish Chamber
became a supplicant to the British Lord Deputy, that
he would graciously obtain the sanction of the English
Sovereign to a series of measures devised for the purpose of preventing the further growth of Popery. 'I
might indeed suppose,' says John Mitchel, an Irishman
who, although a strong Nationalist, was not a Catholic
nor in any manner of religious sympathy with
Catholics, 'that Popery had been already sufficiently
discouraged seeing that the Bishops and regular
clergy had been banished; that Catholics were

excluded by law from all honourable or lucrative employments ; carefully disarmed, and plundered of almost every acre of their ancient inheritances.'

The Irish Parliament of Queen Anne's day was, however, of opinion that a good deal more yet remained to be done for the discouragement and eradication of the faith which was held by six out of every seven of the Irish native population. One clause of the proposed measure was intended to enact that if the son of a Papist should at any time become a Protestant his father might not from that time sell or mortgage his estate, or dispose of the whole or any part of it by will. The meaning of this was, of course, that the moment the son of any Roman Catholic landowner went over to the Protestant Church, his father found himself instantly transformed into a mere occupying tenant of the land, and had no more right or power to dispose of it than if he were a labourer living in a hut on the estate. Another clause provided that a Papist should not be guardian to his own child, and that if the child, no matter how young, should conform to the Protestant religion he reduced by that act his father to the position of a mere occupant for life, and that the child was at once to be taken from the guardianship of his father and placed under the care of the nearest of kin who happened to belong to the Church recognised by the State. Yet another clause declared Papists incapable of purchasing landed estates or receiving any rents or profits arising out of land, and excluded a Papist from the right of succeeding to the property of any Protestant relative. Other clauses declared that the estate of a Papist who was not fortunate enough to have a Protestant heir should be parcelled out in equal shares among all his children or his next of kin, and that Papists must take the oath of abjuration and the sacramental tests in order to qualify them for holding any public office or for voting at any election.

When the Royal assent had been given to the introduction of this measure the process of passing it into law was not accomplished without considerable trouble to Queen Anne herself and to her advisers. Queen Anne was at this time in alliance with the Sovereign of Catholic Austria, and the English Government was bringing active pressure to bear upon the Emperor for the relief of his Protestant subjects from certain disqualifications imposed upon them because of their religious faith. It seemed somewhat inconsistent with these efforts to obtain religious equality in a foreign State, that the Government of Queen Anne should occupy itself at the same time with the introduction of additional penalties for the profession of the Catholic faith in Ireland. Queen Anne's Government easily got over any scruples of conscience which might have arisen in their minds with regard to this apparent inconsistency, and the Irish executive obtained full authority to take all the necessary steps for carrying the new measure safely through the Parliament of Ireland. There was not much trouble in the accomplishment of this feat, and the measure when it

passed through the Irish Parliament was sent on
to England to receive the confirmation of what we
should now call the Imperial Parliament. The
English Parliament not only approved of the measure,
so far as it went, but actually added a new clause,
the object of which was to introduce still further
disqualifications and penalties for the practice of
any religion not recognised by the Sovereign and
the State.   This new clause was directed not
merely against Roman Catholics but also and
especially against the Protestant dissenting bodies in
Ireland.

There was at that time a large and increasing
body of Protestant dissenters in the province of
Ulster, many or most of them men of influence and
comparative wealth, and the new clause declared
that no one in Ireland should be capable of holding
any public office or should be entitled to belong to
the magistracy who had not qualified himself for
the position by receiving the Sacraments according to the rites of the State Church in England.
This was, in fact, only an extension to Ireland of the
Test Act, which had, up to that time, been applicable
only to England and had not been made part of the
system of laws governing the smaller island.   Thus
the only alteration which the English Parliament
made in the measure imposing new disqualifications
on Irish Catholics was the introduction of a fresh
clause imposing further disqualifications and penalties
on Irish Protestant dissenters.

It has been pleaded, in defence of the course taken

by the Queen's Government, that the very introduction of this further clause only testified to their lack of
sympathy with the intolerant spirit which impelled the
Irish Parliament, at such a time, to embarrass Queen
Anne by demanding further measures of persecution
against the Irish Catholics.   In one of George Eliot's
novels we are told of a somewhat sour-tempered old
lady who, when asked by her husband to give him
some more tea, filled his cup so full with the desired
liquid that it ran over and was spilt into his
saucer, thereby conveying to him the intimation that
if he wanted more tea he should have it with a
vengeance.   According to the theory set up by those
who defend the Government of Queen Anne in this
instance the idea was that if the Irish Parliament at
that moment wanted more religious disqualifications
it should have them with a vengeance, and that the
Protestant dissenters in Ulster, who were an important
body, and might be supposed to favour the inconvenient measure in its original form, should be
made to feel that it could be brought to bear on
them as well as on their Roman Catholic fellow-
subjects.

The good Bishop Burnet is apparently inclined
to favour this idea.   According to his view of the
matter, 'It was hoped by those who got this clause
added to the bill that those in Ireland who promoted
it most would now be the less fond of it when it had
such a weight hung to it.'   If any of the advisers
of Queen Anne were cherishing this secret hope in
their minds the hope was doomed to complete

disappointment. Some of the Irish Protestant dissenters did indeed strongly object to the new clause,
but their remonstrance was entirely unavailing. The
desire to impose further disqualifications upon the
Catholic body in Ireland was too strong among the
ruling classes in both countries to give the Irish
Protestant dissenters any chance of asserting with
effect their own claims to religious equality. The
Bill was passed into law, and in due course received
the Royal assent.

During the progress of the Bill through the
Irish Parliament a strong protest against its passing
was made by certain leading Catholics who claimed
their right to be heard by counsel against the
provisions of the measure. During the debates on
the petition which they presented there were many
references made to the provisions of the famous
Treaty of Limerick, which was supposed to have
guaranteed among its conditions the recognition of
religious equality for the Catholics of Ireland. The
controversy which long prevailed over the manner
in which the conditions of the treaty had been set
aside by the ruling powers was still in Queen Anne's
reign a bitter dispute, and was regarded by the
Irish people as one of the greatest grievances ever
imposed upon them by their English conquerors.
Although the facts on which the controversy was
founded do not strictly belong to the history of
Queen Anne's reign, yet the effect which they produced
on the relations between England and Ireland was
still a most serious element of dissatisfaction among

the Irish people and an abiding cause of Ireland's
profoundest discontent with English rule ; and it is
therefore of some importance that a summary of the
whole controversy should be introduced into this
part of the present work. Up to our own days the
Treaty of Limerick, and the manner in which its
conditions were made to fail in their application, is a
subject of eager interest among Irish populations at
home and abroad, and may be heard of again and
again at every meeting of Irish Nationalists in any of
the great cities of the United States, Canada, and
Australia, as in Ireland itself.

The Treaty of Limerick was the agreement by
virtue of which the great struggle William the Third
was carrying on in Ireland against James the Second
had been brought to a close, and William had been
recognised as King of Ireland. The city of Limerick
had held out to the very last against the forces of
King William, and it was especially important for
William to bring the Irish struggle to an end, for the
good reason, among many other reasons, that he saw
in prospect a great war to be undertaken against
what then seemed the ever-increasing power of
France. William was himself in the Netherlands at
the time when the siege came to an end. The city
was defended by the celebrated Irish patriot and
soldier Patrick Sarsfield, who had been created Earl
of Lucan by James the Second in return for the
military services which he had rendered to the King
on English as well as on Irish battle-fields. The
siege of Limerick was conducted by General Ginckell,

a Dutch officer, who had accompanied William the Third to England in 1688, served at the battle of the Boyne, and when William returned to England was left in chief command of William's forces in Ireland.

The besieged garrison held out with such spirit and tenacity, and King William's further purposes rendered it so imperative to bring the Irish war to a close, that Ginckell thought it desirable to enter on some terms of surrender with the defenders of the place. The defenders of Limerick soon made it clear that they would not listen to any terms which did not contain stipulations for the securing of religious liberty to those who might now be regarded as the conquered race. One of the principal conditions of the surrender, therefore, was that the Roman Catholics of Ireland should, in the future, enjoy such privileges in the exercise of their religion as were consistent with the laws of Ireland or as they had enjoyed in the reign of King Charles the Second. Other words of the same article undertook that their Majesties King William and Queen Mary, as soon as their affairs would permit them to summon a Parliament in Ireland, would endeavour to procure for the Irish Roman Catholics such further security as might preserve them from any disturbance on account of their religion.

These were the provisions of the treaty on which the whole subsequent controversy set in. The articles which referred only to the terms and mode of the capitulation need not engage our attention here. Now, it must be said that in stipulating for such measure

of religious liberty as the Irish Roman Catholics had
during the reign of King Charles the Second the
defenders of Limerick were not stipulating for any
great concession. Even in the reign of Charles the
Second there were many severe and utterly ignoble
disqualifications and penalties to which Irish Catholics
were liable—disqualifications and penalties which in
more modern days would be regarded as utterly
inconsistent with the first principles of civilised
government. Still, it is clear that the defenders of
Limerick believed that the acceptance of their
stipulation would give some extension of religious
liberty to their fellow-countrymen to recompense
them for their reluctant consent to the proposals for
capitulation. We may briefly summarise the history
of this whole transaction by saying that the terms of
the treaty were never carried out, that the Irish
Parliament, constituted as we have described it,
declared the concessions made to the Irish Catholics
by the treaty to be entirely outside the limits of the
law, and that not merely were no special concessions
made to the Irish Catholics but that immediately
after the surrender of Limerick both the English
and the Irish Parliaments went on passing further
measures of disqualification and penalty for those
who openly practised the worship enjoined by the
Church of Rome.

Sarsfield and his comrades left the country, most
of them to fight against England on the battle-fields
of the Continent—Sarsfield to give up his gallant life
to the service of France on one such field. Limerick

is still called by Irish writers and speakers the City of the Violated Treaty, and the residents of the place are still proud to show the Treaty Stone on which Sarsfield signed his name to the terms of capitulation. There have been many ingenious arguments set up to justify the disregard which the Sovereign and the Parliament of England showed towards the special conditions on which alone the defenders of Limerick gave up the struggle they had so long and gallantly maintained. It was argued, of course with some plausibility, that the British Commander-in-Chief, General Ginckell, had no authority to make such terms without the sanction and consent of the English Crown and Parliament, and that if Sarsfield and his companions were so unwise as to believe that he had any such authority, they had only themselves to blame for their delusion and disappointment. It has been seriously argued by one eminent English historian that the concessions of religious liberty made in the terms of the treaty were so absurdly generous that no Roman Catholic in his senses could possibly have believed there was any chance of their fulfilment.

These are arguments which fill one with a curious interest, showing as they do how the minds of even grave and responsible historians may sometimes be diverted from the recognition of the plainest principles governing all agreements, by an instinctive sympathy with one or the other of the parties to the agreement. Let us assume for a moment that it was in the power of Sarsfield to maintain his forces still in the garrison long after the treaty had been signed, and after Ginckell had sent away most of his troops on the faith of an honourable surrender, and that King William's plans had thus been wholly marred for the time. It is hardly to be supposed that any English historian would hold Sarsfield to be thoroughly excused for his breach of the agreement by the fact that James the Second had, after some delay, declined to approve of it. When the Commander-in-Chief of a British army, placed in a position of supreme difficulty, is allowed to make an arrangement, greatly to his own advantage, with the opposing force, it is not usual after all is done and the opposing force has actually withdrawn, for him to be told by his Sovereign that he had no right to make any such arrangement, and that the conditions which he accepted are not to be carried out. At all events, one thing is perfectly certain—Sarsfield and his companions believed that they were entering into an agreement which Ginckell had full authority to make and England was certain to carry out, and that except under the influence of such a belief they would never have surrendered the garrison and allowed the Irish war to come to a close.

The Irish House of Lords had even before the Union between England and Scotland shown themselves strongly in favour of an Act of Union between England and Ireland. In 1703, the Irish peers actually issued an address to her Majesty praying that she would be graciously pleased to direct measures for the passing of an Act uniting the Parliaments of England and Ireland. After the

Union with Scotland had been accomplished, the Irish House of Lords renewed the appeal to the Queen, and once again urged her to institute measures for the legislation which they desired to put in motion.   The Duke of Ormond was the Viceroy of Ireland.   Queen Anne and her Ministers paid little or no attention to the urgent appeal made by the Irish House of Lords and supported by at least some members of the Irish House of Commons. Froude the historian has made severe comment on the inaction or indifference of the ruler and her Council.   'No excuse,' he says, 'can be pleaded for Queen Anne's Ministers, or for the English nation whose resolution they represented in meeting these overtures of the Irish Parliament.'

Froude goes on to moralise in eloquent words on the neglect of what seemed to him an auspicious chance for an early and complete union between the Parliaments of the two countries.   'Opportunities occur in the affairs of nations which, if allowed to pass, return no more.   The offered union was thrown away when it would have been accepted gratefully as the most precious boon which England could bestow—was thrown away in the meanest and basest spirit of commercial jealousy. No rational fear of present danger, no anxiety to prevent injustice, no honourable motive of any kind whatever can be imagined as having influenced the persons whoever they were that were generally responsible for the decision.   In fatal blindness they persuaded themselves that the Union would make Ireland rich and that England's interest was to keep her poor. The Queen returned a cold reply " that she would give no particular answer at present, but would take the request into consideration." The consideration never came. The wisdom of the precious resolution was never doubted or reviewed; and from this one act as from a scorpion's egg sprang a fresh and yet uncompleted cycle of disaffection, rebellion, and misery.'

Froude was a man of high intellect, sincere purpose, and a most vivid descriptive power; but nature does not seem to have endowed him with the faculties which create a safe guide in political history. On no other political questions, moreover, is Froude so apt to go astray as on questions which have to do with the relations between England and Ireland. He seems in this particular instance to have allowed his own feelings to carry him as far astray in judging of the motives which inspired the action, or rather the inaction, of Queen Anne's advisers as in estimating the real value of the advice given by the Irish House of Lords. It is not necessary to assume that Queen Anne and her Ministers were governed only by a desire to pander to England's commercial jealousy, and to persuade themselves that England's interest was to keep Ireland poor. Queen Anne and her advisers might well have seen, without any marvellous inspiration of foresight, that a real union between England and Ireland would have been absolutely impossible under the conditions which then existed. They had probably the best reasons also for knowing that the resolutions of the Irish House of Lords, or even of the Irish House of Commons, were absolutely worthless as a representation of the feelings and interests which belonged to the Irish people. By no possible ingenuity of statesmanship could the great majority of the Irish people have been prevailed upon at such a time and under such conditions to accept a legislative union with England. The Irish Parliament, as we have already shown, was a Parliament merely of the conquerors, and had no claim whatever to represent the sentiments of the conquered. Indeed, the Irish Parliament, if such a question could have fairly been put to it, would probably have rejected with scorn and anger the bare suggestion that it had anything whatever to do with the sentiments and the opinions of the Irish population.

The English Parliament under Queen Anne was at that very time engaged, as we have seen, at the suggestion of the Irish Parliament, in passing fresh enactments for the repression of Popery, as it was called, in Ireland, the religion to which the vast majority of the population were still clinging with unabated devotion. The one central idea influencing the actions of the Irish Parliament was to make the Protestant Church absolute in Ireland, and if possible to compel the Irish people to accept its ministrations. Let us do justice even to the members of the Irish Parliament, the representatives of English conquest and of the English conquering race. These noble lords and honourable members had convinced themselves, no doubt, that it would be an immense benefit for the Irish people to be made converts by any process to the Protestant faith, and were quite satisfied that any amount of coercion applied for that purpose would, if only successful, have tended to the moral and material benefit of the Irish people. The same sort of thing has to be said, we may take it for granted, on behalf of every conquering race. The conquerors do not enact their penal laws merely for the wanton purpose of oppressing and torturing the races over whom they have come to rule. They are convinced in their own minds that their religion and their ways are the best for everybody, and that any needful coercion which can be exercised in the hope of compelling other races to adopt them must be amply justified by the possible result. But however the conquerors may satisfy their own minds on this point, the process of coercion is not one which is likely to lead to satisfactory and genuine union between those who exercise and those who have to endure the oppression.

It would probably have been no worse for the Irish if at that time the Irish Parliament had been completely merged in the Parliament of England. No English Parliament, even if it had been composed exclusively of Englishmen, could have been less fitted to represent the majority of the Irish people than the Parliament which was allowed to exercise its subordinate jurisdiction on Irish soil. Froude's eloquent indignation over the supposed loss of happy opportunity by Queen Anne and those with whom she consulted is wholly thrown away. The first condition of a real and enduring legislative union between England and Ireland would have been the abolition of all the laws inflicting penalties on the practice of that religion to which as a nation the Irish people were uncompromisingly attached. Even such a measure, were it possible at the time, could hardly have reconciled Ireland to those decrees which had dispossessed so many of her ancient families in order to bestow their lands and possessions upon the favourite soldiers of successive invaders and conquerors.

The Irish peasant of the West, the South, or the Midlands could hardly wander far from his own hovel without seeing the ruins of some castle which had been in former days the possession of an ancient family whose history was identified with the traditions of the region, or some castle, still in proud repair, which had been handed over by this or that conqueror to a successful follower as a reward for his military enterprise; or the mouldering walls of some abbey where the forefathers of that peasant had worshipped in the days gone by, before English Sovereigns had made it their duty to resist the growth of 'Popery.' Everywhere he turned, the Irish peasant met with evidences telling him that he belonged to a subjected race and was living in a conquered country. The Irish peasant has a natural love of old memories and old traditions. It is a question whether even a system of government

which gave him a fair chance of individual security,
prosperity, and happiness, would have quite made
up to him for the changes forced upon him by the
new owners of the land.   But in those days the Irish
peasant found no chance left open to him of
individual security and prosperity, and he was indeed
one of the most hardly used and impoverished
human creatures on the earth.   Irishmen of means
who were able to leave the country were already fast
flying from it to seek service in foreign armies and
in foreign lands, and those Irish who had to remain
at home found the truth forced on them more and
more with the life of every day that in their
imported rulers they had only enemies, or at the best
had only men who did not care enough about them
even to try to be their friends.   Under such
conditions it mattered little or nothing to the
majority of the Irish population whether the so-called
Irish Parliament was actually merged or not in
that English Parliament to which the laws of the
conqueror made it in any case subservient.

The readers of Walter Scott's novels—and one is
glad to know by the constant publication of new
editions that his novels find still increasing numbers
of readers in our own days—will remember some of
the powerful and painful chapters in ' The Bride
of Lammermoor,' which picture the constant state
of strife between the representatives and followers
of the ancient and dispossessed families, and the
members and followers of those families whom
revolution and conquest had settled in the ancient

homes. But at no time in Scotland had there been anything like the wide-spread unsettlement and re-settlement which conquest had accomplished in Ireland. Scotland had never been a conquered country, and even when her condition was most disturbed by war and revolution she had always maintained her national existence. Her people had never been threatened with extermination.

By the time that Queen Anne came to the throne of England the Irish people had seen so many unsuc-cessful rebellions that they had little heart left for any new attempt of their own, just then, and they clung to the cause of the exiled Stuart Sovereigns mainly because it seemed to promise some hope of a move-ment from abroad against England which might give Ireland a chance of asserting her national claims. The time had not yet come when English statesman-ship could raise its mind to the contemplation of any better means of making Ireland a contented, loyal, and prosperous member of the imperial system than by passing measures to prevent the growth of Roman Catholicism and to provide against any possible rivalry in commerce or manufactures which might tend to the disadvantage of English trade. The conditions under which alone the union with England could have been tolerated by Scotland no English Sovereign or states-man would have thought of conceding to Ireland, and the Irish people had no means of enforcing the conditions by any power of their own. There is no need, therefore, to feel any particular surprise when we read that Queen Anne and her councillors did not

pay much attention to the urgent request of the Irish
House of Lords for some measures to bring about a
formal union between the Parliament of the conquering country and the so-called Parliament of the
conquered people.

CHAPTER XXXI

THE RISE OF ROBERT WALPOLE

DURING the years which we have lately been following a new and a very remarkable figure in political
life was coming to the front. Sir Robert Walpole,
afterwards to become Earl of Orford, was establishing his claim to that position of commanding and
enduring influence which he was destined to assume
in the succeeding reign.

Robert Walpole was the son of an English country
gentleman, and was born in 1676. Robert Walpole,
the father, had represented an English constituency
in the House of Commons, and was owner of a large
estate. Robert, the son, received his education first
at a private school, afterwards at Eton, and then at
King's College, Cambridge. He was the third son, but
both his elder brothers died young, and in November
1700 he found himself owner of the family property.
He had not any natural inclination for study, but he
devoted himself with a characteristic steadiness to
the ordinary course of work during his school and
college days, and he succeeded in becoming at least a
respectable classical scholar. On the death of his
father he became elected as member for Castle Rising,
the constituency which the elder Walpole had repre-

sented in the House of Commons. It may be said that Walpole, the father, was a man much given to the enjoyment of country life and of all the habits then supposed becoming in a country gentleman. One of these habits was an indulgence in the ways of hospitality and in the consumption of good wine, and the story goes that the elder Walpole used to press his son Robert to drink glass after glass on the ground that it would not be fitting for a son to see his father under the influence of what fine writers would then have described as the flowing bowl.

Robert Walpole the younger, seems to have had, from his first entrance into public life, a thorough interest in the business of the House of Commons. He was one of the men to whom parliamentary life becomes at once a natural sphere of activity, and he attended most closely to all the parliamentary work that came within his range. He joined the Whig Party, and made something almost like a display of his devotion to the cause of the Protestant succession. He took part often in debate, and although he had not, and did not pretend to have, any of the gifts and arts that belong to the genuine orator, he soon attracted attention by his capacity for close and practical argument and his faculty for adapting himself to the comprehension of his listeners. The House of Commons was then, as it is now, an assembly where if a man can say anything really well he is sure to find appreciative listeners. Great influence can always be obtained in that House, even by men who never rise to eloquence, provided only that they can display

commanding intelligence, a comprehensive knowledge of the subject in debate, and skill in the array
of clear and coherent argument. A man with such
capacity is all the more likely to make a lasting impression on the House if he shows that he has no
inclination to speak for the mere sake of delivering
a speech, and that he only desires to address the
audience when he really has something to say which
ought to be said.

Walpole soon proved to the House of Commons
that he had in him the making of a political leader,
and the Ministry of the day were not long in finding
out that he was just the sort of man whose services
would be useful to an administration. In 1705 he
was appointed a member of the Council to Prince
George of Denmark, who then held the office of Lord
High Admiral; an office which, it need hardly be said,
had been given to the Prince for no particular reason
but that he was the husband of Queen Anne.
Walpole had not an easy time of it in this position,
and he was not a man who could be content to hold
what may be called an honorary place in any department. He applied himself with so much care and
assiduity and promise of success to this unsatisfactory
office that he won the confidence and approval not
only of Godolphin, but of the Duke of Marlborough.
From this time forth he was recognised by the Whig
Party as one of their leading men, and in 1708 he
was appointed to the office of Secretary at War.
Nor was this official promotion the only testimony
offered to the value of his political services. The

leadership of the administration in the House of Commons was entrusted to him, and he soon proved himself thoroughly equal to the duties and the responsibilities which came under his control.

The House of Commons always shows a marked inclination towards a Minister who can make a clear statement of facts, can set forth his arguments in sentences easily understood, can give his hearers the impression that he thoroughly comprehends what he is talking about, and does not attempt to bewilder them by sudden flights of eloquence. The great orator always has his place and can maintain it in the House; but if a man be not in the true sense a great orator the next best thing for him is that he shall never make any pretension to oratory at all, and shall always impress his audience with the comfortable conviction that they are sure to hear nothing which will put a strain on their minds, and at the same time are sure to get something in return for the attention they bestow. In every political generation we shall find illustration of the fact that a man of this order is more likely, on the whole, to be an effective leader of the House of Commons than one who is endowed with a genuine gift of eloquence. Robert Walpole soon proved himself to be a man of this mould, and everyone could foresee that a great ministerial career was opening for him.

When the impeachment of Sacheverell became a parliamentary question, Walpole was appointed one of the managers to conduct the business on behalf of the House of Commons. Now, Robert Walpole was conspicuous above all things else for what may be called his plain common sense. His keen, shrewd intelligence saw clearly into the real force and weight of contending elements at a time of sudden political storm. He knew very well that there were certain forces of political passion and religious fanaticism supporting the partisans of Sacheverell, with which it would not be quite convenient for a Ministry to contend. Walpole strongly opposed in private the idea of impeaching Sacheverell, but when Godolphin and the other Ministers showed that they were determined to carry out their project, Walpole was not by any means the sort of man to separate himself from his influential friends on a question merely of principle. He therefore performed his part in the impeachment with all becoming earnestness and display of skill. Perhaps his feelings on the subject underwent some change as he found that he had more and more to identify himself with the business of the impeachment. Perhaps the resolve came to him to make the best of an uncongenial position, and to turn the impeachment to the most practical account for the advantage of those by whom it had been instituted. The fact is that he published a pamphlet on the subject, bearing the title of 'Four Letters to a Friend in North Britain upon the publishing the Trial of Dr. Sacheverel.' In those days even a Minister of State sometimes found it convenient to make an appeal to public opinion through the medium of a pamphlet, and Walpole was not a man to neglect any means of serving the interests of the party to which he had attached himself.   Walpole's pamphlet directed itself against the influence of the Sacheverell partisans with characteristic sagacity and skill.

The argument of the pamphlet was that the whole object of those who maintained and worshipped Sacheverell was to establish a conspiracy with the Jacobite party at home and abroad for the purpose of raising the Pretender to the throne of England.   Nothing could be more calculated to discredit the Sacheverell agitation with the more reasonable part of the general public than such a charge as this if it could once be effectively brought home. The majority of the outer public would be likely to grow alarmed at the prospect of any new revolution whatever, having had revolutions enough within recent memory, and of course no true follower of the Church of England could have had any inclination to see a Prince of the House of Stuart brought back from France to rule over England.   But the influences of the time were too strong for any ingenuity of argument or adroitness in the raising of alarm to prevail against them, and, as we have seen, the result of the General Election was that Godolphin and his colleagues could no longer remain in office.

Harley and Bolingbroke came into power, and Harley was so much impressed with Walpole's capacity that he invited him to become a member of the new administration, and strongly pressed the invitation on him.   Harley had been naturally drawn towards Walpole for the same reasons as those which had guided the judgment of Godolphin.   Walpole had shown from his first entrance into public life a remarkable understanding of financial questions, and this was a capacity not common among rising administrators at the time.   There was much beside this which also influenced Harley in his effort to obtain Walpole's co-operation.   Harley had himself no gift of eloquence, and no appreciation of the orator's style even in its highest order.   He was above all things endowed with a faculty for management; he had none of the higher faculties of statesmanship, and was hardly qualified to judge of them or to care about them in others.   He probably saw good reason to believe that in Walpole he could have just the sort of colleague who would suit all his purposes, and would not be likely to hesitate overmuch about fine-drawn distinctions of principle where the work of successful administration was concerned.   Walpole, however, positively declined to join the new administration, and made up his mind to wait for some more suitable opportunity of exercising his capacity for the business of government.

Mr. J. R. Green, in his ' Short History of the English People,' gives a striking picture of Walpole in this earlier part of his career.   Mr. Green describes him as ' a young Norfolk landowner of fair fortune, with the tastes and air of the class from which he sprang.' ' His big, square figure, his vulgar, good-humoured face, were those of a common country squire.   And in Walpole the squire underlay the statesman to the last.   He was ignorant of books, he loved neither

writing nor reading; and if he had a taste for art, his
real love was for the table, the bottle, and the chase.
He rode as hard as he drank. Even in moments of
political peril the first dispatch he would open was
the letter from his gamekeeper.' In another passage
Mr. Green says that Walpole's 'prosaic good sense
turned sceptically away from the poetic and passionate sides of human feeling.' We read in this
passage of admirable description that Walpole
laughed at all oratorical appeals to the loftier or
purer motives of human action as schoolboy flights,
and Mr. Green adds that, 'for young members
who talked of public virtue or patriotism he had one
good-natured answer.' And that answer includes
a colloquial phrase which many readers might have
supposed to be of much more modern, and even of
Transatlantic, origin: 'You will soon come off that
and grow wiser.'

Mr. Green, as might well be supposed, does full
justice to Walpole's powers of administration. 'All
the greater statesmen,' he tells us, 'who have guided
the fortunes of England since Harley's day have been
found in the Commons,' and 'Of these great Com-
moners Robert Walpole was the first.' 'How great
a part Walpole was to play no one could as yet
foresee. But even under Marlborough his practical
abilities had brought him to the front. At the
moment when the House of Commons was recognised as supreme, Walpole showed himself its ablest
debater. Commerce promised to become the main
interest of England, and the merchants were already

beginning to trust to his skill in finance. As a subordinate member of the Whig Ministry at the close
of the war he gave signs of that administrative
ability which forced his enemies to acknowledge
that " he does everything with the same ease and
tranquillity as if he were doing nothing." How great
was the sense of his power was seen in the action
of the triumphant Tories on Marlborough's fall in
1712.'

The Tories proclaimed their sense of Walpole's
importance as an opponent in the most effective
and even dramatic way. From having been one
of the managers of a parliamentary impeachment
he suddenly found himself brought before the
public as the victim of an impeachment. Harley
and Bolingbroke accused the former Ministers of
corrupt dealing with the public accounts. Walpole
undertook the defence of his late colleagues, and conducted the case with so much ability, and such a
force of argument and evidence, that the charges
were believed by almost all impartial persons to be
nothing more than the common general accusations
made against the leaders of a fallen administration
by those who had turned them out of office.

To punish Walpole for his effective defence the
statesmen in power now made a much more direct
and positive charge against himself. Walpole was
formally and circumstantially accused of having
been, while Secretary at War, guilty of ' a high
breach of trust and notorious corruption.' He was
charged with having accepted a sum of about one

thousand pounds as a reward for having passed
certain contracts for forage in Scotland. Walpole
utterly repudiated the charge, and the whole question became the subject of a formal accusation—
it might be called a formal impeachment—in
the House of Commons. Those were days when
political partisanship asserted itself emphatically
where the character of a political opponent was at
stake; and the result of the debate was that a
majority of the House found Walpole guilty and
ordered him to be expelled from the representative
chamber and committed as a prisoner to the Tower
of London. The vote of the House also declared
that Walpole could not be re-elected to serve in the
Parliament then sitting. It has to be recorded,
however, that even the Tory House of Commons,
under the control of Harley and Bolingbroke, did not
show itself quite up to the desired level of partisan
hatred. Considering the strength of the Tory
majority in the House the vote of condemnation
pronounced against Walpole was not very large
numerically, even at its flood tide, and it soon began
steadily to ebb. The resolution proclaiming him
guilty of notorious corruption was carried to success
by a majority of only fifty-two votes. The significance of this fact will be more clearly understood
when it is mentioned that a distinctly partisan
question raised by Walpole himself at the opening of
the session had been defeated by a majority of
126. The difference between the majority in the
one case and the majority in the other may be taken

Q 2

as satisfactory evidence that the charges against
Walpole could not carry conviction with them to the
minds of any reasonable and impartial men.   As the
proceedings went on the majority grew smaller and
smaller.   The motion for Walpole's expulsion from
the House was only carried by 22 votes, and when
the resolution ordering his committal to the Tower
came to be decided, the majority against him had
dwindled to 12.

It is perhaps not too much to say that there was
a certain carelessness displayed in the management
of the contracts which might have justified even the
most impartial member of the House of Commons in
declaring that the whole management of the business
was not such as an ordinary employer would have
endured at the hands of his paid servants.   If some
member of the ruling party had proposed a vote
of censure upon Walpole for the carelessness he had
shown in conducting the financial affairs of his office,
the judgment of history would probably be that
Walpole deserved the censure, but that he was no
worse than most other Ministers who had held the
same office in preceding administrations.   When the
House had taken its final decision Walpole declined to
make any appeal to the consideration of his enemies,
or to offer just then any further vindication of his
character; he was accordingly committed to the
Tower.

At times of recent revolution, and of revolutions still believed to be threatening, it would have
been no very uncommon incident in the career

of a rising statesman to find himself suddenly removed from his place in the House of Commons to a cell in the Tower. But Walpole's was not an imprisonment of the heroic order, and it is probable that most of his opponents then believed that a sentence of imprisonment following a charge of mere peculation would be quite enough to bring the political life of a man like Walpole to an ignoble close. Walpole probably felt well satisfied in his own mind that he could have no difficulty in living down the kind of opprobrium which was put upon him by a decision mainly due to the spirit of partisan hostility. He went to the Tower, and remained there until the prorogation of Parliament, which followed not long after, and then the sentence was supposed to have worked itself out. The prisoner was released, and had nothing to do but to await a favourable opportunity in order to present himself once more as a candidate for a seat in the House of Commons.

The charge made against Walpole was of course only a part of the great attack directed with success against Marlborough. There was much better ground for the charges of somewhat the same kind which were brought up against Marlborough, although even the acts of which Marlborough was accused were not then uncommon or unrecognised practices in the business of such a department as that over which he had control. The substance of the accusation made against Walpole was that he had received, either by himself or through an agent, two separate

sums of money from the forage contractors in his
department. Mr. MacKnight, in his Life of Bolingbroke, gives a clear and concise summary of the
explanation which Walpole set forth for the instruction of his friends and the public after the majority
in the House of Commons had done its worst.
'Walpole explained,' Mr. MacKnight says, 'that a
fifth share in these contracts had been expressly
reserved for his friend Robert Mann; that the contractors chose to pay Mann these sums rather than
admit him into the partnership; that such arrangements were then very usual in the public service;
and that, as Secretary at War, he received no
advantage whatever from the bargains.' It might
well be said that the public revenues were not fairly
dealt with when any such arrangements were allowed
to interfere with the freedom of competition for Government contracts; but at the same time it would
be hard to hold Walpole personally responsible for
defective practices which had been allowed to grow
up in the public service, and from which it could
not be shown that he had derived any personal
benefit.

Mr. MacKnight is naturally a great admirer of
Bolingbroke, whose life he has written; but he can-
didly admits that in stimulating and supporting this
charge against Walpole he did not act with that
honourable fairness which might have been expected
from a great Minister, even though he also happened
to be a vehement partisan. Mr. MacKnight, indeed,
does not hesitate to call the attention of his readers

to certain passages in Bolingbroke's own official conduct which would compare very unfavourably with
the worst of the charges brought against Walpole.
'St. John, too,' his biographer tells us, 'as his correspondence with the Duke of Marlborough shows, had,
while himself Secretary at War, been far from averse
to pocket all the percentages he could obtain ; only
during the preceding year, as Secretary of State, he
had allowed Jack Hill and Mrs. Masham, on account
of the expedition to Canada, to appropriate an
immense sum of public money to their own use in a
manner much more flagrant than—the difference of
circumstances and persons considered—anything that
had been charged against either Marlborough or
Walpole ; and it was with the greatest management
that the House of Commons was at this time prevented from inquiring into this misappropriation of
at least twenty thousand pounds.'   Mr. Green
pronounces the charge of peculation against Walpole
'groundless,' and Burton, while not hesitating to find
fault with the manner in which the business of the
contracts was conducted, believes that Walpole's
defence of his own personal action was well sustained
by the facts.   Army contracts in times of war have
been the frequent source of trouble and of scandal in
the civilised countries of modern times, and we may
be quite sure that the great campaigns of classic
history were not conducted without frequent instances
of nefarious jobbery in the providing of supplies for
the armies.

Within the recollection of living men, various

illustrations of this ignoble historical fact have come
before the world. During the Crimean War such
questions were brought under the notice of Parliament, and led to more than one ministerial crisis. In
the war between France and Prussia, some of the
leaders of public opinion among the French insisted
that the success of the German arms was mainly due
to the fraudulent manner in which the money set aside
for the supply of the French troops was misapplied by
scheming politicians for the benefit of themselves and
their favoured contractors. Much more lately still,
the war between the United States and Spain gave
occasion, even among the victorious Americans, for
many charges of dishonest practice between the
agents of the Government and the competing candidates for Government contracts. At the very time
which we have now reached we find that one of
the most exciting questions brought up in our own
Parliament has had to do with contracts for the
supply of horses to the British troops employed in
the South African campaign. It would not be in the
least degree reasonable to impute any extraordinary
aptitude for corrupt practices to the public men of
Queen Anne's reign merely because of the charges
made against Marlborough and Walpole in connection
with Government contracts, or even because of the
evidence of a careless and indefensible way of doing
business which these charges brought to light.

Walpole was not long in getting out of his
troubles and making a new start on his parliamentary
career. The charges made against him left no real

stain upon his character, and his committal to the
Tower left no darker shadow upon his record than if he
had been called to order by the Speaker of the House
of Commons for some infraction of parliamentary
rules. Any intelligent observer of public life must
have seen, at the time, that the newly-released
prisoner from the cell on Tower Hill was only at the
opening of a great political career. But the history
of Queen Anne's reign has not much further occasion
to deal with the doings of Robert Walpole. It was
only when that reign came to a close and the Hanoverian succession established itself on the throne of
England that the real capacity of the man had a full
opportunity of finding its field of action.

Soon, however, events were to show how uncertain
was the basis on which Walpole's political enemies
were endeavouring to establish their power over the
destinies of England. Walpole, whatever his defects
of character and however lacking he may have been
in an exalted sense of principle, whether politics or
morals were concerned, would appear to have been
sincere in his practical devotion to the Whig Party
and his anxiety for the maintenance of the system
established by the Revolution. He was inferior to
Bolingbroke in those mental endowments which
obtained for their possessor the title of a man of
genius. But he could see into the realities of things
much more clearly than Bolingbroke, and he could
estimate the relative strength of the conflicting tendencies in the political world just then with an accuracy
to which Bolingbroke could make no pretension, and

would not have understood how to appreciate in another man.

Walpole was evidently quite able to see that the principles of the Revolution had established themselves satisfactorily in the minds of the great majority of those British subjects who had anything to do with the movements of political life. It would not have been possible to persuade him that the exiled Stuarts had the slightest chance of being restored to the throne of England. Therefore, even if he had been so far wanting in consistency and in principle as to lend his help towards a Stuart restoration, he was far too sensible, shrewd, and foreseeing a statesman to find himself tempted in the slightest degree by the prospects and the adherents of such a cause. Walpole already saw his way, and was only waiting for his time.

CHAPTER XXXII

ALEXANDER POPE

THE name of Alexander Pope is inseparably associated with the reign of Queen Anne, although most of the works which made him especially influential and popular in the society and the literature of his time were not published until after Queen Anne's reign had come to its close. His fame, however, had been quite assured, and his position as a poet had been won for him by such poems as 'The Rape of the Lock,' 'The Messiah,' 'Windsor Forest,' and the 'Ode to St. Cecilia's Day.' Pope was born in London in the year of the Revolution which dethroned the Stuart Kings and made William of Orange ruler of England. He was of lower middle-class parentage, but was fond to believe that his father could boast of high descent. His father was in business as a linen-draper, some say a hatter, in the Strand; and the young Alexander Pope does not seem to have had anything like a finished education according to the standard of that day or of ours. His poetic gift showed itself in very precocious verse; according to his own account, 'while yet a child' he 'lisped in numbers, for the numbers came.' Some of his earliest poems have a peculiar gravity and stillness about them little resembling the strains of exuberance and emotion generally given to the world by the earliest efforts of inspired youth. Pope had the good fortune, in one sense at least, to attract the attention of Wycherley by some of his youthful poems, and Wycherley became his literary patron, and introduced him to the society of London men of letters.

Pope had much of the temperament which satire and comic literature have in almost all ages associated with the character of the precocious poet. Many of his personal qualities would have needed but little satirical exaggeration in order to construct an effective and life-like caricature of egotistical and dissatisfied poetical aspiration. Pope was always in weakly health, with a feeble and deformed frame. His lack of physical strength and his bodily ailments had done much to make him morbidly sensitive. He was quick of temper, changeful of mood, impatient of restraint or contradiction, ever craving for sympathy, and too often finding the sympathy, even when sincere, wholly unsatisfying. With such a temperament he was naturally too ready to get into quarrels with his friends, and could easily be brought into the mood which made him apt to believe that his friends of yesterday had become his enemies to-day. He quarrelled with men and he quarrelled with women, and some of his quarrels have become famous episodes in the history of literature. Yet his life was, on the whole, one of remarkable prosperity, and he was drawn into close association

with some of the most famous men and women of his
time.

In those days the workers in literature were
brought into intercourse with the leaders of political
and social life more than was usual in most of the
former and most of the later periods of English history.
We do not find Tennyson and Browning, Dickens and
Thackeray, brought into close companionship and
actual co-operation with the great statesmen and
political leaders who conducted or disputed the ruler-
ship of the country during the reign of Queen Victoria.
But Alexander Pope and other literary men as well
were in constant comradeship with such political and
parliamentary leaders as Bolingbroke and Harley,
and the author of a great poem or romance not infre-
quently interrupted or varied his career during Queen
Anne's reign by becoming a great political pamphleteer.   A man like Bolingbroke claimed to be an
author and a thinker as well as a director of State
policy ; a man like Harley loved to be regarded as a
patron of literature, an authority on art, and the
chosen friend of artists and authors.   Pope therefore
lived at a time and came into a social life especially
favourable to the encouragement and development of
rising poetic genius, and he can have known but little
of the hard and bitter struggles which other men, not
inferior in natural gifts, have had to go through in their
efforts to climb that ' steep where fame's proud temple
shines afar,' as another poet has described the attempt.
Few poets have ever been more successful than
Pope in acquiring what may fairly be called a wide

and lasting popularity. Genius of the highest order he certainly did not possess, and some of his most influential critics have not hesitated to assert that he never possessed the true gift of genius at all.

It is not easy to maintain any profitable disputation as to the precise descriptive power, the exact and, if it may thus be phrased, the scientific meaning of words which are employed in the effort to establish certain distinct grades and orders of intellectual capacity. Whether the combination of mental and lyrical gifts, with which Pope was undoubtedly endowed, did or did not amount to actual poetic genius would perhaps be a futile subject of discussion, so uncertain are the standards by which we can pretend to test the existence of that undefined element we call genius. That Pope possessed anything like the highest order of creative genius, that he belongs to the highest rank of poets, nobody in our time would think of asserting, and, indeed, the tendency for several past generations has been rather to disparage Pope than to over-state his gifts of poetry. But it will probably be admitted by all that he created a new poetic form, and that in some of his poems at least we come on passages and thoughts, on imaginings and fancyings, which appear to be entirely original, and can hardly be set down as indicating the possession of anything less than the gift of that genuine poetic fire which we regard as the light of genius. There is, for instance, an exquisite imaginative and creative faculty in ' The Rape of the Lock,' which could hardly be the work of the most felicitous imitation, even supposing that it bore any evidence of imitation at all. There are passages in ' The Messiah ' over which the most casual and careless reader, even though he may have learned from modern criticism to think little of Pope, may be compelled to linger in deep and delightful thought, and in which he recognises the thrill of that touch associated with poetical genius. The very fact that both these poems are professedly founded on literary models is in itself but another proof of Pope's poetic originality. 'The Messiah' was given forth as an imitation of Virgil's eclogue ' Pollio,' and the most delightful passages in ' The Rape of the Lock ' were suggested by a once famous phantasy which had to do with the sprites and other aerial beings sacred to Rosicrucian mysteries. But in both instances Pope only took from his model the mere suggestion for his poem, and treated it entirely and absolutely after his own fashion and according to his own fancy.

In order to make a work of art truly original it is not necessary that the first idea of it shall have come up in the mind of the poet who undertakes to give it a new form. The greatest critics of the ancient and modern world have laid it down as a law that the originality of a work of art consists in the treatment of the materials, and not in the mere conception of the idea the artist intends to work out. Lessing has declared that no matter how often a certain subject has been used before, the latest poet who deals with it is entitled to be regarded as the creator of an original poem if he treats his

subject in his own way and has the gift of modelling
it into a work of art.   Goethe has contended that
'Troilus and Cressida' may be regarded as one of
Shakespeare's most original plays because, although
Shakespeare found his story and its principal
characters in Homer, he treated story and characters
entirely according to the guidance of his own inspiration.   Indeed, if this artistic doctrine, which at first
may seem somewhat paradoxical, were not strictly
true, some of the noblest works of art produced by
the literature of all times would have to be set
down as wanting in originality.   Virgil's great epic
would have to be described as a mere imitation
of Homer, Shakespeare's finest dramas as mere
borrowings from history or legend, and Goethe's
'Faust' as the tenth transmitter of a well-known and
popular story.   The sprites and sylphs and gnomes
of 'The Rape of the Lock' become entirely original
creations as the fancy of Pope has made them live
and move before us.   It is not therefore because of
any want of originality that Pope must be refused a
place among the greatest English poets, but because
his imagination, his intellect, and his constructive
genius did not enable him to create out of any
materials such works of art as those which Shakespeare, and Dante, and Goethe have given to the
world.

Nothing can be more perfect in its way than the
smooth and measured melody of Pope's verse.   One
is sometimes surprised to find that the English
language, which is not in itself essentially musical in

sound, can have been wrought into lines of such harmonious cadence as those which come upon us almost everywhere in Pope's finer poems. The truth has to be admitted that Pope, whether consciously or unconsciously, relied too much on measure of rhythm and melody of sound, and the most sympathetic reader grows a little weary now and then of the smooth and regulated cadence which falls upon his ear as every line is read aloud. Pope had an exquisite gift of phrasing, and we have had occasion to remark before in this history that many of his phrases and his lines have become part of the familiar stock of conversation, and are repeated again and again in our own time by many who have forgotten, or who never knew, the source from which the phrases or the passages have come. Pope's popularity, which was probably unequalled among English-speaking peoples in his own day, and has perhaps been fading ever since, may be made intelligible even to the younger readers of the present generation when their attention is called to the fact that so much of him still lives with us, and comes so often almost unbidden to our lips.

Bentley said with justice of Pope's translation of the 'Iliad' that it was a fine poem, but that it was not Homer. Pope's version of the 'Iliad' is indeed, in all but the story and the personages, curiously unlike the 'Iliad' of Homer. The style of Pope's rendering is too ornate, too elaborate, too verbose, to have any affinity with the simple, strong, inspired style of Homer. But it has to be said for Pope's rendering of the 'Iliad' that he brought home the story of Troy's fall to millions of readers from that time to this who might otherwise have never known the whole story of the marvellous epic. There have been greater English translations of Homer than Pope's, but there was never any other English translation which exercised such a charm over what may be called the average or the popular intelligence as was wrought by Pope's captivating version. In every generation since Pope's time thousands of schoolboys in these countries have learned in the first instance to appreciate the wondrous tale of Troy divine from Pope's translation of the 'Iliad.' Something more even than this may be said. A large proportion of young men have in every succeeding generation been drawn to a study of Homer in his own tongue by the charm of Pope's translation. Many a middle-aged and scholarly man who has learned to appreciate Homer in Homer's own language has frankly owned in his maturer years that it was from Pope's 'Iliad' he first acquired that love of the epic story which could not be satisfied with anything short of a direct acquaintance with the original. To have accomplished such a success as this would be enough to entitle its author to the gratitude of the world, and to a noble place among the world's poetic benefactors.

Pope's translation of the 'Iliad' does not belong to the literary triumphs which adorn the reign of Queen Anne, for it was not published until after Anne's death; and it is only mentioned here as one

of the evidences which go to prove the title to im-
mortality awaiting the author of ' The Messiah ' and
' The Rape of the Lock.'   Perhaps it is not exaggeration to say that if these two poems were the only
productions of their author they would of themselves
secure for Queen Anne's reign a renown in poetic
literature.

Too much of Pope's life and genius was wasted on
futile and deplorable quarrels and on the infuriate
satire in which his anger could not be kept from
expressing itself.   Some of Pope's satirical pieces are
amongst the finest things he ever did, so far as
eloquence and impassioned poetic vituperation and
exquisite melody of sound can make a poem fine ;
and it is hard when we read one of these masterly
satires not to lose, for the time, in our enjoyment of
the thoughts, the images, and the words, our just
sense of regret that such a master of English verse
should have wasted his best powers on ignoble
personal controversy.   The closing lines of ' The
Dunciad,' another of Pope's poems which did not
make its appearance until years after Queen Anne's
death, have been described by critics of great
authority as displaying Pope's imaginative faculty
at its very highest reach.   The lines which picture
the darksome fate to come over the world in punishment for its worship of false poetic gods, the time of
doom when ' art after art goes out, and all is night,'
the time when universal darkness covers the whole
world of thought and intellect, show beyond question
a power of poetic imagination which we rarely find

in those works of the author that are devoted to higher and more noble themes than personal satire.

Pope was only too ready to find offence where no offence was intended, and no warmth of previous friendship could prevent the sudden chill which sometimes came over him when he fancied some friend had done him wrong. As we have already mentioned in this volume, 'The Messiah' was originally published in an early number of 'The Spectator,' and at that time Pope was one of Addison's most devoted friends. When afterwards a quarrel sprang up between them, or when Pope believed he had reason to quarrel with Addison, he assailed Addison in satirical verses all the more bitter and wounding because they professed to come from one who, for the sake of old friendship, would gladly have refrained from uttering a word of condemnation if only the condemnation could be suppressed without injustice to the cause of truth.

Pope's quarrel with Lady Mary Wortley Montagu is one of the standing comicalities of literary history. It must be owned that the poet does not show to much advantage in the stinging verses with which he assailed the lady, and the contrast which he suggests between her diamonds and her dirty smock seems to belong to the order of dispute which might have been popular in the region described by Hogarth as Gin Lane. The fame of Lady Mary Wortley Montagu survived, however, even the satire of Pope. She was a woman of remarkable and original intellect, she had a rare gift as a letter-writer—she wrote

letters which have taken an abiding place in literature
—and the world owes much to her courage as the
promoter of a great and successful experiment, the
practice of inoculation. It was believed at one time
that Pope had been treated with sudden and merciless
contempt by Lady Mary when the friendship which
she always showed him had been misunderstood
by him and he offered himself to her as a lover.
The story went that Lady Mary had been cruel
enough to heap insulting ridicule upon him because
of his personal deformity, and without any excuse
for such an outburst of scorn. There does not seem
any reason to believe that Lady Mary had acted
with such unprovoked and merciless cruelty; but
it is certain that she did in some way wound the
feelings of the over-sensitive poet, and Pope thought
no satirical language could be too strong or too
coarse in which to express his resentment. The
quarrel, and the manner in which Pope conducted
his part of it, and his attempt afterwards to explain
his words away, did more harm in the end to the
man than to the woman. Lady Mary's claims to the
esteem and admiration of the world are not much
affected by any satirical imputations as to the condition of her underlinen; while every true admirer of
Pope must regret that such a poet should have
demeaned himself by so ignominious a display of
enmity in such a quarrel.

When we are considering and endeavouring to
study the development of Pope's poetical genius we
must of course take full account of the conditions

under which its development had to work its way.
We must consider the general character of that
public to which he had to address himself. A great
original poet—a poet of the highest order—follows
no doubt the inspiration of his own genius, and does
not think of shaping his verse so that it may find
a ready acceptance from any particular audience.
The minstrel in Goethe's poem declares that he
sings but as the song-bird sings, without any thought
of public favour or personal reward. It has also
been said that oratory is heard, but that poetry
is overheard. This latter distinction seems to be
scarcely accurate, for it is not possible to think of
the poetry of Homer as something merely overheard
by an audience of whose existence the poet is un-
conscious and to whose attention he is indifferent.
Even the declaration of the minstrel in Goethe's poem
could hardly apply to any but poets endowed with
thoroughly original inspiration, whose only guide and
impulse is the genius that compels them to pour
forth their thoughts. Pope at his very best was not
endowed with this gift of absolute originality. There
was in him a natural tendency to imitation. Some
poetic form had an especial charm for him at one
moment or another, and his poetic faculty shaped
itself accordingly for the time, although the method
by which he made use of his own materials secured
for his work, according to Lessing's principle, a just
title to originality. The form of Dryden had at first
a great attraction for him, and it was only as he grew
bolder and stronger that he came to obey more freely

the impulse of his own inspiration. There are passages in Dryden which show a boldness of imagination and a vigour of expression never equalled by Pope ; but then it must be owned that the finest verses ever produced by Pope are those which show least evidence of the early influence exercised on him by Dryden.

The influence which seems to have had most to do with the moulding of Pope's verse was the influence of that social life to which his verse was chiefly addressed. There was in Pope's time no such reading public in existence as that to which the authors of our own day may hope to appeal. During the reign of Queen Anne, and for long after her reign had come to an end, there was really no reading public according to the meaning which we now attach to the words. The great majority of the people in these countries during that time may be described as men and women who never read books at all. The poorer classes generally had not learned to read, for there was no system of national education going on, and the voluntary efforts made by churches and charitable institutions and beneficent individuals for the instruction of the people could not accomplish much in the way of enlightenment to the common mass of ignorance. Only in the large cities and towns could a writer expect to have many readers, and even in the cities and towns his readers were limited to a comparatively small section of society. The audience to which a book had to appeal in London was confined almost altogether to those belonging to what were called the higher classes, and to those orders of society which looked up to the higher classes for guidance and illumination as to the books they ought to read. The various clubs in London which were frequented by men of rank or by men of intellect, by poets and essayists, by wits and politicians, constituted the audience on whose favourable reception the young author had in the first instance to depend. If such an audience were to appreciate and welcome his early efforts, to pronounce its judgment decisively in his favour, and declare him entitled to a place in literature, then our young author's fame might spread so far as to procure for him a certain proportion of readers outside the privileged circle of society and the clubs. But in no case was it possible for a mere poet to find such a public for his works as he might have found, if he deserved it, in days nearer to our own.

Nothing was more common during the reign of Queen Anne, and long after, than the publication of a book by subscription, as it was called. A young poet appealed to some of his influential friends on behalf of a new volume which he was eager to publish, and the influential friends agreed among themselves, and obtained the agreement of others, to subscribe towards the expense of printing and publishing the volume at so much per copy. Thus the author and the printer were secured in the first instance against loss on the venture, and thus and thus only, in many cases, was there any chance of the book ever coming before the public. Pope himself, when he was preparing his translation of the 'Iliad,' issued an appeal to his friends and the public in general for a list of subscriptions which might enable him to encounter the risk of presenting his translation in printed form to the world.

It must be said that Pope, like many other literary men of his time, got some of his work done for him on the plan which may be described as the farming-out system. When he had shaped a literary project of considerable magnitude he sometimes entrusted the construction of certain portions of it to the hands of men whose skill and capacity might be safely employed for the work, and he gave to the whole composition the benefit of his name. All the more important passages, if we can fairly make such a distinction when speaking of a literary production, were no doubt his own, and in the case of Pope's translations we may fairly assume that all the finer passages were his; but it was not then thought beneath the dignity of a poet or an author of any kind to accept frankly and without concealment the help of a literary co-operation which was nevertheless not formally acknowleged—a co-operation which, if accepted without formal acknowledgment in our days, would be kept a secret even from the most intimate friends of the author whose name appeared upon the title-page.

When Pope was engaged in the translation of the 'Iliad' it must be owned that some manner of co-operation was decidedly necessary for the accomplishment of his task. Pope was not a scholar, even in the sense which the word bore during the reign of Queen Anne. It would hardly be true to say of him as Ben Jonson said of Shakespeare, that he knew little Latin and less Greek; but he certainly had not a scholar's acquaintance with the language of Homer, and he must have helped himself sometimes, as a modern schoolboy might do, with his Latin translation to supply his deficiencies in Greek. It was therefore only natural and reasonable that he should avail himself now and then of the assistance which could be given to him in his work by Englishmen possessed of more scholarship than he could pretend to. Whatever help Pope may have had in this way, it may be taken for granted that the construction, the arrangement, and the final polishing up of the whole rendering were kept in his own hands. Pope may be said to have popularised that peculiar form known as English heroic verse which we find in his translations and in so many of his original poems. It is exquisitely smooth, well balanced and melodious; it often delights and never offends the ear; but it must be owned that the verse sometimes becomes monotonous when it is not broken by vivid descriptions of action or by animated dialogue. Pope appealed to a circle of readers with whom form and phrase ranked higher than nobler and more poetic qualities.

A public chiefly composed of authors, wits, and scholars who take it on themselves to give literary laws to the contemporary world is very apt to fall into ways and dogmas and fashions of its own, and to accept the ordinances of its own school as eternal laws of criticism. Every literary or artistic school or clique established at any time is apt to degenerate into such a mental condition, and to regard mere imitation of the mannerisms which belong to the recognised masters as the best evidence of high artistic culture. This was especially to be observed at the time when Pope was becoming famous among English poets, and it led him, when once he had found his way into the charmed circle, to believe that his whole mission was accomplished when he had obtained its approval and applause. A poet of the highest creative order would never have allowed himself to be fastened down by the rules of a school; but then Pope was not a poet of the highest creative order, and he naturally believed that the supreme seal of approval had been set upon his work when it won for itself the hall-mark of the order to which he presented it.

Queen Anne's days will rank with the highest epoch of English literature, so far as prose writing is concerned; but it can claim no such exalted place in poetic composition, and Pope's poetry may be regarded as illustrating very effectively some of its finest qualities and most of its prevailing defects. There are passages in his best original poems which seem to fill the reader with the sudden hope that the poet is about to break through all conventional rules and to strike a bold original note which shall soar into the most exalted poetic atmosphere. But the reader or the listener is doomed to disappointment, and, according to his mood of mind, is either inclined to turn away from Pope altogether because Pope has not fully satisfied his yearnings, or returns to him with renewed admiration and love because he has gone so near to the full accomplishment of the heart's desire.

It has often been observed that many readers even in our own days have found themselves compelled, sometimes against their own will, to belong to this latter order. They have felt and frankly acknowledged to themselves a certain disappointment with Pope's best efforts, and yet have returned to him, found that his work could never lose its charm for them, and that they could not open a volume of Pope without being compelled to linger lovingly over its pages. In our own time Pope commands a far larger number of readers than Dryden, even among readers who can clearly see for themselves, and are quite willing to admit, that Dryden had a quality of genuine originality which never belonged to Pope, and that Dryden reached poetic heights to which Pope does not seem even to have aspired. Pope has been on the whole one of the most liberally rewarded of men both by the applause of his own time and by the praise of the generations which came after him.

In our own times the number of Pope's readers is but small when compared with the numbers of those who are familiar with the poets of the nineteenth century. But even in our own times it is doubtful whether any poet whose period of production came between the Elizabethan age and the time of Byron, Wordsworth, and Shelley has so large a number of readers as Pope can yet command. Those who still read him may be said to feel something like a real affection for many of his poems. When they open a volume of Pope they are drawn to read on and on, and they put him down with a distinct sensation of reluctance. Many passages in his poems are like dear old friends, or like the loved notes of once familiar music which can never fail to touch the ear. This is the more surprising because of the artificiality which shows itself so much in Pope's mode of construction, and even in the very melody of his verse ; but it is none the less true. Despite all the irritability, the quarrelsomeness, the jealousies which were part of the poor deformed poet's nature, there must have been in him a sincere and loving heart or he could not have maintained such a hold on the affectionate interest of so many generations of readers.

The world is accustomed to think of Pope in association with the shore of that beautiful stream, beside whose ' translucent wave ' he lived so long, in that home which still preserves his name and is made famous by his memory. Perhaps the character of Pope's poetry may be compared not unfairly with that of the river which he loved so well. The poetic stream of his verse was not a Rhine flowing between ranges of hills and beneath antique and legend-haunted castles. It was not that Italian river with the wild wave and headlong speed which Byron celebrated. It was not a Mississippi making its way through a vast continent, from the winter snow of the North to the semi-tropical regions of

the South.   It was like the Thames as it flowed past
Pope's home, beautiful, tranquil, musical, not driven
by tempest, not calling up images of passion and
destruction, but holding always the love of those who
from the first are able to appreciate its charm.

CHAPTER XXXIII

SHADOWS CAST BEFORE

THE health of the Queen had been for some time sinking into a state which caused more and more anxiety among those around her. She had been a victim to attacks of gout, and these began to grow more serious as the months went on. The Queen was growing stout and even somewhat corpulent in figure, and began to show an increasing unwillingness to take any manner of exercise. She was still, however, as anxious as before to go steadily through all the public functions which belonged to her sovereign state, and when she had occasion to be present at some ceremonial in the House of Lords she now had to be carried to her place in a chair. Those who saw her most often felt fresh alarm every day at the visible signs that her strength was failing, and that her course of life was drawing to its close. In the minds of most observers the anxiety occasioned by those unmistakable symptoms of decay was not merely created by a loyal dread that the good Queen Anne might soon have to take her leave of existence. Even among those who felt the deepest and most sincere regard for Anne it was only too well understood that more than the Queen's

life might depend upon the issue of the malady
which was threatening her.   The genuine supporters
of the Hanoverian succession might have cause for
alarm indeed, but then at least they could give
expression openly and freely to their doubts and
fears, and incurred no personal danger because of
their utterances.

But there were others who could not afford to
express in public any of the exciting hopes and disturbing doubts which were created for them by the
sinking condition of the Queen's health.   The Jacobite party began to be inflamed by a new passion
for their cause as they saw the time approaching
when the English people must decide between the
German Prince from Hanover and the heir to the
Stuart dynasty.   The mere fact that the close of
Queen Anne's life seemed drawing near had already
effected something that might almost be described as
a Stuart restoration in the political plans and movements of the Jacobites at home and abroad.   Anne
had not yet reached that period of life when her
death might be looked for as an event near at hand
in the ordinary course of things, and until lately she
had not given any indications of an approaching
break-up.   Therefore the hopes of the Jacobites had
remained for some years without any new stimulant.
The progress of the great war had turned away
attention from the chances of revolutionary intrigue,
for it did not seem in the least degree likely that
while such a struggle was going on the English
people could be induced to listen to any proposals

for a dynastic counter-revolution. But now that the war had come to an end, and at the same time the health of the Queen seemed almost utterly broken, the Jacobites became suddenly inspired by new hopes, and the hopes began to express themselves in deliberate plans and in a secret policy.

There cannot be any doubt that the main-spring of the Jacobite movement was just then in the Ministry of State itself. The two leading advisers of the Queen, Oxford and Bolingbroke, were secretly laying plans to facilitate the restoration of ' the King over the water.' It certainly cannot be supposed that Oxford had any sentimental attachment to the cause of the Stuarts. There was in him nothing whatever of the romantic enthusiasm which can sometimes lead even commonplace men to risk all that makes life dear for the sake of a hopeless cause. No matter what Oxford's personal sympathies might have been, it may be taken for granted that if he had believed the Hanoverian succession to be quite safe and sure he would have held to his high position in office as long as ever he could, without troubling his mind by any vain endeavour for a restoration of the Stuarts. The King, who had been recognised as Sovereign of England by Louis the Fourteenth, and had lately been disavowed and expelled by the Grand Monarch, might continue to be the Pretender and nothing more, so far as the Earl of Oxford was concerned. But nobody could know better than Oxford how strong was the repugnance to the succession of the

family from Hanover which was felt among a large
proportion of the English people everywhere. As
the time grew nearer when the new chapter of history
would have to be opened, the greater seemed to be
the popular disrelish for the introduction of the
unknown Prince from Hanover, about whom and
whose habits the most unprepossessing and discouraging accounts were already beginning to find
their way into England.

The prevailing dissensions among the various
Protestant denominations in Great Britain had
tended much towards a deadening of that horror of
Popery, as it was termed, which had at one time
been a powerful influence in securing the Act of
Settlement. All this was apparent to the watchful
mind of Oxford, and with every fresh piece of news
as to the state of the Queen's health, the question
must have come up for his consideration, how a
sudden crisis in the succession might be got through
with the greatest advantage to his own personal
interests. Bolingbroke, on the other hand, it may
safely be said, was at heart inclined to be a votary
of the Stuart cause. The memories of the Stuart
dynasty had a charm in them which fascinated him.
There was a poetic attractiveness in the very misfortunes of the Stuart family in later times which
appealed to Bolingbroke's sympathy, and contrasted
touchingly with the utterly prosaic character which
common report had already taken upon itself to set
forth as the especial attribute of the Hanoverian
House. Bolingbroke therefore may be regarded as

by temperament and sympathies disposed to favour the cause of the Stuarts, and to consider hopefully the possibilities of a Stuart restoration, while Oxford may be described as inclined to believe, on a comparison of the chances, that a Stuart restoration would give him a better opportunity of maintaining his position at the head of political affairs.

Even already it was becoming evident to those who were brought much into intercourse with the two statesmen that the differences of character and temper between Oxford and Bolingbroke were displaying themselves in jealousies and misunderstandings. The relations between the two men were not those of co-operation, but rather those of actual rivalry. Each man was selfish and ambitious in his own way, but the ambition of Oxford was that of one who, if he had been a member of a civic corporation, would have set his heart upon becoming Lord Mayor, while the ambition of Bolingbroke was that of the man of genius who feels that he is born to rule a State and is resolved to make a name in history. The two Ministers did not trust each other, and Oxford, at least, was not disposed to place much confidence in anybody. At the same time the prospect of a sudden close to the reign served as a fresh stimulant to the rival activities of both the great political parties in the State. The Tories seemed for the time to have won a complete success over their adversaries. They had accomplished a peace and they had secured the favour of the Queen, and the Whigs had been to all appearance thrust into

the background.   The common impression among
Tories of the outside order was that the Whigs
were got rid of once and for ever, but no such comfortable assurance filled the minds of Oxford and
Bolingbroke, and of those in close political association with them.   The Whigs themselves were keenly
on the watch for any possible opportunity to
discredit the ruling party and advance their own
interests.   There were some among them who were
much better able than either Bolingbroke or Oxford,
to estimate accurately the strength of the hold
which the principles of the Revolution had over the
great majority of the people south of the Scottish
border.   The Whigs now began to display a
renewed energy in various forms, and they set
themselves actively to work on the widely prevailing dread of Jacobite plots and the return of
Popery.

The leaders of the party thought that a favourable time had come for impressing the public
mind with some new evidences of their zeal for
the maintenance of the Protestant succession.   An
Address to the Queen was moved in the House of
Lords praying that she would use her influence with
the Duke of Lorraine, in whose territory the Stuart
claimant had taken refuge, to expel the Pretender
from his dominion, and to prevail upon all other
Sovereigns and Princes on terms of amity with her
not to harbour the exiled Stuart in any lands under
their control.   The Address was adopted by the
House of Lords, but not without some reasonable

protest on the part of many peers who could not be accused of the slightest sympathy with the cause of the Stuarts.   These men pointed out in the course of the debate that, as all the countries of Europe were now on friendly terms with the Queen of England, the carrying out of such a policy as that recommended by the Address, would leave to the unfortunate Pretender and the members of his household no patch of European soil whereon they might find a shelter.   Another view of the subject was also pressed very sensibly on the attention of the peers. Suppose, it was urged, that some of the Continental Sovereigns declined, out of mere feelings of humanity, to comply with the request which the Queen was advised to make, how was it proposed that the Queen should enforce practical attention to her appeal ? Was it intended that England should forthwith declare war against any foreign ruler who refused to submit to the dictation of the English Government ?

In due course the Address was presented to the Queen, who happened at the time to be in a condition of health which allowed her to give her attention to the business of the State.   The Queen, in reply, told the House of Lords that she had already made her wishes clear with regard to the harbouring of the exiles who had been mentioned in the Address.   But she added a sentence which could have given little satisfaction to some of the more active and eager among the Whig party.   ' I think, however,' said the Royal reply, ' you will agree with me that if we could cure our animosities and divisions at home it would be the most effectual method to secure the Protestant succession.' The quiet rebuke conveyed in this short sentence had something of queenly dignity in it. It might well have been remembered, too, by those who were disposed to cavil at this mild remonstrance, that the Queen was herself of kindred with the princely exiles whom she was invited to join in hunting out of civilisation.

The fact that the Address was got up mainly as a demonstration of zealous Whig activity for the Protestant succession was made plain enough to all impartial observers by the manner in which the exiled Stuarts had lately been conducting themselves. If any new attempts had been recently made by the followers of the Stuarts to cancel the Act of Settlement; if any intrigues had been going on openly or secretly with foreign Sovereigns; if there had been any rumours of risings in the Highlands or of landings anywhere on the Scottish coast, then there might indeed have been a reasonable explanation for the sudden appeal made by the House of Lords in their Address to Queen Anne. But as a matter of fact the Stuart partisans abroad had been keeping themselves very quiet of late. The Peace of Utrecht, and the pledges which the King of France had found it necessary to make as a part of that treaty, had wrought the most discouraging and disheartening effect on those who had for many years founded their only hopes on the sympathy and protection of the French Sovereign. The truth is that this sudden outburst of activity on the part of the Whig nobles, accompanied as it was by what seemed a demand for a policy of mere persecution, had a good deal to do with the revival of that passionate spirit of loyalty among all the partisans of the Stuart cause abroad and at home which led to the first outbreak of rebellion in the reign which was soon to follow. The House of Lords did not yet abandon their idea of putting a little extra pressure on the Sovereign. A second Address to the Queen was adopted, the purport of which was to express the surprise and regret of the Peers that the pressure put by Anne upon the State of Lorraine had not brought about some more distinct and satisfactory result. To this supplement· ary Address, if it may thus be termed, the Queen only replied by a formal acknowledgment of its reception.

Then the Whig party in the House of Commons thought the time was appropriate for a demonstration in support of that appeal which had been made by their political associates in the House of Lords. An Address was moved in the House of Commons inviting the Queen's attention to the inconvenience which might result to the monarchy from the fact that the exiles of her family were at that time receiving shelter in a region so perilously near to England— these were not the words of the Address, but this must have been its meaning—as the Duchy of Lorraine. Mr. Wyon, in his 'History of Great Britain during the Reign of Queen Anne,' tells us that a sarcastic comment was made in the House on the proposed Address by Sir William Whitelocke, an old Cavalier of eighty years, who 'remembered,' he said, ' an address being carried up to the Protector to procure the expulsion of Charles Stuart from France only a short time before that Prince was invited back to the throne of his ancestors.' The Address was carried, and probably the leaders of the Tory party did not see that any particular object was to be gained by offering it their serious opposition.

Nothing came of the whole performance, and it is only mentioned here as an illustration of the anxiety which the Whig party thought it timely to display for the cause of the Hanoverian succession. It may be added that the mere desire of the Whigs to make public manifestation of such an anxiety was in itself a distinct evidence of the uncertainty and alarm aroused in the popular mind by the increasing illness of the Queen and the prospect of her approaching death. There is something grim and ghastly in the picture thus given to us of the hopes and fears, the partisan rivalries, the personal ambitions just then fixing their attention upon every new symptom which seemed to tell of the Queen's approaching end. There were not many around Queen Anne who loved her, who had been long in companion-ship with her, or had any feeling of tenderness for her. Those who watched over her had no other concern in their minds but the question whether her living on or her dying at once would better serve their political projects. Some painter with the genius of a Hogarth might have pointed the moral of that crisis for the benefit of posterity by the pictorial conception of an imagined scene in the palace of the sinking Queen.

The Whigs did all they could to rouse the country into a condition of ever-growing alarm about the plots against the Protestant succession. The very measures which they took for this purpose had the effect of giving fresh stimulus and new hope to the designs of the Jacobites. When reasonable men set themselves to dispel the alarm by dwelling on the fact that the Treaty of Utrecht had pledged the King of France to recognise the Protestant succession in England, and to do everything he could for the suppression or prevention of Jacobite plots in France, the answer of a Whig politician was sure to be that no sane Englishman could rely upon a French Sovereign's word, and that the moment King Louis saw the slightest chance of repudiating the contract with safety and advantage to himself, he would be only too willing to lend his help to any likely plan for a Stuart restoration. It was a common declaration among the Whigs, at the time, that the Ministers of State round Queen Anne were not merely Jacobites at heart, but that they and their creatures were in constant negotiation with the Stuarts and their partisans abroad, and were preparing for a sudden stroke of policy to bring about a counter-revolution the moment the Queen should breathe her last. Nor is it possible to doubt that the conduct of leading Tory Ministers gave only too much warrant for these accusations. Lady Masham and Bolingbroke were in frequent communication with the Jacobites abroad, and if Bolingbroke had not thus far actually committed himself to any definite scheme for a counter-revolution, it is certain that he was quite willing to listen to suggestions concerning the preparation and furtherance of such schemes, and to consider, as carefully as his impulsive and fitful temperament would allow, their chances of possible success.

Queen Anne herself had not always acted with due caution in her dealings with the family from which her successor on the English throne was to come, or even in her manner of conducting herself towards the representatives of the Hanoverian House. When it was urged upon her that George the son of the Electress Sophia, the Prince who was destined to succeed Queen Anne on the English throne, ought to be invited over to England in order that he might take his seat in the House of Lords as a British peer, Anne would not listen to the suggestion, and showed no favour to any proposition which might indicate a willingness on her part to encourage a visit from the Hanoverian Prince. George himself had become possessed with the idea that the Tory statesmen in office were already doing everything in their power to open the way for a Stuart restoration. George was not well acquainted with the ways of English political parties, and he had little knowledge of the personal characters of Oxford and Bolingbroke, except what he happened to obtain through leading members of the Whig Opposition. Apparently he had come to regard Oxford and Bolingbroke as devoted adherents of the Stuart cause, men who were prepared to risk all that was dear to them in life on the chance of accomplishing a Stuart restoration. Oxford was certainly about the last man in the world to whom such a description could have properly applied. There is not the slightest reason to believe that he would have voluntarily risked any interest of his own with the hope of forwarding the interests of the Stuarts. But to a man of such moral constitution and temperament it was quite natural that the sudden activity of the Whigs in promulgating their alarm about a Jacobite restoration should seem the best possible reason for endeavouring to find out what chances there might be for a successful enterprise of the kind, in order that he might choose his side and take his measures accordingly.

Bolingbroke, according to many contemporary accounts, was beginning just now to be seriously impressed by the gravity of the whole situation. His more intimate friends observed that he had made some change in the free habits of his life, and especially that he had ceased to indulge his love for excessive drinking and could leave the dinner table in almost as sober a condition as that in which he had sat down to it. It does not appear that he was putting much constraint upon himself where his gallantries, as they would then have been gracefully styled, were concerned. But he probably would not in any case have allowed his love-making to interfere too much with the time which he thought fit to devote to his administrative and Parliamentary business. Bolingbroke had certainly committed himself much more deeply than Oxford was ever likely to do to the Jacobite schemes or plots which were going on abroad. But if George the Elector could have been in a position to estimate accurately the forces then influencing the destinies of England he would probably have come to the conclusion that the demonstrative activity of the Whigs themselves was one of the chief sources of encouragement to the hopes of the Jacobite partisans.

Anne seems to have had a strong repugnance to any suggestion, whether prompted by State policy or whatever other motive, which would have brought her into personal association with the Hanover family. It has often been noticed by the historians of royal houses, that a reigning Sovereign is apt to cherish a keen dislike towards the apparent successor, when the successor is not actually a son or daughter, and there are even cases in which the dislike has grown up when the heir to the throne is also the heir of the family. Anne was disinclined even to talk about the Electress Sophia and her son, and showed in this way the habit common to many persons not very strong of will or temperament—the habit of acting as if a refusal to speak of a disagreeable prospect could have the effect of putting the prospect off to a greater distance. This, however, was intelligible enough in Queen Anne's case, because Anne still had a strong sentimental feeling for the representatives of her own Stuart family, and even if she could not cherish any real hope of a Stuart restoration, she yet became more and more unwilling, as the days went on, to accept the actual condition of things, and to reconcile herself to any manner of association with the family which was destined to succeed her own on the throne of England. The Electress Sophia was now in her eighty-fourth year, but was still full of life, was animated with an eager curiosity about everything going on within the sphere of her own interests, and had a surprising faculty for talk. She had ceased to be the reigning Electress, and her son George held the position of active ruler in Hanover.

George was now a man of much more than middle age. He was born in March 1660, and in 1682 he married his cousin the Princess Dorothea of Zell. The story of his married life is one of the grimmest romances of history. He believed his wife to have carried on an intrigue with Count Königsmark, and he obtained a divorce from her, and kept her as a prisoner for many years, until her death, in the Castle of Ahlden, in Hanover, where the tourist visitor is still shown some dismal memorials of her melancholy fate. Her supposed lover had met with a violent and mysterious death. George had held high command during the war of the Succession; and our readers have met in these pages with some accounts of his soldiering. His eldest son, George, had already left his youth behind him, and it was therefore open to Queen Anne to form a tolerably clear estimate of the characters and doings of those whom the Act of Settlement had appointed to succeed her. The Court of Hanover was well known to be always more or less divided by constantly recurring domestic feuds. The Princess Sophia had not much affection left in her for her eldest son, George, whom nature does not seem to have endowed with the faculty of inspiring affection even among the members of his own family. Sophia, however, did all that she could to keep up a decent appearance of domestic concord for the benefit of the outer world, but Queen Anne both sought and found ample opportunity of becoming acquainted with the real condition of affairs in the Hanoverian household.

Meantime the Princess Sophia became much impressed by the accounts which she received from her Whig correspondents in England, concerning the plans which the Tory Ministers were supposed to be preparing for a Stuart restoration. There was an ambitious and even impetuous spirit enclosed in the breast of this old lady, and it is stated by contemporary writers that she had often frankly declared her determination not to die if she could help it before she had signed her name as Queen of England. While the Duke of Marlborough was still in power, he had strongly recommended the Princess to send her grandson George over to England in order that he might make himself popular there, and thus open the way for a general welcome to the Hanoverian family. Marlborough assured the advisers of the Electress that her grandson would have nothing to

do but to settle for a time in London, pay deferential
court to the Queen, make friends of the ruling Ministers, show himself as much as possible in public,
keep himself strictly free from all intermeddling
with political affairs, and that thus he could easily
reconcile the English people to the prospect of the
Hanoverian succession.   Marlborough went so far as
to intimate that arrangements could easily be made,
by which a measure might be proposed and carried
through Parliament for settling on her grandson a
liberal allowance from the funds of the State.   The
Electress was naturally greatly impressed by such
views coming from such an authority.   She entirely
agreed with the policy recommended to her, and
was most anxious to hasten her grandson's departure
for the new field of enterprise in that country to
the throne of which he was some time to succeed.
But the usual lack of concord in the councils of the
Hanoverian family gave her little opportunity of
securing a fair chance for the policy which she was
willing to adopt.

' George the Elector,' as he was contemptuously
called by the Jacobites in England, set himself
stubbornly against the proposed experiment.   He
interposed all manner of delays and difficulties
whenever it seemed likely to take any practical
direction.   All sorts of explanations were thought
of at the time to account for his unwillingness to
sanction the mission for his son.   It was even said
that he was so niggardly in his nature that he
could not be induced to advance the amount of

money necessary to start George the younger on the expedition, even though it might turn out before long to be a very profitable enterprise. The probability is that George the Elector was influenced by a certain quality of hard and narrow common sense, which made an essential part of his character. He had been studying, as well as he could from a distance, the state of things in England, and he felt strongly inclined to doubt whether the visit of any Hanoverian Prince to London just then would not be regarded by Queen Anne as a most unwelcome intrusion.

Some surprise had been created, not only in Great Britain, but also in Hanover, by the fact that the royal speech, which the Queen delivered at the close of one Parliamentary Session, did not contain the usual and formal words in which her Majesty expressed her resolve to support the Hanoverian succession. The attention of the ruling family in Hanover did not fail to be drawn to this somewhat curious omission, and George the Elector probably, and not unreasonably, set it down to the fact that the English Ministers were becoming more and more doubtful as to the enduring efficacy of the Act of Settlement, and were not unwilling to have it publicly known that their hopes were for a restoration of the Stuarts. George the Elector yielded at last so far to the urgency of some of his advisers as to express his willingness that his son, or some other member of his family, should go to England, provided that Queen Anne could be prevailed upon to express a distinct wish for such a visitation. The Electress Sophia was by no means so cautious, and was now, in fact, rather inclined to press the recognition of her family directly on the notice of the English Queen. Some correspondence went on between George and the English Ministers, in which he made it very clear that he had come to believe in the existence of powerful Jacobite plots against the succession of the Hanoverian family. He urged upon the English Government the necessity of bringing strong pressure to bear for the expulsion of the Pretender from Lorraine, and he declared that the leaders of the Jacobites were actually giving out that they had in preparation a plan for effecting a landing on the Scottish coast, while Scotland was undefended by a powerful fleet, and that their efforts would be backed up by the support of some of the Continental States.

Under these conditions, George, or the personage whoever it was that conducted his part of the correspondence for him, represented earnestly to Queen Anne's Government the importance of establishing in England some member of the Electoral family as an additional security to the Queen's own safety, and to the maintenance of the Protestant religion as the creed of the State. The terms of these recommendations made it quite clear to Queen Anne's advisers that George was fully determined not to send his son to England unless and until he should receive a direct invitation from Queen Anne herself. Nevertheless, a report was spread abroad that Prince George, son of the Elector, was coming over to England in any case, and was actually on the eve of his departure from Hanover. This story was brought to the ears of Anne, and the poor Queen, whose recent fits of illness had reduced her to a condition of almost hysterical nervous excitement, was thrown into a perfect passion of anger. The cause of her excitement and her wrath did not arise merely from the idea that the Hanoverian Prince was coming uninvited into her dominions, as if he had a perfect right to take up a commanding position there. The Queen was in that state of mind which comes not uncommonly to those who have reason to believe that the end of life cannot be far away for them. The nearer Queen Anne came to her closing days, the more nervously she shuddered at the thought of death, and the more keenly she felt wronged by any suggestion reminding her that the shadow was upon her. She could only regard a visit just then from a member of the Hanoverian family as a declaration made to her very face that her reign was looked upon as virtually over, and that her successor was actually coming to take his place on the throne.

Queen Anne made her feelings very clearly known to the members of the Hanoverian family. She wrote to the Electress Sophia, to the Elector George, and to the Prince his son, and the letters were despatched at once by State messengers to Hanover. In these letters the Queen assumed the

manner of one whose royal authority is rudely and
wantonly invaded. She told the Electress Sophia
that any attempt to establish in England a Prince
from Hanover, as if by a kind of right on his part,
while the reigning Sovereign was still on the English
throne could only tend to weaken the authority of
the actual Sovereign, and to encourage the
discontent and sedition already prevailing in the
kingdom, because of the strong objection felt by
many to the prospect of the Hanoverian succession.
Queen Anne expressed to the Elector her surprise
that a Prince of his sagacity and judgment should
not be able to see that any seeming infringement of
her royal authority must only have the effect of
imperilling the security of his own hopes and
prospects. She went on to say, she was firmly
persuaded he would not suffer the smallest dero-
gation of his own authority as a ruler; and she
declared, 'I am no less sensitive about mine; and
I am determined to oppose any project which may
interfere with it, however fatal the consequences
may be.'

Queen Anne's letters gave the deepest distress
to the Electress Sophia. Wyon tells concisely and
effectively the story of the two days that followed:
'During three hours of that summer night she paced
up and down the walks of Herrenhausen, descant-
ing upon her affairs to an Irish gentleman named
Molyneux, who was on a visit to the Court with
letters of introduction from Marlborough. The next
day she was unable to leave her bed; but Molyneux

was summoned to her chamber and entrusted with the Queen's letters, that copies might be made of them and transmitted to friends in England. Her health appeared perfectly restored on the following morning. She dressed, and dined with the Elector according to her usual custom, and despatched Molyneux into the town to fetch the copies which had been made. He returned to find the servants of the Electress in tears around the dead body of their mistress, who had just expired in one of the public walks of the park. She had been overtaken by a shower of rain, and in her efforts to reach shelter had perhaps burst a blood vessel.'

Wyon regards it as very probable that Queen Anne's decisive refusal to sanction the Electoral Prince's residence in England precipitated the death of the poor old Electress. But at the time of life which Sophia had reached it is quite easy to understand that any disappointment might have brought about a physical disturbance great enough to hasten death. The shower of rain in the Herrenhausen park, and the hasty attempt to get within shelter, might of itself have been enough to put an end to a life so frail and so long outworn. In any case we can hardly visit Queen Anne with responsibility for the death of the Electress Sophia. Nor was the event one calculated to make any serious mark on the development of English or Hanoverian history. Neither England nor Hanover could have benefited much by her living long enough to interpose a reign, which must needs have been short, between the

sovereignty of Queen Anne and the rule of George
the First.   But there is something curiously, almost
grotesquely, grim and tragic in this story of the
letters sent by the fading Queen of England and the
event which, from whatever cause, followed their
reception by the aged Electress of Hanover.

Sophia the Electress was in many qualities a
very remarkable woman.   She had been beautiful
in her early days, and had retained some of her
charms after she had long left her prime behind.
She had sweet and gracious manners; was able to
bear a brilliant part in conversation even with men
of intellect and culture.   She spoke with fluency
English, French, Italian, and Dutch, and she aston-
ished many a foreign envoy, who was new to her
court, when he found that she could talk with him
in his own language.   Two of her elder brothers
bore names not likely to be forgotten in the story of
England's dynastic and political convulsions.   Prince
Rupert—'Rupert of the Rhine'—was one of these,
and Prince Maurice the other.   Sophia was born at
the Hague, and it has been observed that there might
be some dispute as to whether German or Dutch
ought to be called her native tongue.

When the Act of Settlement was under discussion Sophia did not think it likely she could
survive Queen Anne, and she was not at the time
particularly anxious that her son George should
succeed to the English throne.   She had formed the
idea that George was by nature cast in a mould
which did not fit him for the duties of a constitu-

tional Sovereign, and she foresaw nothing to come
of his succession to the British Crown but a life of
struggle and danger for him and for the country
of his adoption.   For some time she was believed to
hold the opinion that the best way out of the difficulty, for all parties and peoples concerned, would
be that the Stuart Prince who claimed the British
throne should change his religion, quietly adopt the
Protestant faith, thus make himself acceptable to the
people of England, and rule happily over that
country without any risk of provoking a new
revolution.   Indeed, it was fully believed at the
time that this opinion of hers had been made
distinctly known to James Stuart, and that it was
only one of many influential opinions urging him in
the same direction.   The Electress Sophia, as it will
be seen, was not quite fanatical in her views about
religion.   She had accepted some of the ideas which
were beginning to be common, even then, among a
certain class of German scholar, and was inclined to
lay down as an axiom that, as long as princes and
other persons acted honestly and meant to do good,
it did not much matter what their particular form of
religious faith might be.   James Stuart, however,
could not be prevailed upon to regard the subject
from the same point of view, and no advice at this
or any other time could induce him to renounce his
religious faith for the sake of improving his chances
of a throne in England.   When the Act of Settlement became a recognised reality Sophia made up
her mind to accept, in the fullest sense, the

responsibility which it imposed upon her family, and towards her closing years, as we have already mentioned, she came to express the hope that she might not die before attaining the right to have the title of Queen of England carved upon her tomb. And now the end had come, and the pious wish was not to be gratified.

Meanwhile George the Elector appears to have acted with sound common sense in his replies to the letters of Queen Anne. He endeavoured to impress upon the mind of the Queen that he could not possibly find any advantage in an effort to impair her royal authority in England or have any desire to carry out such a purpose. He assured the Queen that his only reasons for recommending his son's visit to England were to be found in the impression he had formed—an impression which had received the support of many qualified authorities—that the visit might help to smooth away any objections still lingering among Queen Anne's subjects to the succession of a foreign family. Thus far George had not shown any of the despotic temper for which his mother gave him credit; but it may be doubted whether his letters did much to win the heart of Queen Anne.

CHAPTER XXXIV

ADDISON'S ' CATO '

WHILE the shadows of some coming events were thus cast before, as we have seen, one event in London deserves description for the literary interest which belongs to it, and the political interest with which it came to be surrounded. This was the production at Covent Garden Theatre of Addison's tragedy 'Cato.' The play may be regarded as the boldest of Addison's poetic efforts. Its production formed a sort of epoch in the history of the English drama. The ambition of the author seems to have been to put a play upon the English stage which should not be a mere attempt at the reproduction of the great Elizabethan drama, and should be free from the influence of the Restoration period. Addison had been urged by many of his friends and admirers to revive high tragedy in a new form, and had felt himself filled with courage and confidence for the attempt. The judgment of succeeding generations may be assumed to have dealt conclusively with the claims of 'Cato' to accomplish such a purpose. Criticism has long ceased to dispute over the merits of Addison's drama, or even to concern itself much about the place it takes in literature, and it can hardly be said any longer to hold a place upon the stage.

We are all now in something like agreement as to the qualities of ' Cato.' We think of it merely as a poem cast in dramatic form, and thus regarded it will be admitted by all readers of intelligence and taste to have many passages of great poetic force and beauty, many noble thoughts expressed in lines of thrilling and melodious eloquence, and some situations which a genius more attuned to dramatic work might have set forth with undying effect upon the stage. English drama was, in fact, at that time passing through a season of eclipse, and the genius of Joseph Addison had not found the spell that was to pack clouds away and welcome the new day. But there were many who believed then that a fresh and splendid era of the English drama began with ' Cato,' and no inconsiderable time had yet to pass before the general decision of criticism had decided that the work, whatever its exalted qualities, was a poem in dialogue and not a drama.

There are some of us now who find Addison's poem, even when regarded merely as a narrative in verse and not as a stage play, less thrilling in its closing passages than the story told in plain prose by Plutarch. Nothing can be more simple than the manner in which Plutarch tells us how ' Cato ' made up his mind to relieve himself of life; how he argued out his own case in his effort to justify himself to those around him, and to carry complete conviction to his inner conscience; how he read his

Plato at intervals, and to little purpose, for the very passages he was reading were a condemnation of suicide; how he fell into sleep and woke again at midnight, sent to the Port for news, and saw his physician; remained awake until the morning birds began to sing, and their music soothed his mind and brought him some sweetness of peace; fell asleep again, and after this interval of rest awoke only to carry out with determined hand his tragical resolve.

The reader—at least the reader of our generation who has read over the story as told by Plutarch —finds the closing passages of Addison's poem somewhat too grandiloquent, overwrought, and rhetorical to express the real dignity of the tragedy, or to touch the human heart. But the public opinion of Addison's day found no fault on that account, and the play was regarded by most critics as a masterpiece of dramatic literature. After Addison's time an unfortunate Englishman, an inferior poet and pamphleteer and a connection of Addison's who committed suicide, left behind him a vindication of his action in the words, written on a slip of paper : 'What Cato did and Addison approved, cannot be wrong.' It is not easy to understand how this admirer of Addison had come to the conclusion that the author of 'Cato' must have approved of self-slaughter because he made the great Roman's death the subject of a dramatic poem. He might as reasonably have declared that Shakespeare approved of suicide because he wrote a play about 'Cleopatra' and another about 'Othello.'

In this history we have less to do with the poetic
or dramatic merits of Addison's play than with the
political sensation which was created by its production.   The fame of the author would have in any
case secured a crowded house, but the fact that
' Cato,' and the announcement of the Treaty of
Utrecht, came on the public about the same time,
added a powerful incentive to popular excitement.
Addison had identified himself with the policy of the
Whigs on the subject of that treaty, and the rumour
had gone abroad through London that the play
was to be made, in some form or other, a means of
invoking a condemnation of the measures which,
according to the Whig estimate, had ended in a surrender to France of all the advantages won by Marlborough for England.   All the leading Whigs were
therefore determined to make the occasion one for
a public demonstration of their sentiments, and for
the awakening of patriotic opinion against the conduct of the Tory Ministers.   Bolingbroke, however,
was not a man likely to submit to any such manifestation without making an effort to turn it aside or
to overpower it altogether.   Never could political
opponents have found an adversary gifted with
greater aptitude for turning everything to his own
advantage. He had become acquainted long in
advance with the resolve of the Whig leaders to
convert this modern version of Cato's tragic story
into a popular demonstration, and he soon made up
his mind that if mortal courage, readiness, and
ingenuity could bring about such a result, the

demonstration should be on his own side. He determined, as the representative of the Tory party, to
point the moral of the tragedy in his own way, and
to the advantage of his political party. A brilliant
and characteristic idea took possession of him—the
idea of adopting the play as a poetic and glorified
expression of Tory sentiments, and proclaiming it as
such from the first rising of the curtain.

When the night came the theatre was crowded
to excess. In the boxes on one side of the stage
were the leading peers and politicians of the Whig
party, while on the other side, to the great surprise
of many in the theatre, both before and behind the
curtain, were the representative men of the party in
power. In the stage-box, to which all eyes were
soon turned, sat Bolingbroke himself—the man who
was universally regarded as the author of the peace
which the Whigs were denouncing as a national
humiliation. In the pit the enthusiasts of the Whig
party were decidedly more numerous than their
opponents; but there, too, as in every other part of
the house, the Tories contrived to have an effective
muster. A phrase borrowed from the vocabulary of
the theatre may, perhaps, be allowed on such an occasion, and it is therefore appropriate to say that the
Tories, wherever they sat, took their cue at once
from Bolingbroke. It is easy to understand how a
temperament like that of Bolingbroke, delighting
in artistic effects, and finding natural enjoyment in
thrilling sensations, must have revelled in the opportunity given by so extraordinary a game as that which

he was prepared to play out to the end. Boling-broke's idea was to proclaim the Tory adoption of the play at the earliest possible opportunity. The Whigs, however, were a little in advance of his purpose, for they began their impassioned applause before a word had yet been spoken on the stage. The Tories, led by Bolingbroke, were equal to the occasion, and followed the first notes of Whig approval by a vehement outburst of applause, which filled the whole theatre with sound, and seemed like the indignant answer to an insolent challenge. The Tory applause might be interpreted to mean : 'You Whigs dare to claim this play which is now to open as a demonstration on your side ; we, the Tories, tell you that it speaks our sentiments, and that, before long, you and the whole country will learn the truth.'

The Whig part of the audience must have been a little put out at first by the unexpected reply given to their demonstration. The common, and not un-natural, idea among the Whigs was that the Tories would set themselves as much as possible against the play from the very beginning, and that a sullen silence would probably greet the opening of the drama. A political leader less full of resource than Bolingbroke might possibly have thought that there was nothing better to do than to remain silent at first and wait for some chance of turning a scene or a passage in the drama to his own partisan account. But the course taken by Bolingbroke asserted the claim of his party from the very outset to be regarded as the true champions of liberty, of patriotic devotion, and of national glory.

The play as it went on lent itself with a curious felicity, or infelicity, to the objects of each of the contending parties. 'Cato' abounds in stately generalisations and in vaguely grandiloquent sentiments. When the lines of the play sounded a lament over the fall of popular liberty, then the Whigs had the best of the applause, and appeared for the moment to have scored a success. In the same manner, when the heroic traditions of earlier days were pictured as fallen into decay, again the Whigs had the advantage, because the audience were reminded of an inglorious peace. But on the other hand, when Cato rose to denounce a military dictatorship, then the Tories carried all before them, for it was brought home to the consciences of many, even among the Whigs, that Marlborough had endeavoured to force on the Queen his claim to be appointed a military dictator for life. Likewise, when some line spoken on the stage could be interpreted as a protest against a policy which would allow the temples of the gods to be desecrated, the Tories had once again the advantage, for could it be denied that Godolphin when in power had authorised the persecution of Sacheverel? But the final and crowning honours of the evening were decidedly won by Bolingbroke, and were the result of a bold and ingenious action which might be called a dramatic masterpiece. Booth, the famous actor, was performing the part of Cato, and when the curtain fell upon the last act, and the tumults of conflicting or at least rival applause were well-nigh over, Bolingbroke sent to Booth a pressing invitation, amounting to a command, to visit him in the stage-box. The great actor came at once, and then Bolingbroke arose, and in full sight of the whole crowded theatre, presented Booth with a purse containing fifty guineas and declared that such was but a poor reward for the service he had done to the State by illustrating with such splendid dramatic effect the protest of liberty against a perpetual military dictatorship. This was the triumph of the night, so far as political manifestations were concerned, and even the Whigs themselves must have admitted that Bolingbroke had won the game.

The event was in itself an effective illustration of the conflict in public opinion created by the Tory policy, and of its culmination in the Peace of Utrecht. In our more modern English history, since the days of the great Reform struggle during the reign of William the Fourth, no event ever brought opposing political parties into such a condition of open hostility. Nothing that even the elders of the present generation can remember, no antagonism of political parties aroused in England during the Crimean War, or between the British supporters of the North and of the South during the American Civil War, or between the Home Rulers and the anti-Home Rulers during Gladstone's later years, had anything like the same outward and visible effect upon social life as that which was brought about in England by the Treaty of Utrecht. Macaulay has described the state of

things in some impressive sentences : ' The ties of party
superseded the ties of neighbourhood and of blood.
The members of the hostile factions would scarcely
speak to each other or bow to each other. The
women appeared at the theatres bearing the badges of
their political sect. The schism extended to the most
remote counties of England.' Of course that schism
had its centre of life and its greatest field of display
in the metropolis. Perhaps the scene witnessed in
the theatre on the night when Addison's ' Cato ' was
for the first time produced might be described as
the crowning ceremony of the great political dispute.
Nothing seems more in keeping with the whole spirit
of Bolingbroke's career than the manner in which
he turned the occasion to the account of his own
party, and transformed what might have been a
political humiliation into at least the semblance of a
complete triumph. The triumph was not to last
long. Perhaps that ' Transformation Scene ' in the
theatre may be regarded as the culminating point
of the Tory success.

With that scene the figure of Addison may be
allowed to pass away from this history of the reign
of Queen Anne. Addison's career, indeed, was not
yet over. The poet and essayist had still much
writing to do, and the politician had to fill high
offices of State. Addison had some years to live
under the reign of another Sovereign. But the pages
of this present work have not much more account to
render of his literary or his political career. As a
politician that career was but a failure, and he can

only be described as a statesman in the sense that he filled some high offices of State. His failure in political and administrative work has not in the slightest degree affected his literary fame. We remember the poet and essayist, and forget all about the member of Parliament and the holder of high office. Few eminent men have ever been more loved than Addison by posterity as well as by contemporaries. He seems to have well deserved the affection which was given to him, for the few faults which he had were nothing worse than weaknesses of temperament, and had no kinship with the ignoble qualities of greed and selfishness, of malignancy and envy and sycophancy, of corruption and of hatred, by which even genius itself is sometimes degraded and made to seem ignoble.

We have spoken already of the quarrel which Pope endeavoured to fasten upon Addison, and it seems only too clear that the quarrel was altogether of Pope's making, and that Addison had neither given reasonable occasion for it nor showed the least inclination to keep it up. Pope had got it into his mind somehow that Addison was jealous of him, disliked him, and was in the habit of disparaging him; and Pope had an undue sensitiveness which left him easily open to erroneous impressions of this kind. The passage containing the supposed attack on Addison is in Pope's 'Epistle to Arbuthnot,' and it describes Addison by the name of Atticus. Probably English literature hardly contains any rhymed passage of the same length from which so many quotations are so often made. Some of the phrases and the lines of this satire on Addison have passed into the ordinary discourse of modern social life, and are reproduced every day in talk and in writing by many who have never known or troubled themselves to think where the familiar words were first to be found. How often do we hear even still of someone who can :

> Bear, like the Turk, no brother near the throne ?

Shall we ever cease to be told of some ignoble person who can ' hate for arts that caused himself to rise'? One can hardly glance over the newspapers of any particular day without learning what it is to 'damn with faint praise,' or without reading the censure of those who are

> Willing to wound, and yet afraid to strike,
> Just hint a fault, and hesitate dislike.

There does not seem the slightest reason to believe that this disparaging picture bore any resemblance to Addison, but the phrases we have quoted and others from the same poem have unquestionably been applied in numberless instances, during every generation since Pope's day, to men whom the description fitted much better than it ever could have done in the case of Addison. The literary world and all who admire brilliant satire may therefore without great want of Christian charity feel glad that Pope flew into a passion with his great contemporary, and composed those lines which have been used with happy effect for the castigation of so many offenders since the time when the author of 'The Messiah' fell out with the author of 'Cato.'

There could be little doubt even from the evidence of the text itself that the satirical portrait was intended for Addison. The line which tells how this personage could 'like Cato give his little senate laws,' fastens the application on the author of the tragedy as if it were a label. Indeed, the story went that in the first version of the satirical poem the name of Addison appeared without any attempt at concealment. The lines so often quoted:

> Who but must laugh, if such a man there be?
> Who would not weep, if Atticus were he?

were written originally, according to this story, with the name of Addison standing boldly out where that of Atticus was introduced in the more recent copy. At all events it is quite certain that nobody at the time had the least doubt as to the object of the satire. There are various explanations given of the reason, or the unreason, of Pope's attack upon his former friend; but the generally accepted account seems to be that Pope took offence because Tickell had begun a version of the 'Iliad' after Pope had undertaken his own translation, and Pope fancied he had reason to believe that Addison had had some part in the preparation or at least the encouragement of this rival effort. There is no valid evidence that Addison had the slightest inclination to back up any attempt at competition with Pope's rendering of the 'Iliad,' but from all we know of Pope's temper it is easy to understand that it would not have required much evidence to fill the poet with the sudden conviction that somebody or anybody had done him an injury. The story of the quarrel will not soon fade from literary records. As the name and the memory of some otherwise insignificant personage are kept alive through unending generations by a portrait which has come from the brush of an immortal painter, so the poor little story of Pope's anger against Addison can never quite fade from recollection while men can appreciate a masterpiece of witty, eloquent, and melodious satire.

Addison married the Dowager Countess of Warwick, and was thus made free of the society of those who used to be called 'the great.' Some of his friends insisted that he never grew quite accustomed to the life which had thus opened upon him, that his shyness became more and more a trouble to him and a bar to his enjoyment of polite conversation, and that he often wished himself back again in the companionship which used to be familiar to him when he was a frequent visitor at some of the London coffee-houses. Others, again, of his former friends insinuated, it is almost needless to say, that he never cared much about his old associates when once he had been made habitually welcome to high society. There is ample evidence, however, to show that Addison was not in any way spoilt by his new associations, and it does not appear that his shyness was more of a trouble to him in aristocratic circles than it used to be among his literary friends—his Bohemian friends as we should now call them.

Addison had really many high qualities for a share in conversation, but these only displayed themselves with happy effect when he was in the society of those who thoroughly understood him and whom he thoroughly understood, who had ideas to interchange with him, and on whom he could always reckon for ready and helpful interchange of ideas. Where there was difficulty in carrying on the conversation Addison was the last man in the world able to lend any help, and the greater the difficulty to be overcome the more absorbing became the shyness which interfered with his efforts to overcome it. In public debate or on ceremonial occasions of any kind this shyness rendered him hopeless, and left him no chance of real success in political life. But there is no reason whatever to believe that his introduction to what Disraeli called the gilded saloons had any harmful influence on his sentiments towards his old friends, or his capacity for exchanging ideas with new associates when he found the new associates congenial and sympathetic. Addison's closing years had an appropriate home in that Holland House which was for many generations associated with letters and art, with wit and humour, with statesmanship and philanthropy, with famous men and gifted women. His name shines as a star in that literary firmament which over-arched the reign of Queen Anne.

CHAPTER XXXV

OLD LAMPS AND NEW

'God said let Newton be, and all was light.' This is the famous line in which Pope described the opening of that new era in science which we associate with the name of Newton. Some of the most momentous discoveries, by means of which Newton opened a new chapter in the history of the world's science, were made before Queen Anne came to the throne, and their author outlived the Queen by many years. But it was during the reign of Queen Anne that he became president of the Royal Society, a place which he held until his death, and Queen Anne had the honour of bestowing a knighthood on him. It may be added that Prince George of Denmark made some atonement to history for his habitual emptiness and his frequent blunders by showing that he had a genuine interest in some of Newton's discoveries, and giving what help he could to the great scientific philosopher in obtaining the means of carrying out his plans. Thus there is ample warrant for associating with the reign of Queen Anne the surpassing glory of Newton's name and career. One does not now readily connect the fame of Newton with the political movements of his time, but his biographers have to record the fact that he sat in two Parliaments as the representative of his University, Cambridge. Newton does not appear, however, to have taken much more of a part in actual parliamentary life than Gibbon did, at a later period, when he had a seat on the benches of the House of Commons.

There is no occasion here to enter into any dissertation on the wonders accomplished by Newton for the development of that science which has to do with the movements of the earth and its relation to the other worlds of matter seen by us as stars in the sky. The discovery of the principle of gravitation would alone mark a new epoch in the history of science. Newton stands as distinctly at the head of England's scientific discovery as Shakespeare does at the head of England's dramatic poetry. The life, the thoughts, and the observations of Newton make the beginning of an era in the world of science. Newton combined the keenest powers of practical observation with that far-reaching, over-arching imaginative faculty which can construct a whole system out of mere suggestive material. The student who becomes absorbed in the contemplation of Newton's marvellous career is naturally inclined to think of a man profoundly and even sternly given up to science, and indifferent to everything but its claims. Newton's own estimate of himself was very different. In some words of touching simplicity and modesty, which are never likely to be forgotten, he said, not long before his death: 'I know not what I may appear to the world; but to myself I seem to have been only like a boy playing on the sea-shore, and diverting myself in now and then finding a smoother pebble or a prettier shell than ordinary, whilst the great ocean of truth lay all undiscovered before me.' The historian of Queen Anne's reign may well be excused if he is unwilling to allow the career of Newton to be claimed altogether by any previous reign, and eagerly lays hold of facts which warrant him in ranking such a man with the other subjects of Queen Anne who have won for the years during which she occupied her throne the renown of a distinct era in the intellectual development of England.

Perhaps the relative positions of Aristotle and Plato in the realms of human thought might be said to admit of comparison, in a certain degree, with the relations between Sir Isaac Newton and Bishop Berkeley in the same field. Berkeley was undoubtedly a great thinker, and in the intellectual regions to which his genius belonged he may be described as a creative thinker. But he was not an observer, and his domain was only of the mind. Pope paid a tribute as eloquent in its own way to Berkeley as the tribute he had offered to Newton, when he ascribed in his famous line 'To Berkeley every virtue under heaven.' Berkeley, like Newton, can be claimed only in a certain limited sense by the historian of Queen Anne's reign as one of the figures which give character and distinction to that epoch.

He lived, indeed, during the reign, and had given evidence of his marvellous powers as a scholar and a thinker, and of his generous and unfaltering devotion to the welfare of humanity. If Berkeley himself had been appealed to for his record, he would probably have said, as the hero of Leigh Hunt's poem did to the angel : ' Write me as one who loves his fellow men.'

Berkeley was an Irishman by birth and bringing up. He was born in the neighbourhood of Kilkenny, in 1685, and was educated at a Kilkenny school, and afterwards at Trinity College, Dublin, where he studied, obtained a fellowship, and remained for many years. He soon gave evidence of his original powers as a thinker and a reasoner, and as the possessor of a certain faculty of imaginative insight or instinct which had something poetical and even unearthly in it, and carried him securely and unbewildered into regions of almost supernatural philosophical inspiration. He became a clergyman of the State Church, and, about that period of the reign of Queen Anne at which we have now arrived, he came to London in order to arrange for the publication of some of his earlier philosophical works. In London he was introduced to political, literary, and fashionable society by Swift and Steele. Through Swift he made the acquaintance of Lord Peterborough, who was then engaged on a diplomatic mission abroad, and from Peterborough he obtained the appointment of chaplain and secretary. We need not follow his career any farther, for little more of it belongs to the reign of Queen Anne. It was in the highest sense an active and even an adventurous career, for Berkeley had great projects for the spreading of the Gospel among the savage tribes of the Bermudas and among the Indian races of the North American continent, and he devoted years of his life, and a large amount of his fortune, to the establishment of teaching institutions for these regions—institutions which he founded, directed, and watched over for a long time himself. To the world in general Bishop Berkeley—he was afterwards raised to the bishopric— is best known as the author of the theory that there is no such thing as matter, in the sense of a substance having an existence independent of the faculties which are capable of perceiving it; or, at all events, that there is no possibility of proving the existence of any such independent substance. It is easy to understand that such a proposition opened itself naturally to all manner of ridicule from those who had not taken the trouble to understand it, and from many who were not capable of understanding it even if they had taken the trouble to try. Byron's famous two lines are of course only the outburst of a jocular mood, for Byron did not really believe, whatever many of his readers may have done, that he had wholly settled the question. Often as these two lines have been quoted they will bear quoting again. In ' Don Juan ' Byron says :

> When Bishop Berkeley said there was no matter
> And proved it, 'twas no matter what he said.

Bishop Berkeley's theory was designed to be and

may yet prove a complete refutation, on philosophical and even on what might be called scientific
grounds, of the doctrines of materialism which at
that time were beginning to identify themselves more
or less definitely with the doctrines of atheism. The
development of exact science had been leading many
great thinkers into the belief that where science
could not reach there was nothing to be reached,
and where man could not prove anything there was
nothing to be proved. The theory of evolution,
which has become such a power in modern thought
and life, was then finding its earliest systematic
development among some of the German philosophical
writers. The object of Berkeley was to deny and
refute the main proposition on which this theory
rested. Berkeley contended that there could be no
proof of the existence of matter, except such as we
find in our own perceptions. God had given us, he
argued, the senses by which alone we could realise
the existence of matter or know anything at all
about it, and therefore there could be no possible
proof of the existence of matter independently of the
evidence supplied by our own senses. So much of
Berkeley's doctrine may almost be set down as self-
evident. Of course it may be said that Berkeley
went still farther than this, and positively asserted
that there is no such thing as matter, and that the
supposed reality to which we give that name is
nothing but a figment of the senses and perceptions.
But the essential condition of Berkeley's theory is
found in the declaration that there is no possibility

of proving the existence of the substratum which we call matter, independently of the evidence given by our own senses, and then Berkeley calls upon the philosophers of materialism to tell us what was the power which endowed mankind with those senses and perceptions by means of which alone we can form any idea of material substance.

The argument Samuel Johnson used with so much apparent effect when he stamped his foot upon the ground and proclaimed that he had thereby refuted Berkeley's theory, only proved of course that Johnson had not been at the pains to understand the meaning of Berkeley's proposition. Berkeley was contending that the existence of matter cannot be proved without perception, and Johnson believed himself to be giving a conclusive reply when he demonstrated that perception can testify to the existence of matter. There is but little controversy on Bishop Berkeley and his theory nowadays, and the materialistic philosophy of the present time does not as a rule set up any doctrine positively denying the existence of a Divine Creator and a world outside our knowledge of nature. But it is not too much to say that wherever a negation of this kind is distinctly put forward it can have no more formidable antagonist than that which is found in the doctrine maintained by Berkeley. An element of inappreciable value is added to the historical dignity of Queen Anne's reign by the fact that it saw Berkeley's entrance into the field of philosophic science.

The reign of Queen Anne is of course associated

rather with letters, with politics, and with arms, than with pure science, either physical or metaphysical. These pages have already described most of the men who won fame in political life, in literature, and on the battlefield. The age was especially remarkable for the number of writers it produced, of whom it might fairly be said that their literary achievement only just fell short of entitling them to a place among the great masters of literature. One of these was assuredly Dr. John Arbuthnot. Johnson goes so far as to declare that Arbuthnot was 'the first man among the eminent writers in Queen Anne's time.' Macaulay speaks somewhat more moderately; but he pays a tribute to Arbuthnot's style hardly to be surpassed when he says that 'there are passages in Arbuthnot's satirical work which we cannot distinguish from Swift's best writing.' Thackeray warms into genuine enthusiasm when he comes to tell of Arbuthnot's gifts, accomplishments, and sweetness of nature.

Johnson's commendation of Arbuthnot is practically justified by the fact that the most famous of all Arbuthnot's works was for a long time commonly ascribed to Swift. This is the book by which Arbuthnot has established his highest claim to a place in history. He has created in it a typical character destined apparently to live for ever. We can hardly imagine a change in human progress which would be likely to efface John Bull as the accepted representative of the Englishman. It is not a mere caricature; it is not a masterpiece of mere satire; it is a faithful embodiment in one humorous personation of all the characteristics generally supposed to make up the typical Englishman. Droll and comical it is, and was intended to be; but we know on classic authority that truth can be told in jesting, and we must all have seen for ourselves how a perfectly recognisable portrait of a man can be produced by a pencil which purposely and deliberately exaggerates all the more marked characteristics of the person thus humorously represented. The most sensitive or most self-satisfied Englishman is ready to admit that the John Bull figure, as we now know it, embodies fairly enough, from the humorous point of view, the traditional and national peculiarities of the being whom we have agreed to recognise as a type of English civilisation. There has been some dispute as to the original invention of the name John Bull; but it is certain that the 'History of John Bull,' brought out in 1713 by Dr. Arbuthnot, first introduced the name and the character to the literature of England and the recognition of the world. The book was a political satire, and its principal object was to stir up the growing dissatisfaction of the English people with the objects and the progress of the war maintained by England and her allies on the question of the Spanish Succession.

Arbuthnot was a Scotchman by birth, and a physician by profession. He had settled in London, had risen to great practice in his profession, had been made one of the physicians to Queen Anne, and, as we shall see later on, was in attendance upon her during her last illness. He had an inborn capacity for literature, and, while following his professional work in London, he had made the acquaintance and entered into the pursuits of most of the eminent poets, prose writers, wits, and politicians who illuminated the reign of Queen Anne. Pope and Swift were among his intimate friends, and he is understood to have worked with Swift in more than one literary undertaking. The 'History of John Bull' creates a number of typical figures, most of which have been universally accepted as humorous although, of course, extravagant presentations of the national characters which they profess to embody and illustrate.

The book sets out to tell the story of a certain lawsuit between John Bull, the clothier, and Mr. Frog, the linen-draper, on the one hand, and Lord Strutt on the other hand. Mr. Frog, the linen-draper, is intended to personify England's Dutch ally, although, in the lapse of time, the name of Frog came to be employed by satirical and insular Englishmen as the fitting epithet for the nation with which John Bull and the Dutchman were engaged in unfriendly argument. Lord Strutt is meant for Philip Duke of Anjou, and Louis the Fourteenth is brought in under the uncomplimentary appellation of Lewis Baboon. The Archduke Charles comes off easily as Esquire South, while the Duke of Savoy becomes Ned the Chimney-Sweeper, and the King of Portugal is Tom the

Dustman. The Duke of Marlborough, whom the satire was meant especially to discredit, figures in the unattractive character of Humphrey Hocus the Attorney. John Bull, we are told, is 'an honest, plain-dealing fellow, choleric, bold, and of a very unconstant temper.' It is explained for our instruction that this lack of constancy in honest John Bull's temper was chiefly caused by the effect produced upon his spirits by the uncertain weather which belongs to his climate and country. 'His spirits,' we are told, 'rose and fell with the weatherglass.' John Bull is described as engaged in a sort of perpetual rivalry with Lewis Baboon. It was not that he had any reason to feel jealous of Lewis, for he was well able to encounter him at any moment, and under any conditions, 'at back-sword, single faulchion, or cudgel-play; but then he was very apt to quarrel with his best friends, especially if they pretended to govern him. If you flattered him you might lead him like a child.'

It will easily be seen how satire of this description was meant to work its way. John Bull had no reason to be jealous of Lewis Baboon, but he could easily be led away by those who flattered him, and he could thus be drawn into believing without any adequate evidence that poor Lewis Baboon was secretly plotting to do him some serious injury. Another touch of the description had a distinct application to the alleged mismanagement of public accounts, which was brought as a charge against Marlborough by those who were eager to see an end of the war. We are told of John Bull that 'No man alive was more careless in looking into his accounts, or more cheated by partners, apprentices, and servants.' It was not that Mr. Bull was incapable of managing his financial affairs if only he would turn his attention to the subject, but he liked to lead a quiet and jolly life, and was too apt to trust overmuch to those whom he believed his faithful servants. He was 'A boon companion, loving his bottle and his diversion; for, to say truth, no man kept a better house than John, nor spent his money more generously.'

It should be said that the full title of the work is 'Law is a Bottomless Pit; or, the History of John Bull.' The opening chapter, which deals with ' the occasion of the lawsuit,' tells us how a great quarrel broke out in a certain neighbourhood on the death of the late Lord Strutt, in consequence of the fact that the deceased nobleman had been prevailed upon by some roguish person to settle his estate upon his cousin Philip Baboon, to the great disappointment of his other cousin Esquire South. The reader will have no difficulty in seeing how the 'History of John Bull' is made to fit in with or to symbolise the events and the personages in the great quarrel concerning the succession to the Spanish crown. Among the chief tradesmen, with whom the late Lord Strutt was accustomed to have dealings, were John Bull and Nick Frog. The young Philip Baboon has a grandfather, Lewis Baboon, and both John Bull and Nick Frog get it into their heads that Philip Baboon, the new Lord Strutt, will take away his custom from them and give it to his grandfather. They therefore serve him with notice that, unless he gives them sufficient security that he will not thus withdraw his custom from them in favour of his grandfather, they will at once take an action against him, and will thus involve him in expense, and as his estate is much embarrassed, this must plunge him into difficulties, from which it will not be easy for him to extricate himself.

Thus the story of the lawsuit opens, and it is from first to last a most amusing, clever, and telling burlesque of the events and personages engaged in the war arising out of the Spanish succession. John Bull's wife may be taken to typify the British Parliament, by whom the war was urged upon John Bull, the British people. Mrs. Bull had been the main cause of her poor husband plunging into the lawsuit. 'Don't you hear,' she asks him indignantly one day, 'how Lord Strutt has bespoke his liveries at Lewis Baboon's shop? Don't you see how that old fox steals away your customers, and turns you out of your business every day, and you sit like an idle drone with your hands in your pockets? Fie upon't! Up, man; rouse thyself! I'll sell to my shift before I'll be so used by that knave.' So the lawsuit was got up, and a number of other tradesmen, who also believed they had been injured by old Lewis Baboon, were glad of an opportunity of joining against him, provided that Bull and Frog would bear the charges of the suit, and so Ned the Chimney-sweeper of Savoy and Tom the Portugal Dustman put in their claims. The cause was placed in the hands of Humphrey Hocus the Attorney. This Hocus, as we have seen, was meant for the Duke of Marlborough, whom his political enemies used to accuse of having fostered the war for his own personal advantages. 'Hocus,' says the author, 'was an old cunning attorney; and, though this was the first considerable suit that ever he was engaged in, he showed himself superior in address to most of his profession : he kept always good clerks, he loved money, was smooth-tongued, gave good words, and seldom lost his temper : he was not worse than an infidel, for he provided plentifully for his family; but he loved himself better than them all : the neighbours reported, that he was henpecked; which was impossible by such a mild-spirited woman, as his wife was.' This last touch told, of course, most effectively in the mind of the public, because the temper of the Duchess of Marlborough, and the dominion she exercised over her husband, and over others too, made a subject of common talk among all classes of society.

We need not follow the history of this lawsuit any further. It is one of the most famous pieces of satire known to the literature of the modern world. The satire is of an extravagant order and sometimes becomes utter burlesque, but like all really artistic burlesque it retains enough of the lineaments and

proportions and characteristic peculiarities of the
originals to leave one in no doubt as to the subject
of each caricature.   All the conspicuous political
figures of the reign come into the story.   The reader
who takes it up for the first time at the present day
will find himself carried away by its humours, just as
he might be if he were studying some masterpiece of
satire intended to show up the leading personages in
the political life of our own day.   The figures in the
narrative all appear to live and move, and where the
author has any opportunity of giving a passage in
his own style he discourses to his readers in clear,
simple, perfect English.   The ' History of John Bull '
was for a long time published with the works of
Swift, and many believed that Swift took a leading
part in the composition of the narrative.   It is quite
probable that Swift may have given suggestions and
offered advice in the construction of the work, but it
may be taken for granted that Dr. Arbuthnot was its
author in the fullest sense of the word, and every
other writing which we have from his pen gives
additional evidence as to his capacity for the production of such a piece of unsurpassed satirical
humour.   There are obvious reasons why Arbuthnot
might not just then have wished to be known as the
author.   Arbuthnot the man long outlived the reign
of Queen Anne.   His fame as an author will live
with the fame of the reign.

William Congreve, till then the greatest of English dramatic authors since the Elizabethan era, had
done all his best work before Queen Anne came to

the throne, and we hardly associate him now with
the literary period of Pope and Swift. But he published a volume of poems in 1710 and a complete
edition of his works appeared in the same year. Sir
Samuel Garth, poet and physician, lived through and
beyond the age of Anne, but his lamp had ceased to
burn at its brightest when Anne succeeded, while
that of John Gay was only just beginning to burn
with its real power when the reign was coming to
a close. Thomas Brown, whom Addison describes
as ' of facetious memory,' a man who had some
genuine powers of imagination, of humour, and of
poetry, seems, as Dr. Johnson says, ' to have thought
it the pinnacle of excellence to be a merry fellow,
and therefore laid out his powers upon small jests
and gross buffoonery.' He died while the reign was
still young. These later names are mentioned here
because they must be regarded as having contributed something to the splendid store of literature
which enriched the age. In one sense the mere fact
that the historian does not lay any stress upon his
claim to regard them as part of the literary constellation of the Queen Anne era only adds another
tribute to the order which that constellation must
hold in the literary firmament. We may fairly ask
what must be the renown of that literary age when
those who are most anxious to maintain its renown
can freely admit that the best works of such men do
not belong to its epoch?

This chapter professes to tell of old lamps and
new. It has described some of the older lamps

which were still enlightening the reign of Queen
Anne and were yet to burn into that of the succeeding
family. Before the life of Queen Anne had quite
come to a close some new lamps had just been
lighted which were destined to illumine for ever the
art and the literature of England. Not long before
Anne became Queen a boy named William Hogarth
was born in London who may be said to have
created by his own almost untaught genius a school
of British art for himself, and who has never had
any rival in the kind of work he dedicated to the
ordinary every-day life of the England living around
him. So obscure were the conditions in which this
boy began his existence that it is not quite certain
whether he was born in 1697 or 1698, and there is
even some dispute as to whether his birthplace was
in the parish of St. Martin, Ludgate, or in the parish
of St. Bartholomew. His family appear to have
come from Westmoreland and his father was the
third son of a poor hard-working yeoman.

William Hogarth's father is said to have been a
self-educated man, and he had apparently given
himself an education considerably better than that
which was at the time likely to be found among
men of his class. This man made his way to
London, and settled there, and succeeded in obtaining employment as corrector of the press. He
does not seem to have made by his labours any
income which could enable him to give his son
William a promising start in life. The boy appears
to have been brought up with no better prospect

than that of earning his living by some mechanical
occupation. He was bound apprentice to a silver-
smith, and was set to work in that part of the
business having to do with the engraving of arms
and ciphers upon plate. Even this occupation,
however, had something artistic in it, something
akin to art, and encouraging to the tastes of a boy
whose natural inclination must have found congenial
employment in any work not belonging to merely
mechanical handicraft.

From the beginning of his apprenticeship
Hogarth set himself to acquire a knowledge of
drawing. One of his biographers tells us that 'he
felt the impulse of genius, and it directed him to
painting, though little apprised at that time of the
mode nature had intended he should pursue.' The
special turn of his genius soon made itself evident.
His earliest attempts at drawing displayed themselves
in the form of caricature.

We are told that while Hogarth was still early
in his apprenticeship, he went one Sunday with two
or three comrades to make a country excursion in
the neighbourhood of Highgate. The day became
very hot; the boys had tired themselves with
their tramp, and they turned for rest into a country
alehouse. While they were there a quarrel arose
between two wayfarers who, like themselves, were
enjoying the holiday after their own fashion, and
were having a rest and a drink in the public room
where young Hogarth and his companions were
seated. One of the disputants struck the other

with a quart pot on the head and cut him rather severely. The face of the unlucky man thus injured became so grotesquely distorted by pain and wrath that it made a ludicrous show, which was far too tempting to be resisted by the embryo caricaturist who was a spectator of the incident. Young Hogarth carried a pencil and paper with him ready at any moment to dash off a sketch of something which might attract his notice on his holiday ramble, and he instantly jotted down a droll likeness of the man's face as it thus appeared in comical convulsion. Hogarth, in fact, drew a picture in a few happy touches of the injured man, of his antagonist, and of some among those who were looking on. The remarkable peculiarity about the sketch was that while it was downright caricature in every detail, the faces bore a striking likeness to their originals, and the fidelity of the portrait-painter, if a boy with a pencil and a piece of paper may be thus described, was recognised with uproarious delight by most of the assembled company. Let us hope that the boy's successful attempt at caricature had the effect of restoring good temper and good fellowship to the quarrelsome pair whose dispute had brought about so sudden a development of art.

It is said that this incident first turned the mind of the young Hogarth directly to that particular field of art which nature had designed for his cultivation. The story is accepted as true, by some at least of Hogarth's biographers, and it is quite within the range of probability that some such incident may have quickened the artistic instincts of the boy into a recognition of his genuine capacity. In any case the story has quite as much probability in it as most of the stories have which profess to enlighten us as to the earliest revelation of genius in the career of a great man.

One new lamp must be mentioned, although it had only just begun to burn within the lifetime of Queen Anne, and did not until after her death give any of its light to literature. Samuel Johnson himself compels us to associate his name with that of Queen Anne, although he was but a little child in her time. He has left us a picture, the more charming and the more real for its very vagueness, of his one meeting with the Queen. Anne kept up the old fashion of touching for the king's evil, and Johnson's mother, fearing at one time that her child was threatened with the malady, carried him to London, where he was actually touched by the Queen. Boswell tells us the story, which has since been told over and over again in all languages. It gave Johnson some pleasure to recall his childish memory of this interview with royalty. He used to tell his friends that he had a confused but somehow a sort of solemn recollection of 'a lady in diamonds and a long black hood.' This one association of Johnson with Queen Anne and the picture which it calls up to the mind may be held to justify the introduction of Boswell's hero into the present chapter. There is something peculiarly interesting and even touching in the picture. The representative—titular representative at least—of the age just about to close is besought to give a kindly touch to one who is destined to be a representative of the age about to open, and she lays her hand upon him graciously and bids him to be well. The meeting might be held to typify in a certain sense the contact between sinking superstition and rising knowledge.

CHAPTER XXXVI

WALES UNDER QUEEN ANNE

WALES is one of the component parts of the British Kingdom concerning which, up to the present, we have had little or nothing to say in the course of this history. The truth is that Wales did not make herself prominent during Queen Anne's reign, and that the movements going on in that part of the kingdom had not much to do with the political events of the time. Wales had a clearly distinct nationality of her own, a literature of her own, and religious struggles and tendencies of her own ; and she took her full share in the events going on at home and abroad, in the battlefields, and in the political developments. But she did not give the British statesmen of the time much occasion to trouble themselves about her condition, or to withdraw their attention from foreign wars in order to secure her acquiescence in the policy of the Empire. Wales, in fact, had settled down into an era of apparent tranquillity after a long history of warlike struggle.

At the time when Queen Anne came to the throne Wales was as thoroughly and securely a part of the Sovereign's dominions as Lancashire or Cheshire. Yet she was all the while as completely

independent in her social habits and in her ways of
thought as if she had been some far remote colony
willingly accepting the rule of the British monarch.
The Celtic nationality could not have expressed itself
more clearly and emphatically than it did among the
inhabitants of Wales.   The student of history will
find in Mr. Green's 'England' an admirable, complete, and most interesting account of the successive
vicissitudes of struggle, conquest, and subjugation
through which Wales had passed before she thus
settled down to become a part of the kingdom.   Mr.
Green's narrative, forming but a few pages of his
historical volume, is of course only a rapid and
closely condensed summary of the events which it
describes ; but it is instinct all through with
sympathetic feeling and with appreciation of the
traditions and sentiments which inspired the Welsh
nationality.   The underlying and unconquerable
strength of what we may call Welsh independence
was found in that sentiment of nationality, and when
English legislators had learned to respect it and give
it a fair field for its development there was no reason
apparent to the Welsh people why they should not
become contented and loyal partners in the business
of the British Empire.

The poetry, romance, and general literature of
Wales bear a striking, and indeed a very natural,
resemblance to the poetry, romance, and general
literature of Celtic Ireland.   The Welsh legends
remind the reader in all their essential characteristics
of that early Irish literature which is undergoing a

remarkable revival in our own days.   The wonderful,
the supernatural, the marvellous are common features
of every Irish and Welsh legend and seem to be
accepted in both alike as ordinary, familiar, and
recognised elements of human existence.   This
peculiarity is common to all the Celtic races, but it is
to be especially noticed in the legendary lore of
Celtic Ireland and Celtic Wales.   The inner movements of Welsh history, whether religious or political,
were movements of thought against thought.   While
men in England were disputing for the maintenance
of this or that political party, men in Wales were
contending for the superiority of this or that school
of thought and of belief.   The Welsh were on the
whole a practical people always, notwithstanding the
wild and fanciful character of their native literature ;
and although their legends made little difference
between the possible and the impossible the Welsh
people themselves were quick to recognise and to
accept, where the practical work of life was concerned, the difference between what they could and
what they could not accomplish.   One might therefore fairly describe the manner in which Wales agreed
at last to accept her position under English
Sovereigns as an agreement to the effect that so long
as Wales was allowed to think and feel and pray
and worship according to her own independent
national ways, she would be willing to merge her
political independence in the general composition of
the British State.

Wales had for a long time sent her representatives

to the sort of Parliament which had grown up as a system in England, and one of the most famous figures in English history is that of Algernon Sidney, who, although not a Welshman, was at one time the representative of Cardiff in the British House of Commons. Wales was always proud of the fact that according to a settled institution the eldest son of the reigning Sovereign took his title from the Welsh division of the kingdom. During the rule of the Commonwealth Wales was not allowed even a semblance of fair representation in the English Parliament, such as it was. In the series which is called 'The Story of the Nations' there is a very instructive and interesting volume on Wales by Mr. Owen M. Edwards, and in his book the author tells us that Wales during Cromwell's time 'was led and ruled with a rod of iron. Its members of Parliament were generally strangers, some of them having risen from the ranks during the wars—their ability and their energy were beyond question. The characteristic charges brought against them were not timidity or lack of ability to govern, but the exuberance of masterful activity, even highway robbery.'

We learn without surprise that the instincts of the Celtic peasantry brought them into perpetual revolt against the persistent efforts to convert Wales into a mere agglomeration of the English counties. Whether Wales was ruled merely by the right of conquest, as in Cromwell's time and in earlier days, or was allowed her fair share of representation in the existing Parliament, the result was much the same, so

far as the Celtic spirit, the Celtic language, and the
Celtic usages were concerned.   The conqueror, whatever his power, cannot make subjugated peoples forego or forget their nationality and their languages, so
long as the rule of iron is still not strong enough to
deprive these peoples of their memory.   With the
Revolution and the reign of William the Third there
came to be something like a genuine Parliament
established in England, and the true principles of
parliamentary government received, as we have seen,
further development during the reign of Queen
Anne.   There was a singular combination of the
ideal and the real, of the practical and the dreamy,
in the Welsh national character.   Not the opposing
Protestant sects in Scotland herself could argue and
dispute more perseveringly and more passionately
than the Welsh religionists on questions of pure
theology.   But the fierce disturbances to which such
disputations so often led in Scotland were seldom
known to manifest themselves in Wales.

The Welsh, like the Scotch, had in general a great
liking for the study of law, and, after the Revolution
of 1688, Wales sent to the English courts some of the
ablest lawyers known to the period.   The author of
the book on Wales to which we have just referred
observes that 'Welsh lawyers were the most unscrupulous and the most able instruments of the
tyranny of the restored Stuarts.'   But he adds,
'Welsh lawyers, on the other hand, helped to secure
the independence of jurors and to draw up the Bill
of Rights.'   In the political struggles between Whig

and Tory the feelings of Wales went on the whole
with the Tory side of the controversy, and showed
for long a lingering inclination towards the cause of
divine right.   But at the same time it has to be said
that Wales gave many able representatives to the
Whig side in Parliament, and, indeed, the general
character of the Welsh nationality was too shrewd,
too inquiring, and too thoughtful to put up with one
pattern of representative when questions were under
discussion to which a practical and a political answer
would have to be given.   There was a strange lack
of affinity between the general character of life in
England and life in Wales during the reign of Queen
Anne.   Notwithstanding the splendour of intellect
which distinguished England during her reign, it
must be owned that the general character of English
life was somewhat prosaic and commonplace.   Even
the poetry of England at that time seldom soared to
any great height of imagination, and when it
endeavoured to appeal to the loftiest emotions seemed
unable to make the effort except through the process
of imitating the grand old classic authors.   The
literary schools of Queen Anne's day do not appear
to have set much store by such English authors as
Chaucer and Gower ; and even Shakespeare himself
was not so thoroughly appreciated as he had been in
former days and was again in later days.   In Wales,
on the contrary, there was an almost universal and
deeply rooted sympathy with the past—its dreams,
its legends, and its music.   It would have been impossible to find an intelligent Welshman in whose

soul the old-time history of his country was not kept alive. There must have been some quality in the nature of the typical Welshman which enabled him to combine the poetic and the practical without any sacrifice of one to the other.

During Queen Anne's reign the migration of Welshmen into English cities and towns not far removed from the Welsh borders had not set in to any considerable extent. The feeling of trade rivalry or jealousy which has been felt in later days by many English classes towards the intrusive Welshmen, who will persist in setting up business places of their own in Manchester or Liverpool and interfering with the profits of the local traders, had not yet begun to be felt, and there was but little interest taken by the England of Queen Anne in anything that Welshmen might think, or write, or do. Welshmen enlisted in the English armies and served in the English fleets; Welsh officers distinguished themselves on foreign battle-fields; and Welsh intellect won many triumphs in science and in letters; but the English public in general, and even English historians of the time, took little account of contemporary Wales. There appears to have been a surprising absence of curiosity—if such a word may be considered appropriate—about the ways and the doings of Wales. That part of the island, with all its unsurpassed beauty of mountain and lake, river and valley, had not then become a show-place for English tourists. The keen poetic sympathy which the writings of many Englishmen about Wales at a later time awakened among the public in general, had not, during Queen Anne's reign, aroused English attention to the land of legend, mystery, and beauty, which lay on the other side of the Welsh border. To us of the present time, who have seen whole schools of English writers devoting themselves to the revival of Welsh legend and romance, it seems strange and hard to understand how the varied English literature of Queen Anne's era should have failed to find any interest in the history, the traditions, and the characteristics of Wales. Perhaps this lack of interest was owing in some degree to those practical qualities in the Welsh nature which we have already mentioned.

The Welsh held out for centuries against England's efforts at supremacy—held out again and again with an absolutely desperate stubbornness; but at last there came a time when the leaders of the Welsh people and the Welsh people themselves seem to have made up their minds that it would be useless to argue with the inexorable any longer. Wales had, of course, no exiled royal family, as Scotland had, in whose cause she felt compelled to fight to the last, and she was never treated as an absolutely subjugated and vassal land with no rights whatever left her to claim, according to the principles of rule which were applied to Ireland. The fact at all events is certain that at a definite period of her history Wales gave up the work of resistance and resolved to make the best she could of the actual conditions and of the place assigned to her in the British imperial system.

But this practical resolution did not in the slightest degree tend to make the Welsh people submit to any process of denationalisation. The Welsh nationality remains as distinct a fact in our own time as it was in the days when Wales was yet carrying on her wars with England. English states-manship had to give up after a while any serious idea of interfering by legislation with the common use of the Welsh language, and at last was even prevailed upon to make a thorough knowledge of the native tongue a necessary condition of certain classes of appointment in Wales. The Welsh people kept on singing their national songs, studying their national literature, and celebrating their national festivals as if the country were an independent State. One result of all this was, as we have said, that the Wales of Queen Anne's time received little notice at the hands of English politicians, historians, and essayists. There were men in Wales at the time leading rival schools in theology, carrying multitudes along with them by the force of their earnestness and their eloquence, making converts and proselytes here and passionate enemies there; and it may be taken as more than probable that the very names of these leading Welsh disputants were positively unknown to many members of Queen Anne's successive ad-ministrations. Controversy in Wales was for the most part a dispute between rival schools of belief and rival systems of education, and arguments such as these did not of necessity call for any intervention on the part of the central Government. It is not likely that Bolingbroke or Oxford ever gave himself many anxious hours of thought concerning the possible consequences of this or that religious revival, this or that new illustration of national sentiment in Wales.

Mr. Edwards tells us that 'Political feeling in Wales at the beginning of the eighteenth century can be seen from two books which have to this day universal popularity in Welsh peasant homes.' Before dealing with his description of these two works, it is well to mention the fact that Mr. Edwards sets before us his story of Wales as practically consisting of two parts; in the first half of which, he says, 'I tried to sketch the rise and fall of a princely caste; in the second the rise of a self-educated, self-governing peasantry.' This latter class 'with stronger thought and increasing material wealth, rules Wales to-day'—such at least is our author's estimate of the force which prevails in modern Welsh history.

We return, then, to the two books which, according to his judgment, best enable us to understand political feeling in Wales at the opening of the eighteenth century. The first of these is Ellis Wynn's 'Visions of the Sleeping Bard,' which appeared in 1703; and the other is Theophilus Evans' 'Mirror of the First Ages,' published in 1716. We cannot do better than quote some passages from the author's description of these two books. 'Ellis Wynn gave

the affrighted Welshmen so realistic a description of
hell that it has haunted the imagination of the country
ever since. Its scenery is Welsh—the scenery of
those wild Merioneth mountains which rise in terraced
grandeur above the home of Ellis Wynn and of
the regicide John Jones. Among its inhabitants are
statesmen closely associated by Welsh peasants, for
a century, with the evil one. Its gaping jaws had
already received Oliver Cromwell; they were hunger-
ing for Louis XIV. The grasping landlord and the
indolent tenant, the unworthy minister and the sedi-
tious sectary—all that were condemned by the conscience of the time find a place in the loathsome
dungeons on the hot lurid precipices of the poet's
hell . . . . The book helped to give Wales the politics of the moderate Tories of the reign of Queen
Anne—that the Queen maintained right and the
Church truth; that France ought to be feared, and
that Dissenters, especially Quakers and Independents,
should be the care of the Justice of the Peace. Theophilus Evans, in a style that gradually obtained
the perfection of homely simplicity, told his countrymen their early history, how great they had been,
how many lands they had governed, and how much
they had lost. The imagination of children, by many
a mountain hearth, was fired by the visions they
saw in the "Mirror." The supine inaction of the
first half of the eighteenth century was the seed time
of many ideas.'

We can hardly suppose that the English statesmen, or even the English poets, of Queen Anne's time

found any opportunity of realising Welsh national
feeling by the study of the Celtic *Inferno* which
Ellis Wynn had given to literature, or that they
had bestowed many glances at the 'Mirror of the
First Ages' which Theophilus Evans was offering to
the gaze of the world. Mr. Edwards tells us how
the movement for a system of national education
began among Welshmen early in the eighteenth
century, and how the religious awakening began,
'which so profoundly affected the national character
before the century was to end.' One result of that
religious awakening was, as he explains, that 'the
life forces that were drawing men irresistibly to the
whirlpool of the French Revolution failed to attract
Wales.' We are left to understand, therefore, that the
Wales which we now know—intelligent, educated,
prosperous, peaceful, and intensely national—developed itself without much outside help throughout
all the storm and stress of political movements in the
other parts of Great Britain.

A writer must naturally feel reluctant to quote
once again the very familiar dogma about the happiness of the land which has no history. It may,
however, be said with some special application that
the happiest and most productive era of Welsh
national life was just that time concerning which
British history, at all events, has the least to say.
Wales had for centuries a very stormy history of her
own—a history which no chronicler can overlook,
but when studied from the higher point of view it is
seen to be a comparatively barren record of battle,

invasion, and national convulsion. Just at that period when English historians have little or nothing to tell us about what was happening in Wales—when, in fact, the ordinary reader of English history might find there no evidence that Wales had any genuine national existence—the process of self-reliant, independent development was going on, which has made Wales one of the most enlightened and prosperous parts of the British Empire. Statesmanship might find an important lesson to learn in the story of that quiet national development. Wales has not been converted by force of arms or of laws into a little imitation England on the other side of the Welsh border line. She has maintained her language, her customs, her forms of worship, her ways of thought ; while she cordially accepts every new development of science, art, and letters, and has indeed won a high place as a contributor of fresh ideas to all these expressions of human intellect.

Mr. Edwards mentions casually in his summary of the story of Wales during the early part of the eighteenth century that two false impressions began, just then, to spread about among Englishmen and Welshmen. ' One was the Welsh belief that the Englishman had the ingrained insolence of a guilty robber. The other was the English belief that Taffy was a Welshman and that Taffy was a thief.' There can be no doubt that Taffy was, at one time, regarded very much as an intruder by the English trading communities among which he made his appearance, and that John Bull was looked upon by many classes in Wales as a very obstinate, grasping, and overbearing sort of person. But it must be borne in mind that, so far as we can judge from writers of the period in both countries, the Englishman did not then habitually adopt the language of eulogy and brotherhood when speaking of his Scottish fellow-subjects, and that the Scotsman did not always indulge in words of affection and admiration for his English brother. Nor do we learn from the literature of the day that the 'tyrant Saxon' and the 'Irish Papist' usually spoke of each other in terms of reciprocal admiration.

The one important fact which impresses itself upon the mind in the story of that part of Queen Anne's dominions, is that Wales was quietly and steadily developing a national life of her own concerning which the other parts of the British kingdom were taking but little account. There was not any other division of the kingdom which was growing more happily into all the conditions of prosperity than that small division of the imperial system which appears to have been making so faint an impression on the minds of English historical writers. Self-reliance and independence—independence, that is to say, of thought and habit and national movement—were the characteristics of the Welsh people at the period when England was actually trembling under the throes of the anticipated change in the royal succession, and the struggles of rival political parties to make use of the crisis for their own ends. We do not find that the struggles of these political parties had any perceptible influence on the conditions and the fortunes of the Welsh people. There was no political or sectarian party in Wales which appears to have engaged itself openly or secretly in any plans for a counter revolution for the restoration of the Stuart dynasty. The Welsh people seem to have taken it for granted that the Act of Settlement would be carried duly into effect in the ordinary course of things, and that life for them would go on in much the same way under the reign of a Hanoverian Prince as it had gone on under that of a Stuart Princess.

Nor was this quiet contentedness any indication whatever of a want of patriotic feeling, of an indifference to the general prosperity of the kingdom, or a lack of sympathy with the national hopes and feelings of their English fellow-subjects. The people of Wales were thoroughly in union with their English fellow-subjects on all that concerned the real interests of the kingdom, and had no more desire for a separate political existence than might have been found in any one of the English counties. Nor, on the other hand, did this state of quietude come from sluggishness on the part of the Welsh, or stolid preference for an untroubled and stagnant condition of life rather than any effort which might bring about an interruption of life's routine. The Welsh were divided all the time by many questions which had to do with religious worship, with education, and with intellectual development, and were debating them as earnestly and with as much sacrifice to individual interests, here and there, as if they had involved the fate of a dynasty or the predominance of a ruling party. There is something profoundly interesting in this quiet story of Wales's national and intellectual growth making its way unnoticed amid the fierce rivalries and tumultuous commotions of contending political parties in other parts of Britain. A people which could thus hold the noiseless tenour of its way without haste and without rest, might well be regarded as a perpetual source of strength to that governing system which it had made up its mind thus firmly and thus cordially to accept. Wales had indeed by this time won her title to be regarded as a component part of the British Empire.

CHAPTER XXXVII

RESTORATION HOPES REVIVED

THE great question of dynasty seems by this time to have been actually opened up once again. There can be no doubt that the adherents of the Stuart Prince at home and abroad had convinced themselves that a crisis had arrived which was in every sense favourable to a restoration. The Stuart papers which have found their way into publicity make it certain that a definite scheme was on foot for the bringing back of the exiled family to England and the prevention of the Hanoverian succession, and that some of those around Queen Anne were directly and actively engaged in this project. Bolingbroke had clearly made up his mind, by this time, that the hour had arrived for him to take a distinct side in the dynastic struggle, and that his place must be with the advocates of the Stuart Restoration. Lady Masham was heart and soul in the same cause.

Queen Anne herself was much distracted by conflicting inclinations and an internal contest of opinions. There cannot be the slightest question that her wishes went thoroughly with the objects of the Restoration party, and that in any case she regarded the Hanoverian succession with almost unqualified dislike. If she could have prevailed upon the Stuart claimant to change his religion and proclaim himself a convert to the Protestant faith, she would have entered unreservedly into the projects of Bolingbroke and Lady Masham. But whatever may have been Anne's weaknesses, whatever may have been her inconsistencies of opinion on other subjects, she was conscientiously devoted to the Protestant Church, and she was anxious to play the part of a thoroughly constitutional Sovereign. In any case, it was impossible to induce the Stuart claimant to renounce his faith for dynastic advantages. Anne therefore found herself compelled to choose between her feeling for her family, and her devotion to her own faith and to her duties as a constitutional ruler.

The intrigues which were in movement between the partisans of the Stuarts at home and abroad could not possibly be carried on in absolute secrecy, and the supporters of the Hanoverian succession were well informed as to the nature and extent of the political organisation which was preparing for a counter revolution. One immediate result of all this was that some of the leading Tories who had held out against the Whigs on all other questions found themselves forced to choose between the Whigs and the Stuarts, and the Queen's sinking health compelled them to see that the choice must be promptly and definitely made. They therefore allied themselves openly with the Whigs for the one purpose of maintaining the Hanoverian succession. Almost all the Bishops ranged themselves on the same side, and the result was that in both Houses of Parliament motions were made against the Government, and debates took place in which it was clearly manifested that the Whigs had strong Tory support in their attacks upon the existing Tory Government.

Oxford had been for some time endeavouring, with little success, to play a double part. He had not the courage or the heart to take one side or the other boldly and finally. He was always thinking of his own personal interests, and trying to come to a definite conclusion as to the side which promised him the highest advantages and the greatest security. Lady Masham was doing her very best to turn the Queen's mind wholly and resolutely against Oxford, and Bolingbroke was helping her with all his power. The Queen, as we know, had no personal liking for Oxford from the beginning, and of late she had been growing more and more to feel a positive dislike for him. Many of Oxford's ways were offensive to the Queen, and Lady Masham never failed to direct the Queen's attention to any peculiarities of his bearing and his conduct which might be likely to offend her. Oxford, like most other men of his time, was somewhat given to indulgence in what used to be called the pleasures of the table, and Lady Masham was always sure to suggest to her royal mistress that her chief adviser was sometimes under the influence of liquor when he appeared in the royal presence. Anne had often complained that Oxford's manners to her wanted the deference which she was entitled to expect, and she was quite ready to accept the explanation given by the royal favourite that his peculiarities of manner occasionally arose from the fact that he had been drinking too much, and did not quite know how he was deporting himself or what he was saying. Oxford had but a poor opinion of the Queen's intelligence, and he had not in him that quality of noble toleration which would have made many a man endowed with a far higher intellect than his, generously considerate of the Queen's deficiencies and appreciative of her good qualities. Moreover, it had for a long time been quite certain that the reign was drawing to a close, and the knowledge of this fact, which would have made a man of different mould from that of Oxford only the more anxious to show to her his personal deference and sympathy, had the effect upon him of increasing his disregard for a Sovereign who could no longer be of much advantage to his personal interests and ambitions.

Oxford, in fact, was not good enough or bad enough to play a successful part at a time of supreme political crisis. Had he been thoroughly sincere and single-hearted he would have taken his side, one way or the other, before events had advanced so far, and it might have happened that the party to which he gave his conscientious adherence would have come out triumphant at the end. Had he been thoroughly insincere he might have seen the right moment for throwing in his fortunes with the winning side, and would thus have secured his own success. But he was always endeavouring to maintain a creditable appear-

ance in the eyes of the two great political parties;
he was always endeavouring to maintain the reputation of a statesman and a man of honour; and
between the proverbial two stools there could only
be the proverbial fall to the ground. He made fair
promises to the Jacobites abroad, with whom he was
in frequent correspondence, and he made fair promises
just as frequently to the Hanoverians abroad; but he
never could come to any resolve as to the moment
for a definite choice of sides. The reader who looks
back on the history of the crisis from this distance
of time is apt to wonder how men like Bolingbroke,
and even like Oxford, could possibly have had any
faith in the chances of a Stuart restoration. It
seems to us now as if the whole tendencies of
England's constitutional growth had rendered it impossible that such a counter revolution could take
place, and that the country would ever settle down
again to a system of rule such as that which had
existed in the days of the Stuart Sovereigns.
England would seem to have positively outgrown
the conditions of those days, and the principle of
divine right might well have been regarded as a mere
anachronism.

We have said that the great majority of the
Bishops had proclaimed themselves resolute supporters of the Hanoverian succession. But there
were some exceptions, and among these the most
remarkable was Francis Atterbury, Bishop of
Rochester. Atterbury had for some years been the
most conspicuous champion of the High Church

party amongst English divines, and was generally re-
puted to have prepared for Sacheverell the powerful
pleading, the eloquent appeal, by which Sacheverell
defended himself against his impeachment. In Wyon's
account of the reign of Queen Anne we are told that
Atterbury 'had been during ten years the most
popular preacher in town.' Wyon tells us that
Atterbury's discourses were 'remarkable for the
exquisite polish of their style and replete with a
sober and chaste imagery.' And that these discourses 'were committed to memory and were delivered with all the additional graces that a fine
voice, a well-studied action, and a very handsome
person can bestow.' He had been regarded as the
prompter of more than one ingenious pleading as
well as that of Sacheverell. In the once famous controversy which took place on Bentley's ' Dissertations
on the Epistles of Phalaris,' Atterbury was understood to have inspired the reply to Bentley which
bore the name of Charles Boyle of Orrery, to whom
Atterbury had at one time acted as tutor. Macaulay
says that Atterbury had a mind 'inexhaustibly rich
in all the resources of controversy.' At the time
which we have now reached he had been made
Bishop of Rochester and Dean of Westminster. The
general impression then was that in the natural
order of things Atterbury might well look forward to
a still higher position, and was likely to be elevated
to the primacy.

The events, however, which were already fore-
shadowed, put a stop to the chance of his promotion

to such a rank. Atterbury was devoted in his heart
to the cause of the Stuarts, the legendary picturesque-
ness of which would have had a natural charm for a
man of his temperament and turn of mind. Atterbury
had the courage of his convictions, and if all those
who thought with him and possessed any influence
to support their purposes had been endowed with a
spirit equal to his, it may be taken for granted that
the Hanoverian succession would never have been
allowed to establish itself without a severe struggle.
Even at the last moment, as we shall presently see,
he was found ready to encourage and to demand a
policy of open resistance to the coming change.
Fortunately for England's domestic quiet there were
not many of those around the Queen, even among
the men and women who were unquestionably plotting
for a Stuart restoration, in whose hearts there was
anything like the resolve which would have inspired
the action of Atterbury. If his advice had been
followed it could only have led to a hopeless struggle
and a futile waste of life; but at a time when so
much hesitation, so much duplicity, and so much
personal self-seeking distracted the counsels even of
the leading statesmen it is impossible not to feel
something like admiration for the one great partizan
of the Stuart cause who saw his way to risk everything upon the momentous issue.

Certainly the part which Atterbury was willing
and eager to play does not appear quite suitable to
the position of a Christian prelate, and especially to
that of a Bishop belonging to the Protestant Church

established in England. Atterbury would appear to have been born out of his rightful time, and ought to have found his appropriate place in the mediæval days when an impassioned prelate might have becomingly pointed to the soldiers of a crusade the right road to victory. By the side of so prosaic a figure as that of Oxford, for instance, the form of this irreconcilable and undaunted Bishop of Rochester looks singularly commanding and picturesque. The mere fact that he did take such an attitude at such a time is another evidence that the zeal for the Stuart cause had not yet become a mere memory or a mere tradition in England, and that men like Oxford had still some reason to feel uncertain whether they were quite safe in committing themselves too hastily to the support of the Hanoverian succession.

It may easily be understood how the advice and the influence of a man like Atterbury must have stimulated Bolingbroke in his desire to shake himself altogether free of any companionship with the hesitating Oxford, and to give rein to the impulses of his own ambition. Even Bolingbroke, however, was not prepared to go so fast and so far as Atterbury's inclinations would have prompted. Bolingbroke saw quite clearly that there was no probability of bringing over the English Tory squires to the proposals for a Stuart restoration, so long as the representative of the Stuart cause professed the religion of the Church of Rome. There can be little doubt that if the Stuart Prince could have been prevailed upon to adopt the faith of the Protestant Church, Bolingbroke would have promptly declared for the cause of the Jacobites. It did not even seem certain that in such a condition of things there would be any necessity for a formal repeal of the Act of Settlement. The provisions of that Act were obviously and avowedly constructed for the purpose of preventing any Prince or Princess of the Roman Catholic faith from succeeding to the throne of England. In the minds of those who were opposed to the Hanoverian succession it seemed quite clear that the Act of Settlement could in no wise interfere with the accession of a Prince who stood nearest in relation to the reigning Sovereign and who proclaimed himself a member of the Protestant Church. Bolingbroke was, in fact, quietly arranging his measures so that as far as possible the control of the troops of the Cinque Ports, and of various important cities and fortresses, might be put into the hands of men who were known to be in favour of the Stuart cause, and could safely be relied upon to act under Bolingbroke's directions.

It was commonly believed, at the time, that Oxford himself was influenced so far by his desire to please the Queen and to keep open his chances of gaining the favour of the Jacobites in the event of their success, as to inspire a letter written by the Abbé Gaultier to the Stuart Prince telling him that before he could have any real hope of succeeding to the throne it would be absolutely necessary for him to renounce his religion, or at least to proclaim such a renunciation. The letter, which was said to have been inspired, if not dictated, by Oxford, warned the Stuart Prince emphatically that Queen Anne could do nothing for him so long as he remained a member of the Church of Rome. Bolingbroke was for some time confident in his persuasion that the son of James II. only required to have it made clear to him that he must either give up all chance of the crown or renounce his religious faith. The philosophical sceptic could not bring himself to believe that a man with any ambition could value religion, or at least the mere outward profession of one form of faith rather than another, so much as to make it a reason for throwing away his last chance of wearing a crown. The Stuart Prince, however, held firmly to his resolve, and wrote a letter in reply declaring that he could not abandon, or disavow, or conceal, his religious convictions for the sake of any earthly advantage, and adding his belief that his strong resolve ought to be rather a recommendation of him to the minds of the British public, who could not but see that no trust could be placed in the promises or the pledges of any man capable of sacrificing his deepest religious convictions for the sake of being chosen king. Bolingbroke began to see that he could have little to hope for from any further committal of himself and his influence to the Stuart cause, just at that moment, but he was by no means clear that the prospects of the Hanoverian succession were so unclouded as to give him any warrant for definite and proclaimed adherence to its side. In a letter written by him he described with some frankness the state of mind into which the approaching crisis had brought him and many of his adherents. 'As to what might happen afterwards, on the death of the Queen,' he declared, 'to speak truly none of us had any very settled resolution.' During part of the time, too, Bolingbroke was much occupied by the immediate impulses of his own ambition to make himself the first man in the realm, and to get rid once for all of the rivalry with Oxford, whom he thought it was now in his power to put definitely aside.

One illustration of Bolingbroke's purpose was given which deserves to be specially mentioned. A motion was brought forward in the House of Commons by Sir William Windham for leave to bring in a Bill having for its object to prevent the further growth of schism, and for the better security of the English State Church. Sir William Windham was one of Bolingbroke's confidential associates, and it was to him, in fact, that the letter was addressed, a passage from which has just been quoted. The object of the Bill which Windham asked leave to introduce was to revive and put into regular practice a clause in the Act of Uniformity, providing that no schoolmaster or tutor should be allowed to give instruction to pupils unless he had previously signed a declaration of absolute conformity with the doctrines of the Established Church. This clause had not been superseded by any subsequent Act, but it had been allowed to fall into something like entire disuse; and many schoolmasters and tutors all over England, who were known to be religious Dissenters or Nonconformists, had been teaching their pupils according to their own views, and without having made the prescribed declaration of conformity.

While the Whig party had official power there was naturally no inclination shown by the Government to enforce the most tyrannical of the enactments which sought to make avowed adhesion to the doctrines of the State Church a necessary condition to the full rights of citizenship. Sir William Windham's Bill was allowed to pass through its earlier stages without any serious opposition; but when it approached its third reading the Whig members of Parliament became aroused to a sense of the duty which their political creed enjoined on them, and they made manifest their determination to oppose the further progress of the measure. The Bill sought to enact heavy penalties upon all instructors who ventured to teach without having previously obtained a licence from a Bishop, and such a licence was not to be granted in any case unless where the applicant could produce a certificate showing that he had received the Sacrament according to the form ordained by the State Church.

In the course of the debate which took place many of the Whig members dwelt with just emphasis upon some of the results which must inevitably come from the adoption and the enforcement of such a measure. One of these results, as it was pointed out, would necessarily be to compel a large number of English parents to send their sons into foreign countries for their education. Thus there would be created a whole class of young Englishmen who would learn the ways, the habits, and the principles of foreign peoples, and who, if they did return to their own country, would return there with anti-English, or at least un-English, training, habits, and prejudices. The Tories replied to these and all other such arguments by the old familiar diatribes about the dangers to Church and State, to good order and morals, and to society in general, of allowing Papistical idolaters, and heretical Nonconformists, to go about the country instructing the youth of England in evil ways. The Tory members rallied in all their strength to support Windham's Bill, and the result was that the measure passed through the House of Commons by a large majority. Then, of course, the Bill had to go up to the House of Lords, and about that time, as we have already more than once had occasion to observe, the cause of religious freedom had a better chance in the hereditary chamber than it would have had in the chamber which was at least nominally representative.

Bolingbroke took a decisive part in recommending the measure to the House of Lords. The impression at the time was that in the introduction of this measure he saw a favourable opportunity for putting his rival Oxford into a position of extreme embarrassment. Bolingbroke had probably something to do with the preparation of the measure, or, at all events, with giving his friend Windham the idea of bringing it forward just then. Oxford was as usual unable to make up his mind. He had been playing the double part too long, and he could not rally resolution enough at a sudden crisis to make him choose his

ground.   Looking cautiously to the future, he could
not see his way to renounce altogether the good
opinion of the Whigs who might be counted on as
certain to have the ascendency if the Elector of
Hanover should come to the throne.   But, at the
same time, he could not regard the chances of the
Jacobites as wholly desperate, and if he were to vote
against the measure he must give up, at that critical
moment, his last hope of reckoning on the support of
the Tories.   During the course of the debate a direct
appeal was made to him for his advice as to the
measure, and he could find no better way out of the
difficulty than by declaring that he had not yet had a
full opportunity of studying the Bill, but that when
he had considered its provisions he would then vote
according to the best of his judgment for the civil
and religious interests of the country.   Such a
declaration as this about a measure which had already
been the subject of debate in the House of Commons
was a practical abdication of his position as a leading
statesman.   He did not, however, make good even
the poor and evasive promise by which he had
endeavoured to get himself out of the difficulty.   He
did not show himself again in the House of Lords
during the remainder of the time occupied in the
consideration of the measure, and he gave no vote
one way or the other.

The Bill passed its third reading in the House of
Lords, and became law.   A protest, signed by thirty-
three peers, was entered on the minutes of the
House embodying the obvious objections enlightened

men of any party must, even then, have felt to the
adoption of a measure reviving some of the most
tyrannical provisions belonging to a system of legislation already beginning to be regarded as behind
the age, and unworthy of a State which boasted a free
government. It is satisfactory to know that this
curious freak of constitutional reaction remained a
curious freak in legislation and nothing more, and
never was allowed to come into real operation. By
a singular chance it so happened that the time appointed for the new Act to begin its working as a
law proved to be the very day when the reign came
to a close, and when Bolingbroke and his Tory colleagues ceased to manage the affairs of the country.

There was no inclination for the revival, at least
in England, of the old-fashioned machinery of religious
persecution. After four years of merely nominal
existence the Act was formally repealed, and it is
mentioned here chiefly for the purpose of illustrating
the strange lack of political principle in Bolingbroke's
character which allowed him, for the mere sake of
some supposed temporary advantage, to play the part
of a religious fanatic, and to sanction and even to
stimulate an act of religious persecution fitted only
to be the work of the stupidest bigotry. There can
be little doubt that the one great advantage Bolingbroke saw in the support he gave to this measure
consisted in the awkward dilemma it forced upon
Oxford, while at the same time it enabled Bolingbroke to posture before the Tory squires as the
resolute supporter of that State Church which Oxford

had not the courage either to maintain or to disavow.

Bolingbroke soon made up his mind that the time had come when the sitting of the Parliament then existing might well be brought to a close. No further advantage to his plans could be found in any prolongation of the Session, and he was growing utterly tired of the strain put upon him by his efforts to maintain the leadership of one party, and at the same time to avoid a total disruption with the other. If he could have seen his way to bring about such a disruption without peril to his own interests and disappointment to his own ambition, it would have thoroughly suited his spirit and his temper to make open war at once upon the Whigs. But then there was the Hanoverian succession looming in sight, and the Hanoverian succession would certainly mean, for a time at least, the restoration of the Whigs to power, and Bolingbroke did not feel in the least disposed to cut himself off deliberately and decisively from all the possibilities of the coming reign.

We can only understand the political conduct of Bolingbroke during this part of his career, by adopting the theory that while actually engaged as a leader in the political struggle his soul lived altogether in a philosophical region far removed from the parliamentary battlefield. He seems as one who found that he had to play the political game, and whose temperament compelled him to get the very best of it—since his love of the contest would not allow him to keep out of it—but who could not bring himself to regard the rules of the game as anything more than conventional arrangements devised to test the skill of the competing players. For all that ordinary men value as religious and political principles he appeared to have no manner of reverence. The Tories adopting the cause of divine right and the State Church, and the Whigs going in for constitutional government and the Hanoverian succession, he only regarded as if they were rival chess players, of whom one takes the red pieces and pawns, while the other takes the white. The game was delightful: he knew himself to be a skilful player, he was determined to win if he could; and he saw that he must abide by the rules of the chess-board for the one reason among others that if he did not do so he could not be permitted to hold his place in the competition. We can no more think of him as inspired with devoted loyalty to Queen Anne, or with a high-flown yearning for the coming of George the Elector, than we can think of his having any sentimental preference for the white king or the red queen, if he were settling down to a game of chess.

Meanwhile the career of his rival Oxford was rapidly drawing to a close. The world will probably never know for certain what the final reason was which induced Queen Anne to deprive Oxford of his office at the time when she made known to him that he must never more be officer of hers. There were reasons enough in any case to have prompted her to such a decision long before. She must have been perfectly aware that he was playing fast and loose,

so far as he could, with both the great parties in the
State. She must have known very well that he
never possessed the intellectual capacity needed for
the chief minister of a great country in a season of
peculiar political trouble. She had of late more than
once expressed herself freely to some of those around
her with whom she was most intimate, and let them
know that she had no longer any faith in Oxford,
either as an adviser or as a friend; that she found his
manners and his habits unbearable, and that she was
very anxious to get rid of him. Yet she kept putting
off the moment of decision from month to month, from
week to week. Possibly the delay was caused in a
great measure by her reluctance to put Bolingbroke
into the leading official position, and her fear that if
she were to get rid of Oxford she could hardly avoid
the necessity of putting Bolingbroke in his place.
Bolingbroke's views on religious subjects were intolerable to her; his habits of life, his libertinism, his
love of social orgies were utterly repugnant to her.

Perhaps it may have been that Queen Anne's final
decision to free herself from Oxford at any risk was
but the result of some sudden impulse, some chance
provocation, some incident rendering the gradual
accumulation of Oxford's offences too great to be
borne any longer by her sickly frame and her
shattered nerves. No doubt Lady Masham had much
to do with the final decision. There had been disputes between Oxford and Lady Masham, in the
Queen's own presence, which must have done much
to make the situation unbearable to Anne. On one

occasion, it was commonly stated at the time, Lady Masham declared that Oxford had never been of any service to the Queen, and Oxford had retorted that he had helped certain persons to rise in the world, and that he would soon leave them as low as he had found them.   It was said, too, that he had strongly objected to a proposal on the part of the Queen that a liberal annuity should be conferred on Lady Masham out of the State funds.   The Queen suddenly came to a final determination, and on July 27, 1714, Anne summoned her Council around her and told them that she had determined to dismiss Oxford from his office.   She explained to the Council her reasons for this decision, and seems to have displayed great frankness in her explanation.   She declared that Oxford had of late got into a way of neglecting all the business of the State.   She described him as wholly wanting in punctuality, and said that she could never reckon upon his coming at any appointed hour.   It was reported that she distinctly accused him of coming often into her presence after he had been indulging too much in drink, and of behaving to her in a manner which wanted the respect due to a Sovereign from a subject.   Queen Anne seems to have on this occasion displayed a vehemence of temper and an energy of expression not to be expected from one who during her reign had on the whole borne her faculties so meekly.   Her mind was made up, and Oxford was ordered to return the staff which was his badge of office as Lord High Treasurer.

Oxford appears to have taken his dismissal and his disgrace with more serenity and dignity than might have been expected. He wrote a letter to Swift concerning a request Swift had made to him, and he told his friend, in words displaying an evenness of temper almost heroic, that he believed it was no longer in his power to exercise any official authority, and that his tenure of office must have actually come to an end before Swift's request had reached him. When the news of Oxford's dismissal became known in London it was the occasion for much rejoicing among many who had little or nothing to do with political party. Oxford had of late become very unpopular, and there was a widespread impression that he had made use of his high position as a Minister of State to increase his income by investments in various doubtful speculations.

Perhaps, on the whole, nothing in Oxford's official life became him like to the leaving of it. Statesmen of far nobler character than his have allowed themselves to indulge in futile demonstrations of disappointment and anger when some sudden political reverse has reduced them to private life. Oxford endeavoured to find some consolation for his wounded feelings by actually attempting to construct a short poem on the ingratitude of princes, which he was courageous enough to send in confidence to Swift. Oxford had yet some years to live, and had to go through a trying time on the opening of the new reign. He passes now out of the domain of this history, and we need only say of him that the closing years of his life were spent in quietude, and with a revival of a scholarlike interest in the curious collection of books and manuscripts which made the foundation of the Harleian Library, afterwards arranged and completed by his son. Perhaps the one noble monument of his career is to be found in that collection of books and papers.

CHAPTER XXXVIII

THE GAME LOST

'THE hour and the man' are words expressing an association of ideas which finds illustration in almost every historical crisis. The hour of crisis at the close of Queen Anne's life seems to have brought with it just the man demanded by the occasion. While the Queen was sinking more and more, the counsels of most of those who were near her seemed to be perplexed and distracted by an increasing uncertainty. This was especially manifest among those who were more or less avowedly in favour of the Stuart succession. Bishop Atterbury indeed did not give way to any uncertainty, and was quite clear in his mind as to the course which ought to be pursued. His earnest advice to his friends was that the death of the Queen should be followed at once by the proclamation of King James III. as Sovereign of England, and he declared himself quite ready to take the leading part in the proclamation. He did not, however, succeed in filling the hearts of his Jacobite friends with his own courage or his own confidence, and whatever may have been Bolingbroke's personal inclination to the cause of the Stuarts he could not make up his mind to such a venture. Much speculation has been indulged in by historical writers as to the possibility of a Stuart restoration if the advice of Atterbury had been followed. But the mere fact that Atterbury was not able to inspire his friends with a full faith in the feasibility of his project is decisive evidence that he was not the man of the hour.

Among the Whig leaders, on the other hand, the man of the hour appears to have been found. Amid all the doubts and distractions of the time it was natural that the eyes of the leading Whigs should have turned to one of their peers, who, although he had not taken an active part in politics lately, was known for his absolute integrity, his clear head, and his steady nerve. This was Charles Talbot, Duke of Shrewsbury. Born in 1660, he had been brought up as a Roman Catholic, but had become a Protestant and took an earnest part in the Revolution of 1688. After William III. had been made King of England, Shrewsbury was appointed one of the Secretaries of State. He did not hold that office long, but resigned of his own accord. In 1694 the office was again offered to him and accepted, and his peerage as an earl was then raised to a dukedom as a tribute to the valuable services he had rendered to the cause of the Revolution. He was a man of very engaging manners, and won universal estimation for his high principles, his unselfishness, and his sincerity. Macaulay in his 'History of England' says of him that 'before he was of age he was allowed to be one of the finest gentlemen and finest scholars of his time. He was early called the King of Hearts, and never, through a long, eventful, and chequered life, lost his right to that name.'

Shrewsbury had borne an important part in the negotiations with France for the treaty of peace. During these negotiations he had shown some distrust of Bolingbroke's policy, and it was commonly believed that Bolingbroke found him a good deal in his way. An outward appearance of friendship was kept up by the two men, but their characters and purposes were so widely different that anything like common action between them was not easily maintained. Shrewsbury always endeavoured to impress counsels of moderation upon both Bolingbroke and Oxford during the time of their growing and manifest rivalry. Mr. Wyon in his history gives it as his opinion that 'before the genius, the character, the years, and the fame of Shrewsbury the brilliant and eager Secretary felt himself rebuked.' One is reminded of Macbeth's words about Banquo—

> There is none but he
> Who's being I do fear; and under him
> My genius is rebuk'd; as it is said
> Mark Antony's was by Cæsar.

Probably the rebuke which Bolingbroke's genius felt in the presence of Shrewsbury arose from the fact that Bolingbroke's keen perceptions recognised in Shrewsbury the constant presence of those high qualities of disinterestedness and noble devotion to principle which he well knew were wanting to his own character. Shrewsbury was one of

Bolingbroke's official colleagues, for at the time we have now reached he was Viceroy of Ireland. The serious crisis threatened by Queen Anne's illness had led to Shrewsbury's being summoned over from Dublin to take part in the councils of the Ministry. Shrewsbury's arrival in London made him more than ever an object of distrust and dislike to Bolingbroke. It was of course Bolingbroke's ambition to succeed Oxford as Lord High Treasurer, and the mere presence of Shrewsbury seemed to him to bode something detrimental to his ambitious hopes. The idea, no doubt, came into his mind that Shrewsbury might obtain the place which had been taken from Oxford, and, as Mr. Wyon puts it, 'he could not treat Shrewsbury as he had treated Oxford.' 'The grace and gentleness of Shrewsbury's manners,' Wyon says, ' disarmed all opposition ; his sweet temper conciliated even the fiercest of politicians ; his age, his rank, and the great services which he had rendered to the Revolution when William of Orange was seated on the throne rendered him an object of respectful interest to the generation which had grown up since that great event first startled the world.'

Meanwhile the crisis was drawing to an end. The trials the Queen had to go through before the dismissal of Oxford was finally resolved upon, and at the time when it was put in force, were too much for her physical weakness and her shattered nerves. Her own words to one of her physicians were that she felt sure she could not survive the

A A 2

shock which the crisis had brought upon her. On the morning of Friday, July 30, she had an attack of apoplexy and remained for some time absolutely speechless. It was clear to all around her that the end was close at hand, and that no time was to be lost in making arrangements to meet the danger that must have to be faced. A meeting of the Privy Council had already been summoned for that day at Kensington Palace. The constitution of the Privy Council was in its principle much the same in the days of Queen Anne as it is in our own time. The usage was that only those members of the Privy Council were to attend one of its meetings who had received an official summons to take part in the consultation. Perhaps it would be better to say that the Privy Council of that time represented the whole body of the administration as we now have it, and that the members summoned to attend its meetings held the position which the members of the Cabinet occupy in our own time and have occupied during recent reigns. Therefore, when summonses were issued for the meeting of the Council on the memorable July 30, 1714, there was no expectation in the mind of Bolingbroke that any Privy Councillor would present himself to take part in the consultation who had not received the formal summons inviting his presence. But at the same time there was no law or rule of any kind forbidding the attendance of any Privy Councillor who chose to present himself at such a meeting. Here then arose a contingency against which Boling-

broke had never provided, or even thought of
providing; and as often happens at such critical
moments, the one possibility never taken into
consideration proved to be decisive of the whole
result.

There are few scenes in merely political history
more dramatic and more momentous than the
scene enacted at that meeting of the Privy
Council at Kensington Palace. Bolingbroke, of
course, was early in his place. The Duke of Ormond was present and other Jacobite Peers as
well. It was understood that the Council would
have to come to some decision as to the name of the
Minister who should be recommended to the Queen
for the place of Lord High Treasurer from which
Oxford had been dismissed. The Duke of Shrewsbury was one of the earliest among the peers who
presented themselves in the Council chamber. His
presence was no doubt expected by Bolingbroke,
and he was entitled to receive the formal summons
which was the right of a Minister holding such a
position.

But before the members present in the Council
chamber had time to get to any of their business, an
addition was made to the numbers present which was
totally unexpected by Bolingbroke and those acting
in combination with him. The doors of the Council
chamber were suddenly thrown open and the Duke of
Argyle and the Duke of Somerset entered the room.
To many of the peers then present the entrance
of these noblemen must have seemed little short of

a daring intrusion. There was, however, nothing
to be done. There was no way of expelling the
intruders, for they had a strict constitutional right,
by virtue of their titles, to present themselves at the
meeting. The Duke of Argyle quietly explained to
the Council that the Duke of Somerset and he had
heard the news about the dangerous state of the
Queen's health, and that although not specially
summoned to attend the meeting of the Privy
Council they had felt themselves bound to hasten
to the meeting in order that they might be able to
afford some advice and assistance at a crisis so
much fraught with danger to the State.

Now the Duke of Somerset was a man of the
most commanding position, and was, so far as rank
and property and influence went, one of the most
powerful noblemen in the kingdom. He had many
intellectual and personal defects, which often rendered
him positively ridiculous. The haughtiness of his
manners, his preposterous pride in his rank and his
dignity, made him the sport of satirists, and many of
the anecdotes told, truly or falsely, to illustrate his
overweening and grotesque arrogance, have passed
into history, and are in constant circulation even in
our own days. Of him the story was told, at a later
day, that when his second wife once playfully tapped
him on the shoulder with her fan he sternly admon-
ished her against such familiarities, and told her that
' my first wife was a Percy, and she never took such
a liberty.' That first wife was a woman of great
political and social power, a bulwark of the Whigs.

She was believed by the Tories at one time to have an immense influence over the Queen, and was an object of especial detestation to Swift. Whenever the Duke had occasion to travel in England all the roads he had to pass through were cleared by a body of outriders whose duty it was, not merely to protect him against obstruction or delay, but to take care that none of the lower orders were allowed to gladden their vulgar eyes by gazing at his august person.

But however extravagant he may have been in his pride, and however ridiculous he may have made himself by displaying it, he was undoubtedly a nobleman of immense territorial and political influence, and when he had openly attached himself to the cause of the Hanoverian succession there could be no question that he was regarded by both parties as a tower of strength to that cause. Moreover, he was undoubtedly a man of honour and of steadfast principle; a man whose word when once it had been given could safely be relied upon, whose very pride made it impossible for him to condescend to any acts of duplicity or any violation of a given promise. His voluntary appearance that day in the Council room was evidence enough for Bolingbroke that he must have some definite political purpose in coming there, and that he was not likely to fail in carrying his purpose into execution.

The other uninvited member of the Council was one whose name and character have been made familiar to us by poetry and romance as well as by

political history. The Duke of Argyle is described
by Pope as one

> The State's whole thunder born to wield,
> And shake alike the senate and the field.

We know that Pope's eulogies of his friends were
sometimes a little too enthusiastic, but it is certain
that Argyle was regarded as one of the most eloquent
speakers in the House of Lords, and he had undoubtedly read and studied much for a man whose
professional occupations did not afford many opportunities for intellectual culture. Argyle was a soldier
by profession, and had taken part in many great battles
and sieges. His name has already been mentioned in
this history, when the story of the campaigns under
Marlborough was told. Unnumbered readers have in
modern days known him chiefly, perhaps only, through
the pages of Walter Scott's novel, ' The Heart of
Midlothian,' where he is pictured as the generous
and resolute protector of poor Jeanie Deans, when
she makes her immortal pilgrimage to London to
plead for her sister's pardon with Queen Caroline.
Scott, however, shows us only the higher and nobler
side of Argyle's character, and is not called upon to
take any account of the weaknesses and defects which
marred to a great extent the better qualities of the
man. We learn from many of Argyle's contemporaries that he was haughty, imperious, and self-
asserting ; and his enemies declared that the maintenance of his own influence and his own commanding
position was his chief object in life. He had changed
his political opinions more than once on some

apparently sudden impulse, and the general impression was that no party or cause could rely upon him
if his own personal interest and ambition were to
lead him the other way. Some of his ancestors had
given up their lives for the sake of their political
convictions. His grandfather was the subject of
Ward's famous picture in Westminster Palace, ' The
Last Sleep of Argyle.' Few modern paintings are
better known to the general public than this, which
pictures the last rest of that Argyle before his execution. The father of that Argyle, too, laid down his
life on the scaffold, and a still earlier representative
of the family fell at Flodden.

But the Argyle with whom we are now dealing
was not supposed to have any tenacity of opinion
which would be likely to conduct him to the scaffold.
That he was a man of courage nobody could doubt,
for he had won the high praise of Marlborough by
his gallant action at Ramillies, Oudenarde, and Malplaquet; but neither his friends nor his enemies
believed him to be one who would sacrifice his own
interests and his own ambition for the sake of any
political cause. He had played fast and loose for a
time with the great questions which were agitating
the country, but he had of late given his adhesion
openly, and even ostentatiously, to the Hanoverian
party. The mere fact that he had done so made it
clear, even to those who liked him least, that he
must have felt completely satisfied as to the success
of the Hanoverian cause, and that he was thus
satisfied was strong evidence that the cause was

likely to succeed.   When Bolingbroke and Ormond saw Argyle in the Council chamber they must have known that a decisive stroke was about to be made on behalf of George the Elector.

The appearance of the two uninvited and unexpected visitors was not the only, or even the chief, surprise for Bolingbroke and his friends.   The supreme moment of the crisis came when the Duke of Shrewsbury arose, and in impressive tones tendered on his own behalf, and on that of the members of the Council generally, his thanks to Somerset and Argyle for their courtesy in coming to the meeting, and formally accepted their co-operation.   The new comers then took their places at the Council table, and Bolingbroke must have thoroughly realised the meaning and the significance of the whole event.   That two Whig peers of so great position and influence as Somerset and Argyle should have presented themselves unbidden at such a Council meeting on such an occasion would of itself have made it clear that these two men must have regarded themselves as representing a power too strong to be carelessly dealt with.   But when Shrewsbury took it upon himself to welcome their presence and to accept openly their co-operation it must have seemed certain to Bolingbroke that the whole proceeding was part of a premeditated and prearranged policy which felt itself in a position to overbear all resistance.   Bolingbroke must have seen, at that moment, that the Whig statesmen knew themselves to be absolute masters of the situation, and that the Jacobite game was up.

Thus far all the received accounts of this important political episode are in general agreement as to what took place in the Council chamber. But with regard to what followed there is some difference in the reports. According to one story, when the Peers had formally settled down for consultation, Somerset and Argyle demanded the latest reports of the royal physicians as to the Queen's health, and having received them and studied them, proposed to the Council that the Duke of Shrewsbury should be recommended to the Queen to fill the place of Lord High Treasurer. Bolingbroke, according to this statement, did not venture to take on himself the responsibility of resisting the proposal. It was clearly borne in upon his mind that the crisis was actually over, that the Hanoverian succession was secure, and that it would be utterly unwise of him to offer any objection to a proposal which had so much influence to support it. Of course it was well known that it was his ambition to obtain the place of Lord High Treasurer for himself, and perhaps, up to that moment, it may have been his confident expectation that his desire would be realised. But when the men who evidently believed themselves entitled to assume a dictatorial position could take on them to recommend the name of the Duke of Shrewsbury, Bolingbroke was not likely to put himself in the ignoble position of one who betrays at the same time his ambition and his weakness by offering a futile resistance.

According to another version of what passed in the Council chamber it was not either Argyle or

Somerset, but Bolingbroke himself who proposed that Shrewsbury should be recommended for the Treasurer's office. The suggestion is that when Bolingbroke heard the welcome offered by Shrewsbury to the two uninvited Whig peers he made up his mind at once that the crisis was over, that there was no more question as to the chances of the struggle, and that as he could not resist the success of the Whig party the best course he could take, for the sake of his own influence, was to put himself at the front of the rising movement and make, of his own accord, the proposal which would most certainly be made and carried whether he approved of it or not. This version is accepted by many writers in the earlier days of the Hanoverian dynasty, and by some in our own time who are well qualified to form an opinion. Mr. Lecky, for instance, regards it as quite probable that Bolingbroke may have thought it well to accept and anticipate the inevitable by making the proposition himself. Such a course of action on his part would undoubtedly have been quite in keeping with all that we know of Bolingbroke's character. He was not a man to throw up the cards because he saw that the chances of the game were going against him. His was a fighting spirit, and his impulse was ever, like that of Macbeth, to try the last. When he saw that the whole scheme had been prearranged, and that it must have its way, nothing could have been more in accordance with his impulsive and self-asserting temperament than that he should make up his mind at once to maintain at

least the appearance of being a leader in the struggle,
and should take on himself to initiate the course of
action which otherwise his adversaries would be sure
to adopt as their own.   The proposal, by whomsoever
made, was adopted without further discussion.

The Council appointed a deputation of the Peers,
with the Duke of Shrewsbury among them, to seek
an interview as soon as possible with the dying
Queen.   Anne consented without delay to receive
the deputation, and when its purpose was made
known to her she gave the Lord Treasurer's staff
into Shrewsbury's hands, and spoke a few words in
that voice which had always been sweet and musical
—that voice which was one of her few personal charms
—and even to the last retained its melodious tone.
The words she spoke were few indeed, but they must
have made a deep impression on those in whose
hearing they were spoken.   As she put the symbol
of office into the new Lord Treasurer's hand she
enjoined him to use it for the good of her people.

With the appointment of Shrewsbury to the office
of Lord High Treasurer the crisis may be said to
have come to an end.   Bolingbroke must have known
by this time that, so far as the purposes and plans
of the Jacobites were concerned, the battle was
lost.   The men now placed in power acted with
promptitude and energy.   Summonses were sent out
at once specially inviting the attendance of every
member of the Privy Council living in or near
London.   The Council thus summoned held a meeting on the same afternoon.   That meeting would have

been made memorable, if for no other reason, by the fact that one of those who took part in it was Lord Somers, the great lawyer and Whig statesman who had rendered splendid services to the rule of William the Third, and had been famous before that time as one of the advocates who defended the Seven Bishops. Lord Somers was now in feeble health, had grown old beyond his years, and was supposed to be physically incapacitated for any part in public affairs. When he received the summons he realised the full importance of the occasion, and overmastered so far his infirmities of frame and nerves as to hasten to the place of council and put his judgment, experience, and authority at the service of the dying Queen.

The Council took prompt and decisive action. Several regiments were concentrated in and near London. Troops were recalled from Ostend, and the fleet was ordered to be in readiness for sea. General Stanhope, who was both soldier and statesman, was put in full authority over all the military measures that might be thought necessary by him in order to anticipate any attempt at a Jacobite revolution and to secure the safety of the succession. One of his first duties was to hold possession of all the outports and to enable the Ministry to have at their command such a military force as might be wanted to make good the arrests of important personages if any such measures should prove to be necessary. Stanhope, in fact, was entrusted with all the powers of a military dictator, and was a man well qualified to exercise such powers with firmness and judgment. The Whigs had won the game, and there was nothing left for the losing party but to pay the forfeit quietly, and avoid as much as possible any unseemly demonstration of disappointment.

There was still one at least of the Jacobites who did not despair. We have already mentioned the course of policy which Bishop Atterbury was prepared to advocate and to carry into action. Atterbury actually came to Bolingbroke and strongly urged him to make arrangements for the proclamation at Charing Cross of James Stuart as King of England, the moment the breath should be out of Queen Anne's body. Atterbury had the full courage of his opinions, and he offered to head a procession in his lawn sleeves for the purpose of supporting the proclamation if Bolingbroke would only accept his advice and give orders to have it put in force. Bolingbroke, however, was not the man to lead or even to concern himself much about what he now knew to be a forlorn hope. For him the cause of the Stuarts was already lost, and his temperament and animal spirits did not allow him to take any interest in lost causes. But he did not by any means accept the idea that there was not something still to be done for his own party and for his own advancement. It was thoroughly characteristic of him to find new ambitions and new schemes arising out of the very ashes of extinguished hopes and plans. We know from the letters which he wrote to Swift, at the very time of the crisis, that

he was already meditating plans for the utter
confusion of the Whig party, no matter how soon
the Hanoverian Sovereign might come and take possession of the kingdom. Bolingbroke's firm belief
appears to have been that he could convict the Whig
statesmen of having been all the time engaged in
treasonable and secret machinations for a Stuart
restoration. He declares emphatically that he will
show up the Whigs as 'a pack of Jacobites,' and
cheerily adds 'that shall be the cry in a month, if
you please.'

No doubt Bolingbroke had good reason to know
that the statesmen of that time were not all and
always exactly what they professed to be. He had
himself played fast and loose with Jacobites and
Hanoverians to the very end, and he knew that
Oxford had done the same sort of work although in
a somewhat different way. He was well aware that
Marlborough, who was now recalled to England to
support the Hanoverian succession, had at various
periods of his career entered into private negotiations
with the Jacobites. He might therefore have had no
difficulty in persuading himself that the Whigs were
no better than their rivals, and that it needed only a
bold and loud-spoken accusation against them to fill
the mind of the public with the conviction of their
guilt. Bolingbroke was by this time perfectly
willing to accept the Hanoverian succession, and to
serve the new Sovereign to the best of his ability.
His brain was occupied only with the conception of
plans which should keep his enemies out of office and

allow him to become the head of the new administration. Condemn as we must the selfishness of the man, his utter lack of patriotism, and of political morality, it is impossible not to feel a sort of admiration for the indomitable courage and the inexhaustible animal spirits which no defeat could reduce to mere prostration.

CHAPTER XXXIX

THE DEATH OF THE QUEEN

THERE is hardly any dramatic situation described by history which lends itself more than that we are now surveying to the tempting and futile speculation as to what might have happened if only this or that had been done which was not done. There were three great separate and it might almost be said rival influences working each for its own ends in three countries, and two of them at least working also against each other in the one country. In England the Hanoverians and the Jacobites, or the Whigs and the Tories, were watching each other's movements with a vigilance which dared not rest, each anxiously looking out for the moment or for any chance that might enable it to take advantage of the other. In Hanover the recognised heir to the throne of England was waiting with a kind of stolid patience for the hour when the message was to come which might either be a summons to England or an advice to stay at home and not risk the chances of a dangerous game. In France the representative of the Stuart cause was still eagerly hoping for the news that a struggle had begun in which he was willing to venture all.

We may take it for granted that George of Hanover was not willing to peril or sacrifice much for the sake of gaining a throne in England. George, as we have shown more than once in this history, had as much physical courage as any man could have, and had proved on more than one battle-field that he was as ready, when proper occasion required, to risk his life as the most chivalrous of knights-errant could have been. But George was a slow and prosaic personage by nature, who loved above all things to lead a life of comfort, to have his own way and indulge his own whims, and he took no pleasure whatever in unnecessary enterprise. It does not appear that he had from the first any great wish to become King of England, and it can hardly be supposed that he had imagination enough to inspire him with a sense of the historic grandeur with which such a dignity must invest him. But a certain heavy obstinacy in his nature would have prevented him from submitting tranquilly to defeat in any game he had positively undertaken to play. If the public voice of England had distinctly and decisively pronounced against George, the Hanoverian Elector would very probably have felt rather relieved on the whole by the declaration, and would have been well content to settle down to his old ways and his Hanoverian life. Throughout the whole of the struggle quietly going on in England there seems to have been but little account taken of the attitude of George, and no one thought it possible that the final

settlement was likely to be affected by any sudden
and voluntary movement on his part.

On the other hand, as we have seen, there was
much speculation as to the possible action of the
Stuart Prince. The Pretender, as he was commonly
called, was not in the enjoyment of a quiet and
comfortable position like that held by the Elector of
Hanover, and it might be well worth his while to run
the greatest risk for the sake of establishing himself
on the throne of England. Moreover, the utmost
uncertainty prevailed as to the strength and the
policy of the Stuart party in Scotland, and many
leading English statesmen were even then looking
out for the possibility of a Stuart uprising, some
such uprising as Scotland was actually destined to see
twice over before very long. The whole situation
showed itself distinctly dramatic and full of the
most thrilling possibilities. If we can imagine some
intelligent student of history becoming acquainted
for the first time with the conditions of the struggle
up to the moment we have now reached, and knowing nothing of what happened afterwards, we shall
probably come to the conclusion that such a student
would have anticipated anything rather than that
quiet and prosaic termination of the crisis which
England was so soon to see.

Meanwhile the Queen was sinking fast. She
passed through many alternations of fever and of
chill. At times her suffering seemed to be chiefly
from the pains of gout; she had fainting fits now
and then, and there were intervals during which her

mind utterly wandered. She was troubled also with
an abscess in one of her legs, caused by erysipelas,
and she had to be subjected to a special course of
treatment before the discharge arising from this
source could be effectually checked. It would be
almost needless to say that during the whole time of
her illness, and whatever might be the symptoms by
which it made its existence manifest, the blood-
letting process, the method of dealing with disease
most in favour everywhere at the time, was liberally
used. There were able physicians in attendance
on the dying Queen, one of whom, as we have
already said, was Dr. Arbuthnot, who would be
remembered for his great medical skill if he were
not better remembered for his remarkable literary
gifts. But even the most genuine and accomplished
physicians of that day and of a much later day
seemed to be under the impression that there was
hardly any human malady which ought not to be
dealt with by the copious letting of blood.

On July 30 the Queen felt much better, and she
told her attendants that she was well enough to get
out of bed and prepare to receive the members of her
Council. The Queen did actually get out of bed, but
the corpse-like paleness of her face and the extreme
feebleness of her movements so alarmed her
attendants that they sent for Dr. Arbuthnot at once,
and Arbuthnot directed that her head should be
shaved. While this operation, the exact purpose of
which does not seem quite clear to the unskilled
reader of to-day, was going on the poor Queen fell

into a fainting fit, declared by the doctors to be apoplectic, and she lay senseless and speechless for nearly two hours.

The Council on this day was holding one of its meetings at the Cockpit. Suddenly a message came from the Palace at Kensington with the announcement that the Queen had fallen into a most dangerous state. All the members of the Council present hastened to Kensington Palace, assembled there in the chamber appointed for their reception, and sent for Dr. Arbuthnot to give them the latest news about the Queen's actual condition. Arbuthnot came to the Council chamber, and several other physicians came with him; but once again the proverbial difficulty arose, and the doctors disagreed. There were three sets of opinions: Arbuthnot held that although the Queen's state was beyond all doubt most critical, it was not beyond hope, and that there was good reason to believe in the possibility of her recovery. Another of the physicians, Sir Richard Blackmore, who like Arbuthnot had made for himself something of a name in literature, was of opinion that, although the Queen could not recover, she might yet hold out for another day or two. Blackmore had at least one colleague present who quite shared his opinion, while another doctor declared that Anne could not live for five minutes.

It happened unfortunately that the most distinguished and trusted physician of that age, John Radcliffe, was not able to be in attendance on the Queen at that critical hour. It is not likely, indeed, that the attendance of Radcliffe could have done much to prolong the life of the sinking Queen; but his absence just then was regarded by those around the Queen as something in the nature of a public calamity. The absence of Dr. Radcliffe was not owing to any negligence on his part, but merely to the fact that he was lying ill at Carshalton, suffering severely from an attack of the gout; and although he was privately sent for, yet he was not informed of the Queen's actual condition in time to be of any service. Mr. Fitzgerald Molloy, in his interesting and well-arranged book 'The Queen's Comrade,' quotes a letter written by Dr. Radcliffe which we cannot forbear from reproducing in these pages both on account of the remarkable frankness of its expressions and the peculiarities of its grammar and style. 'However ill as I was I would have went to the Queen in a horse-litter had either Her Majesty or those in commission next to her commanded me so to do, but the people about her—the plagues of Egypt fall on them—put it out of the power of physic to be of any benefit to her.'

Dr. Radcliffe was at this time near to the end of his own life. He had effected so many cures in bad cases of gout and smallpox that the public had come to have an absolute faith in his capacity for conquering most forms of disease. He had unquestionably inspired the medical faculty with some new ideas which have since vindicated themselves triumphantly in the scientific treatment of human maladies. He was, however, distinctly wanting in the courtliness

of manner which commends itself to most patients—
he was, in fact, an Abernethy of an earlier date.   He
had been in attendance upon Anne before she became
Queen, but his blunt ways and his roughly humorous
sallies were so disagreeable to her that she struck his
name off the list of her physicians, and had never
been attended by him since she came to the throne.
This very fact made it all the more painful and bitter
to Radcliffe that the private summons to him to
visit the Queen in her last illness did not reach
him at a time that would have made it possible for
him, with whatever trouble and danger to himself, to
render her any service in his power.   A report got
about that Radcliffe had been summoned in good time
but refused to attend the Queen, and the story went
that he had actually been threatened with personal
violence because of his supposed disloyalty, at once
to his Sovereign and his profession.   Radcliffe, it is
certain, took much to heart the unjust and offensive
reports thus spread abroad, and his feeling of the
injustice affected him deeply during the short time
which was yet to run of a life that had been valuable
in many ways outside the sphere of his distinguished
medical career.

Among the many rumours which passed out from
the bedside of the dying Queen, one in especial
created much public interest, and has been accepted
by some historians as absolutely deserving of cre-
dence.   According to this story, the latest hours of
the Queen's life were disturbed by frequent paroxysms
of anguish finding expression in the repetition of

the words 'Oh, my brother—oh, my poor brother!'
Of course those who repeated this story accepted and
described it as conclusive evidence that the Queen
was thrown into agonies of remorse because of the
part she had taken in preventing the son of James
the Second from obtaining the Crown of England.
The story had much to recommend it to the Tories
as well as to the Whigs. It was welcome to the
Tories because it enabled them to say that the Queen
in her dying hours had felt deeply penitent for the
opposition she had given to their schemes, and that
at the last moment she would if she could have acted
on a different resolution. It was acceptable to the
Whigs because it gave them another opportunity of
magnifying in the eyes of the new Sovereign the office
they had performed in securing the Hanoverian succession against the latest efforts of its enemies.

But when the whole story is submitted to close
and careful inquiry, it is seen that it rests on no
genuine foundation whatever. It was of course just
the sort of story which would be likely to find
ready belief among the general public. There was
something dramatic or melodramatic in it which
easily caught hold of the ordinary imagination. It
seemed the natural close to such a life as that of the
good and kindly-hearted Queen Anne that her last
hours should be distracted by conscience-stricken
remorse for the manner in which she had allowed
her brother to be excluded from his chance of
succession to the throne. Even among those who
were entirely opposed to the claims of the Stuarts

there was something that touched many hearts in
this story of the poor Queen's death-bed penitence.
It has to be said, however, that the whole statement
rests on no clear and direct evidence claiming any
serious consideration from the writer of history.
Even if there were no actual reasons for regarding
the whole report as improbable, we have, to begin
with, the fact that no trustworthy witness is known
to have given direct authority for such a report.
But there is much more to be said against the story
than can be found in merely negative evidence.
It cannot be questioned that throughout all the
later years of her life Anne felt greatly troubled
because of the part she had taken and had felt
herself obliged to take against the father who had
been most kind and loving to her and whom, so far
as we can judge, she had never ceased to love. But
her feelings towards her father may very well have
been quite different from any which she could have
had towards the Stuart Prince whom all the world
now believes to have been James the Second's son.
Anne had never in her life set eyes on the living
claimant to the Stuart succession. She was one of
those who fully believed in the warming-pan story,
and repudiated the idea that the child about whom
the fierce controversy arose was the son of her father
and his wife.

Wyon declares in his history that ' not a word of
hers has been recorded by any person who had any
degree of intimacy with her which might seem to
indicate that she had changed her opinion.' Wyon

goes on to justify this remark of his by some indirect
evidence which is well worthy of notice. 'For nearly
a quarter of a century,' he tells us, 'the Duchess
of Marlborough was the friend of her bosom and
the chief repository of her thoughts.' In 1742 the
Duchess published a volume containing an account
of her relations with Queen Anne. This work, Wyon
says, 'was composed in a frame of mind so spiteful
that had her Grace been able to charge Anne with a
wish to alter the law of succession established by
Parliament she would most certainly have done it.
But there is not a line from which it can be inferred
that Her Majesty entertained even the slightest
affection for the Pretender.' Then, again, Wyon's
history reminds us that a year after the death of
Anne one of Swift's letters contained the sentences
we quote. 'Whoever knew anything of the Queen's
disposition must believe that she had no inclinations
at all in favour of the Pretender. She was highly
and publicly displeased with my Lord Bolingbroke
because he was seen under the same roof with that
person at the opera when his lordship was sent to
France. Her Majesty said that he ought immediately to have withdrawn upon the appearance of
the other. And at her toilet among her women, when
mention happened to be made of the Chevalier, she
would frequently let fall expressions of such a nature
as made it manifest how little she deserved those
reproaches which had been cast upon her on that
account since her death.' Swift, as Wyon points
out, was the close friend and correspondent of Lady

Masham, the Duchess of Ormond, Dr. Arbuthnot, and many others who had been in constant attendance upon the Queen in her last hours, and it is not likely that he would have ventured on making such statements within a year after Anne's death if he had believed there was the slightest chance of their receiving a contradiction from any of those who were best qualified to bear testimony on the subject.

We can well believe that the Queen's latest hours must have been darkened by many sad and penitential thoughts, even though it is not shown that she felt remorse for the course she had pursued with regard to her brother. During the intervals of her malady, when she had the full possession of her senses, Anne must have felt herself overshadowed by many a darkening memory. It is not to the guilty that the near approach of death most often brings repentance and remorse. Probably the men and women who have least to reproach themselves with are just those who feel most keenly, when threatened by death, the regret for golden opportunities neglected, the grief for good left undone which might have been accomplished, the racking self-reproach for wasted years, for evil allowed to succeed where conscientious resolve and energy might have secured the triumph of good. There was nothing of the heroine about Anne, but she was undoubtedly a woman who had a conscience and a clear moral purpose throughout her life, and was therefore just the sort of woman to feel bitterly, in her closing hours, that she had sometimes disobeyed the dictates of her conscience and had allowed herself weakly to be led away from her moral purpose. These are the troubles of a nature which has capacity enough to see always the right course, but not strength and patience enough to hold that course when threatening difficulties stand in the way.

If the moralists who illustrate the evils of ambition by pointing out to us the special troubles which come with exalted station had not utterly exhausted their subject long before Queen Anne came into the world, their preachings might have found a new argument in the story of her life. If Anne had been born to a quiet and irresponsible position she might have had as little to reproach herself with, when the close of her existence was drawing nigh, as any mortal could well expect to have in this world of ours. She would in all probability have fulfilled her duties as daughter, sister, wife, mother, and head of a household in such a manner as to leave her little ground for conscientious self-reproach when coming death began to cast its shadow on her. But the temptations which came in the way of poor Anne, and sometimes led her astray from the path her conscience bade her to follow, came almost altogether from the peculiarities of her exalted and exceptional position. She had to choose, at a critical moment of her life, between the father who dearly loved her—the father whom she dearly loved—and what she believed to be the interests of the country over which she was called to rule, and of the religion to which she was devoted.

No impartial reader, whatever his religious faith or his political belief, can say that Anne was not justified in the choice she made when once she had convinced herself that there was no way of compromise. But it must be evident to everybody that a woman of Queen Anne's nature and character could not by the mere act of choice set herself for ever free from moments of bitter and agonizing uncertainty as to whether she had really made the rightful decision. The very best qualities of the woman would only have left her more liable to those visitations of torturing doubt and even of occasional self-reproach. We cannot, says Goethe, leap over our own shadow. Anne had not that strength of character for good or for evil which can form a resolve once for all, at a moment of portentous crisis, and never again return to any mental discussion of the question.

Then, at the very moment of her entering on her royal station, Anne had become the victim of a conscientious struggle which remained with her to the end of her life. Her own judgment and her own feelings did not allow her to approve of the policy that carried on the war against France. If she had been a despotic Sovereign it may be taken for granted that she would never have allowed England to accept the supposed inheritance of such a war. But she felt that it was her duty to maintain the part of a constitutional Sovereign and to act upon the advice of her Ministers and her Parliament. She made up her mind conscientiously to maintain that part ; but the business of constitutional sovereignty was a new thing then in the world's history, and had not received that hallowing sanction of time and usage which gives it unquestioned supremacy over the individual judgment or inclinations of the ruler. There are abundant evidences to show that during the progress of the war the mind of Queen Anne was often troubled by doubts as to whether she had done right in accepting the policy which carried it on. It may be taken for granted that such doubts as these grew only the more pressing and the more painful as the sinking condition of Anne's health began to indicate more and more the near approach of death.

The end was now near. Saturday, July 31, 1714, was the last day when Anne was able to have any interchange of ideas with her attendants, her physicians, and the Bishop of London, Dr. Robinson, who was often with her at that time. Late in the evening she became delirious, and shortly after seven o'clock on the morning of Sunday, August 1, 1714, the struggle was over, and the reign of Queen Anne had come to an end. The last Sovereign of the House of Stuart had passed away from the throne of England. The ante-chambers of the palace were soon crowded with Ministers of State, Privy Councillors, and officials of various kinds. The Archbishop of Canterbury and the Lord Chancellor were among those in attendance. Every preparation was instantly made for proclaiming King George the First and for carrying on the work of administration until the new Sovereign should present himself in person to his new subjects. A list of eighteen noblemen who had been appointed, with the approval of the late Queen, to act as Regents with the seven highest officers of State during the interval between the death of one Sovereign and the arrival of the other, was read aloud. The announcement of the names of those who had thus been summoned to act in conjunction with the State functionaries occasioned some surprise at the time and much comment afterwards. The list seems to have been made up fairly enough of Whigs as well as of Tories, but it did not contain the names of Somers or of Wharton, both of whom might well have been thought entitled to a place in such a Regency. But the one omission which created most comment was that of Marlborough's name. One reason suggested for this omission was the fact that Marlborough was still abroad when the list was in course of preparation; but then it was certain that Marlborough had been summoned back to England, and it was understood that he had set out on his journey home. The impression generally prevailing was that Anne herself still retained in her latest hours her feeling of resentment towards Marlborough, and that she was unwilling to sanction his appointment as one of those invested with authority to govern the kingdom during the interval between her death and the arrival of her successor.

A proclamation was prepared announcing the death of Queen Anne and the accession of King George the First, and during the course of the day the proclamation was read aloud at the historical places in

London and Westminster, with all the usual pomp and ceremony belonging to such an occasion. The royal funeral took place on the night of August 24, when the last mortal remains of Queen Anne were entombed in a vault in Westminster Abbey, close to the burial-place of Charles the Second, of William the Third, of his Queen Mary, and of Anne's husband Prince George of Denmark. Nothing remained but for George the First to enter his new kingdom and take unchallenged possession of his new throne.

Thus came to an end the reign and the life of England's last Stuart Sovereign. England had yet to see two successive efforts made by Princes of the House of Stuart to recover possession of the English throne. Each effort proved futile for its own purpose, and only brought with it the loss of gallant lives on the one side and on the other. The cause of the Stuarts has now passed altogether into history. There is even at the present hour something that might be called a Stuart sect, although hardly perhaps a Stuart organization, in these countries. There are still men and women who cherish a faith in divine right and in the Stuart succession, and refuse to give any public adhesion or recognition to the sovereignty of the House of Hanover; who keep up anniversaries and celebrations of their own in their own way, and proclaim their belief that a foreign Princess is the legitimate Sovereign of the British Empire. This little sect of Stuart votaries has comprised in our time many sincere, highly educated, and most honourable men and women, and had amongst its

numbers more than one member of the House of
Lords. There is something touching, something
which ought to defy ridicule, in this unconquerable
devotion to a lost cause. But, so far as human
foresight can inform us, the dynasty of the Stuarts
came to an end when Queen Anne passed out of life.

There was no reason why those who loved Queen
Anne, if any such were then living, should have
grieved for her sake over her comparatively early
death. Dr. Arbuthnot wrote that no wearied
traveller ever could have longed for rest more sincerely than Anne, in her later years, had longed for
the close of her life. All those whom she really
loved had been consigned to the grave before her
time came. The late Arthur Penrhyn Stanley, Dean
of Westminster, used to give an account of an ex-
cavation which once had to be made under his
direction among the tombs of Westminster Abbey.
Nothing could be more pathetic, he said, even at that
distance of time, than to see the tomb of Anne near
to that of her husband and around it all the coffins
of the children she had borne, not one of whom
lived beyond the age of childhood. She had not
secured any lasting attachments outside the range
of her own family; she had not the qualities
which win attachment from those who are not of
kin. There is no reason to believe that she left
behind her any sincere, unselfish mourner, and that
very fact is itself more truly tragic in a death-bed
scene than the profoundest grief of the survivors could
be.

That easy form of moralizing which has been going on since sovereignties and crowns came into use among mortals, the moralizing which loves to dwell upon the lesson that happiness belongs no more to kings and queens than to peasants and paupers, might again find effective illustration in the closing hours of Queen Anne. That reign of hers had been a great era, destined to be remembered in history for ever. She had been Queen of England at a time when England won some of her greatest triumphs in war and in peace, in literature and in science. She had done many good deeds herself, and had attached her name to some noble works of charity. Yet she died without husband or child, brother or sister, to kneel and pray beside her deathbed, and without any one devoted friend to listen to her latest words. While she was passing away the public out of doors, and even those who still watched over her last moments, were thinking not of her but of the Sovereign who was to succeed her, the changes which his coming might bring with it, the fortunes of this or that political party which might be endangered or shattered by the change. The dying ears of the Queen might have caught the sound of some of the noisy preparations for the coming of her successor which were already agitating London. The mind of one who has studied her history feels only a sense of relief when he reads that the Queen sank into unconsciousness before her death.

CHAPTER XL

RETROSPECT

THE reign of Queen Anne is beyond all question entitled to take a distinct place in history. It does not stand as one in a succession of reigns, but forms in itself an epoch. It is the coming of the new order, and does not merely mark the passing away of the old. The new order may indeed be said to have been initiated by the reign of William the Third, but it only came into actual existence and made its life manifest with the reign of Anne. The one condition which mainly distinguishes the new order from the old in the constitutional history of England is the recognised supremacy of Parliamentary government. Of course there was a system of so-called Parliamentary government existing in Great Britain and Ireland for long ages before the Stuart dynasty had come to an end, or even had made a beginning; but then it was only a Parliamentary government in name, and had none of the essential qualities belonging to the institution we now recognise as the governing power in these countries.

So far back as the reigns of the earlier Henrys the principle was adopted by which a certain number of men were chosen to represent the interests of the

whole community, and to advise with the Sovereign
as to the laws and regulations necessary to be made
for the general welfare. This arrangement developed
into a representation by knights, citizens, and bur-
gesses, and thus by degrees the Parliament composed
of Lords and Commons came to be established. But
a Parliament ruling with anything like the authority
now belonging to the institution only came into
existence with the Revolution and the reign of
William the Third. Then it became definitely settled
that the Sovereign must obtain supplies by the
vote of the House of Commons, and so it was
made impossible for the King to dismiss his Parliament according to his own mere will and pleasure.
Thus the Parliament ceased to be an assembly whose
whole business consisted in advising the Sovereign
as to the course which ought to be pursued for
the general welfare of the State. As the power of
voting supplies was made to rest with the House of
Commons there was a distinct control given to the
representative assembly which the Sovereign could
not resist or refuse to acknowledge without a breach
of the constitutional law. This authority in the
representative assembly came to be fully recognised
as a working part of the governing system during
the reign of Queen Anne. Such was, in fact, the
first establishment of what we now recognise as the
principle of Parliamentary government.

In Queen Anne's reign, and during many of the
reigns following, the system of representation was
utterly inadequate to its supposed purpose, and

the great majority of the community had no voice whatever in the election of the representative chamber, and therefore had no share in the making of the laws. But during Queen Anne's reign the Houses of Parliament, and more especially the House of Commons, came to be a recognised power in the ruling of the State with which every Sovereign must bring himself into something like accord. The era of rule by the mere will of the monarch was over and done with, and the House of Commons became one of the three elements of government. The time had not yet come, and did not come until a much later reign, when it was to be definitely settled once for all that the Sovereign must act only on the advice of an administration called into power by a majority of the House of Commons. But the reign of Queen Anne saw for the first time the recognition of the principle that the Sovereign could no longer act without regard for the authority of the representative chamber. The mere fact that such an authority was thus established and recognised gave to the House of Commons new motives for existence. Parliamentary debate became with Queen Anne's reign one of the great moving forces in the system of constitutional government.

The House of Commons created a platform from which the statesman and the political orator could address the whole community. A man with a gift of eloquence knew that if he could obtain a seat in that assembly it rested only with him to make his gift a power in the State and to win for himself a fame throughout the land.   There was no other avenue to influence and to fame so secure for the capacity that deserved success.   It became a part of the ambition of every great family to have some one at least of its members in that chamber of debate, where genuine eloquence could wake an echo throughout the whole country.   The Parliamentary career became a distinct object of ambition to numbers of men who might otherwise have had nothing to call them from a life of mere indolence or pleasure. During the reign of Queen Anne some of the greatest Parliamentary orators known to our political history made their mark in the House of Lords or in the House of Commons, but more especially in the House of Commons.   Every reflecting student of history might easily have foreseen at the time that the influence and the power of Parliament were destined to grow greater and greater, and that no matter what the succeeding Hanoverian Sovereigns might think on the subject, the representative assembly was destined to become the chief ruling power in the British Commonwealth.

Queen Anne, to do her justice, seems to have recognised from the beginning the growing influence of Parliament, and more especially of the House of Commons.   Although she was not a woman of great intellectual capacity, and although she cannot be supposed to have given profound study to the principles of State government, yet it has to be said in bare justice to her that she seems from the first to have had a clear understanding as to the business and the duty of a constitutional Sovereign.   We have seen again and again in this history how Queen Anne, on some important occasions, allowed herself to bend her own will, her own prejudices, and even, it must be added, her own conscientious convictions, to the earnest representations of the Ministers whom she recognised as the advisers appointed for her guidance by the Parliamentary constitution.

The reign saw also a new and important stage of advancement in the great movement for religious equality.   During many previous generations the struggle had merely been one for ascendency between the Church of England and the Church of Rome. When the one was in power the other was oppressed and persecuted, and there were but two contending parties in the controversy.   Before Anne's reign a new development of the question had arisen.   A large and increasing number of men and women who were devoted adherents to the faith of Protestantism as opposed to that of Rome, found themselves unable to submit their religious beliefs and practices to the absolute decrees of the State Church.   The Protestant Dissenters and Nonconformists began to assert themselves boldly and coherently, and to claim their right to maintain their own religious discipline and their own forms of worship independently of any decrees issued by the Established Church of England.

Here, then, was an entirely new question to perplex and disturb the community.   Public opinion had outgrown the simpler code of earlier days, which proclaimed the block or the stake as the approved and appropriate way of dealing with heretics of any order. The difficulty in the way of the downright religious persecutors was, of course, much increased by the fact that the Dissenters and Nonconformists declared themselves devoted to the Protestant faith, and insisted that not they but the members of the State Church were straying from true Protestant doctrine. The Dissenters and Nonconformists were numerous and influential, and they had amongst them some men of the highest capacity for controversy, whether in the pulpit or with the pen, who were not to be reduced to silence or inaction by any terrors the law could bring to bear against them. The trouble which the constituted authorities had in dealing with these controversial Nonconformists was much increased by the fact that the whole system which the Revolution had set up proclaimed itself to be a system of civil and religious liberty. The Nonconformists were well entitled to ask what advantage they, as ordinary citizens, had gained by the overthrow of Rome's domination if the State Church of England were now to be allowed to deal with them just as the authorities of Rome might have dealt with those who disputed its doctrines and denied its supremacy.

We have seen through the course of this history how time after time the Government of Queen Anne made attempts to punish and to suppress every form of Protestant Nonconformity, and how the most energetic attempts only seemed to add to the strength and increase the numbers of the Nonconformists.

Even within the fold of the Church of England itself there were, as might have been expected, numbers of able and influential public men who could not sustain the administration in such a course of policy. The age was beginning, at least in these countries, to outgrow the idea that the prison cell and the scaffold were the convincing arguments with which to sustain the religious doctrines favoured by the ruling classes. We have seen also how in the House of Lords itself the attempts made to enforce Protestant conformity by penalty and disqualification were more than once resisted and defeated. More than once the House of Lords showed itself superior to the representative chamber in enlightenment and in foresight where questions of religious liberty were brought up for consideration. The explanation of this fact is not difficult to find. Members of the House of Lords were not dependent for their position as legislators on any declarations of public opinion. No popular movement could deprive a too liberal minded Peer of his seat in the House of Lords. But a popular movement might well deprive a member of the House of Commons of his place in the representative chamber.

At that time, and for long after, the representative chamber was representative only in a very limited and figurative sense, and the vast majority of British subjects in these islands had no more to do with the election of a member of Parliament than their wives and children might have had. The electoral body was itself a privileged class, and could not possibly be regarded as entitled to speak with the voice of the British people. Therefore, if any question arose which brought a majority of the privileged electoral body into temporary combination, a member of the House of Commons might be very likely to lose his seat because he had acted with the independence and enlightenment which a member of the House of Lords could display with impunity. All these various controversies inside and outside the Houses of Parliament had the effect of arousing the attention of the whole people to the existence of the great principle of religious equality. Even the fiercest and most passionate debates and disputes could not fail, when the rage of the controversy had passed away, to leave behind them some instructive lessons as to the reality of that principle and the inevitable success of its claims.

Many generations, indeed, had yet to pass before the lessons of the great controversy, which had become a political question in Queen Anne's reign, came to be fully recognised in legislation. But it is not too much to say that the true doctrine of religious equality—the doctrine that no one shall suffer penalty or disqualification because of his religious faith —was for the first time set up as a constitutional principle during the reign of Queen Anne. The full meaning of the principle was not proclaimed or even perceived by many of those who were most earnest and most influential in maintaining the civil rights of Dissenters and Nonconformists in the days of Defoe. But these men had consciously or unconsciously

carried the movement far enough to make its further
progress evident and inevitable.   Many of the State
Church Protestants who advocated, at that time, the
emancipation of Dissenters and Nonconformists would
have utterly refused to champion the extension of
the same principle to Roman Catholics or to Jews.
Many or most of the Dissenters and Nonconformists
themselves would have drawn just the same distinction between their own claims and the claims of
their fellow subjects who belonged to the Hebrew
faith, or who worshipped at the altars of the Church
of Rome.   But from the moment when it was
asserted as the principle of a political party that
absolute conformity to all the doctrines and practices
of the State Church was not necessary in order to
qualify a British subject for citizenship, it must
have been foreshown to many minds that the emancipation of the Roman Catholic and of the Jew was
but a question of time.   The reign of Queen Anne is
entitled to the historical honour of having opened
this new chapter in the story of England's progress.

The reign of Anne had not much to do with the
work of what we should now call Imperial administration.   England had hardly yet grown to be an
empire in the modern sense of the word.   The
conquest of India had scarcely begun, and although
England had colonial possessions, the manner of
maintaining them and of keeping them in good order
was not of much concern to the administration at
home.   Some man of intellect, enterprise, and high

purpose, like William Penn, established a colonial
province of his own and managed it to the best of
his power with the approval, or at least the toleration,
of the Government in England. Some adventurous
company took possession of new ground at a distant
part of the globe and set about enabling its members
to make fortunes there, and Queen Anne's statesmen
adopted it and recognised it as part of the Queen's
dominions, but did not usually make the method of
its management a direct concern of their official
departments. The whole business of statesmanship
was therefore much more limited in its operations
than it began to be in the succeeding reigns, and it
may fairly be said that the functions of a Government
during the reign of Queen Anne were to look after
the prosperity of the British Islands and to fight the
French. The fame of the reign rests chiefly on its
accomplishments in literature and in war. We have
already given such account of what was done in
these two fields as to render any further description
unnecessary in this retrospect. It may be said,
without undue boldness of assertion, that no coming
period of English history is likely to bring forth a
greater military commander than Marlborough, or
greater writers of prose than the writers who created
the English literature of Marlborough's time.

In the drama and in the fine arts the age of
Queen Anne has not much to boast. But that age
certainly has an architecture all its own. That
architecture does not seem to have come into being
from the inspiration of any one great man or any

school of men.   There was really no great architect
whose name is associated with the history of the
reign.   There was no man whose fame will go down to
all time in connection with that reign in companionship with the names of some poets and many prose
writers who created for it a characteristic literature.
Yet it is certain that the architecture of the reign
has a character peculiar to itself, and is still the
object of artistic admiration, and of a frequently
rather inartistic imitation.   It is enough to make
mention of Queen Anne houses and Queen Anne
streets in order to conjure up in every mind the idea
of an architecture quite distinctive and essentially
picturesque.   It was no doubt to a certain extent an
adaptation from foreign models; but the adaptation
was so completely and so artistically brought into
harmony with the English climate and English
conditions of life, with the manorial fields of English
landscape and the streets of English cities, that it is
still regarded as essentially characteristic of the
country and the people over whom good Queen
Anne came to reign.   A Queen Anne country
mansion seems to be the appropriate home for Sir
Roger de Coverley; a Queen Anne house in town
might claim to be regarded as the fitting abode of
Addison or Steele.   When Thackeray made up his
mind to have a house built in the Kensington region
to suit his own ideas and his own tastes, he had it
built after the most approved models of the age of
Queen Anne.   In days still later, and chiefly under
the inspiration of William Morris, who was an artistic

decorator as well as a poet, a reaction set in against the
disheartening and unlovely monotony of the stucco-
fronted houses, jammed close to each other—and
each exactly resembling the other—which had come
up for the disfigurement of the life of cities in the
early days of the Victorian reign. The reaction
made itself manifest for the most part in a brave
artistic attempt to restore to our cities and towns
some of the best qualities of the architecture which belonged to the reign of Queen Anne. That reaction
had beyond all question a most healthy and enduring
effect, and we can see that its spirit still lives in the
architect's work here, there, and everywhere throughout the cities and the country places of these islands.

Macaulay speaks of that ' vile phrase, the dignity
of history.' The great author was thus expressing
his reprobation of the sort of criticism which at one
time used to condemn the introduction of trivial
details and commonplace illustrations into any
historical narrative, as beneath the solemn gravity
of a branch of literature which had a Muse all to
itself as its representative. Let us hope that it may
not be considered quite beneath the dignity of
history if we mention that the silver ornaments and
vessels used in Queen Anne's reign had a peculiar
value and a special hall-mark of their own. Some
discussion has lately been revived on the subject of
Queen Anne silver, and an interesting article in
' Country Life,' a well-known periodical, told us in
the September of 1901 something about the Queen
Anne mark. This mark, we read, ' consists of the

figure of Britannia holding a trident, the lion's head erased—that is, cut off—the maker's initials, and the date letter.' The writer further tells us that 'since this series of marks was impressed only between 1696 and 1720 any piece of plate bearing them may be roughly said to belong to the Queen Anne period, since the expression is not necessarily limited strictly to the mere period during which Queen Anne reigned, but may be fairly taken to include a few years before and after. The most characteristic part of the Queen Anne mark is the date letter. Practically every one of those letters is extremely illegible, consisting of a crabbed kind of black letter, usually, but not always, a capital. Ever since 1716, the London date letters have been very bold and clear, and the presence upon a piece of silver of one of these old-style letters gives positive proof, if it be genuine, that it is not more recent than the Queen Anne period.'

Perhaps the mere fact that a discussion has arisen on the subject of Queen Anne silver, and on the question how to ascertain whether some prize relics are genuine in their value or not, may be taken as an excuse for reminding the reader that a peculiar kind of silver work was one of the characteristic creations of Queen Anne's reign. Perhaps, having gone so far in disregard of the dignity of history, we need not restrain ourselves from going still farther and mentioning the fact that especial value still attaches to the coins which are known as Queen Anne's farthings. We learn from an authoritative source that the common patterns of 1713 and 1714 are worth one pound sterling each; that the patterns with Britannia under a canopy, and Peace on a car, are worth two guineas each; and that the patterns with Peace on a car and without Britannia are still more rare and valuable, and are worth five pounds each.

The reign of Queen Anne may be regarded as the parent age of the newspaper, according to our modern acceptation of the journalist's work. There were newspapers existing in England before Queen Anne's day, but these were for the most part the brief and abstract chronicles of events given to the public as time and opportunity allowed, and no particular sheet continued very long in circulation. But with the age of 'The Guardian,' 'The Examiner,' and 'The Spectator' began the development of that newspaper press dealing in commentary and in criticism as well as in the mere narration of events. It may be observed as a curious and significant fact in the history of our journalism, that 'The Spectator,' which had little or nothing to do with political questions, accomplished perhaps more than any other journal of the same time towards the creation of a keen public interest in the reading of criticism and commentary on political subjects. A class or community when once taught to take delight in the reading of daily essays on the fashions, the social habits, and the morals of the time would not be likely to remain long without demanding a regular supply of essays on politics and parties. We have already in these

volumes given some account of the journals, political
and other, published during the reign of Queen
Anne, and in this retrospect we merely desire to
take account of the fact that the reign which saw
the first genuine and practical recognition of the
power of parliamentary debate saw also, and perhaps
as a necessary accompaniment, the opening of that
newspaper system which has since become one of the
recognised institutions and powers of the modern
State.

The great work of what may be called philan-
thropic legislation can hardly be said to have come
into existence during Queen Anne's reign. There
were philanthropists, lovers of their kind, then as at
all other periods of history; but the idea that legislation in itself had anything to do for the unrepre-
sented classes, beyond the enforcement of the criminal
law, had not yet become part of the ordinary legis-
lator's creed. The practice of keeping negro slaves
in England was not declared illegal by a British
court of law until more than fifty years had passed
away after the death of Queen Anne. We can find
in books and in pictures of Anne's reign many illustrations of the fact that negro slaves were still to be
seen at that time in English households. Nothing
could seem more outrageously antagonistic to all the
principles of Christianity, of the moral law, and of
civilization than such a practice, and yet it was
regarded by the British public of Queen Anne's days
as an ordinary and unobjectionable part of the social
usages of the time—a time when writers like Pope,

and Addison, and Steele were the leading favourites of English readers.

The criminal laws were still not merely oppressive but outrageously cruel, and the most trivial offences against property were liable to punishment by death, and were so punished, without arousing the slightest general feeling of indignation and abhorrence. We have already spoken of the prison discipline which was maintained and enforced every day while Queen Anne was still reigning, and told how the use of the lash to men and women who were imprisoned under sentence of the law was looked upon as an interesting incident affording a natural amusement to educated spectators. The State concerned itself but little in providing means for protecting the poorest classes against actual starvation. Private benevolence and charity were left to do the best they could, out of their own resources, for supplying food to the destitute, so that they might eat of it and live. There was private charity in those days as well as in ours, and there were kindly-hearted men and women ever ready to do their best for the maintenance of the very poor; but the subject did not appear to be one with which any State system was bound to trouble itself overmuch. There was no system of national education, at least in England—Scotland was much more advanced in its ideas as to popular education at that time—and many writers of good repute still encouraged and fostered the common notion that, on the whole, the poor were rather better off without education than with it, for the reason that the

reading of books would only be likely to make poor
people discontented with the lot to which it had
pleased Providence to call them. Down to a very
much later period in our history the prevailing idea,
even among men who might have known better,
was that compulsory education was a sort of thing
which might be well suited to despotically-governed
countries like some of the German States, but was
not suited to the habits and the doctrines of free-
born Englishmen.

We have already described the condition of the
streets in the great cities and towns of England, and
the utter absence of any systematic protection for
the safety of the most respectable citizens who might
have to make their way through the public thorough-
fares after darkness had set in, or indeed before it
had set in. In the country districts no care whatever was taken by the authorities, at least in any
systematic fashion and by any legalised appliances,
for the safety of travellers and of ordinary residents,
and highway robbery by armed desperadoes was so
common an occurrence as to attract but little notice.
For a traveller to be stopped and robbed as he was
approaching within sight of the London suburbs was
regarded as a sort of mishap, like the advent of a
storm, making one of the ordinary chances likely to
come in the way of enterprising persons who thought
fit to move at their own risk from one part of the
country to another.

It must also be evident that a high standard of
political morality and consistency was wholly un-

known at the time when Queen Anne came to reign over these islands. We have seen again and again in the course of Queen Anne's reign that some of the most eminent statesmen in England were habitually acting parts which at a more modern period would have been universally regarded as infamous. Men high in office who were pledged to the support of the Hanoverian succession were constantly engaged in secret intrigues with the Jacobites and with the exiled Stuart family. Among the Ministers who sat in council with the Queen were some who concerted measures with her for the maintenance of the established dynasty, and on leaving the council chamber found means to acquaint the Jacobites with all that had been done, and to suggest efficient measures for a Stuart restoration. Much of this was perfectly well known to the colleagues and friends of those Ministers and to the public in general; but no one seems to have thought any the worse of those who thus played false with the Sovereign to whom they had pledged their allegiance. Such a course of action was only looked upon as one of the political manœuvres a clever man might naturally be expected to have resort to, for his own private advantage and for the benefit of the political party to which his personal inclinations were given. Much of this curious disregard of political morality was undoubtedly due to the fact that the Sovereign herself was well known to be at heart in sympathy with the interests and the cause of the exiled Stuarts.

However that may be, it is quite certain that this
system of double-dealing pervaded the whole political body at the time we are describing, and that
the professions and the practices, even of a man
holding office, were not supposed to have any
necessary cohesion or correspondence. In our own
times it is quite well understood that the managers
of a political party are free to enter into temporary
arrangements and compromises with the managers
of the opposite party. We do not regard it as
anything dishonourable or even inconsistent that the
members of a Government which has just brought
in some measure for the consideration of Parliament
should enter into private arrangements with the
leaders of the opposite party for the purpose of
offering certain conditions, by the acceptance of
which it might become easier to carry into legislation
the more important parts of the new scheme. Such
a policy is now looked upon as belonging to the
regular business of an administration, and the statesman is not supposed, and is justly not supposed, to
have committed any act of treason to his principles
or his party if he is known to have suggested or
accepted any slight compromises not affecting the
main principle of the measure he is anxious to carry
through the two Houses of Parliament. During the
reign of Queen Anne it would seem as if the private
dealings of a statesman in office with the Jacobites
at home and the Stuarts abroad were not to be
judged according to any more severe principle of
political morality. The fact that Bolingbroke, and

Oxford, and Marlborough himself, were sometimes engaged in such transactions was looked upon very much as we should now look upon the conduct of a Minister who was willing to enter into terms of agreement with the Opposition, or the Irish National Party, or the representatives of some independent commercial interest, in order to make smooth the course of a complicated measure.

The plain and obvious fact is that we have risen to a higher standard of political morality in our times than any which was thought of in the days when Oxford and Bolingbroke were Ministers of the Crown. We must judge men like Marlborough, Oxford, and Bolingbroke according to the accepted political standard of their own days, and not according to that set up by the moral code belonging to more modern times. The age of chivalry, with all its splendid virtues, and its errors of an imperfect civilization, had passed out of existence at the time when Anne came to rule, and the new era of development was then only opening on the social and political life of Europe.

The age of Queen Anne must therefore be regarded as a distinctly new chapter in the history of England's political and social life. The monarchical system itself was then, and only then, beginning to take that shape which has enabled it to become a powerful instrument in the development of political liberty and of progressive social institutions. England owes in great part to the influence of that age the fact that she was relieved from the terrible necessity imposed upon France of having to pass through the ordeal of a tremendous revolution. The reign of Queen Anne must always be regarded as one of the great historical eras forming the land-marks of England's progress in civilization. The woman herself, with whatever good qualities, was but a very passive and inconsiderable influence in the promotion of such a work; but her name is made immortal if only by the mere fact that it was her happy fortune to be England's figure-head at such an epoch. Her name will pass into history with the name of Queen Elizabeth, and with the name of Queen Victoria.

INDEX.

CHA

Charles, Archduke—*cont.*
Position after Almanza, i. 305
Proclaimed Emperor, ii. 43
Proclaimed King of Spain, i. 163, 305
Reception in Madrid, ii. 40
Charles I. devotees, i. 5
Charles II. character, i. 5
Charles II. of Spain, death, i. 44
Charles XII. of Sweden, ii. 1
Marlborough's Mission to, ii. 4, 8, 10, 12
Policy, ii. 6, 8
Sketch of, i. 54
Chelsea, as station for boats, i. 252
Chocolate houses, i. 225
Christ's Hospital, i. 220
Churchill, Arabella, i. 60, 107
Cibber, Colley, as actor, i. 233
'Richard the Third,' i. 234
Cicero on refinement in choice of words, i. 283
Clarendon, Edward Hyde, Earl of, i. 2
Clive at Council of War, i. 119
Clubs, i. 222, 224
Coaches, hackney and private, i. 237, 238
Cobden, Richard, i. 7
Cocoa Tree Chocolate-house, i. 226
Coffee-houses, i. 225
Coleridge, 'Ancient Mariner' quoted, i. 247
Cologne, Archbishop of, Elector of Germany, i. 99
Ally of Louis XIV., i. 106
Colonial Government, growth of, ii. 396
'Comet of a Season,' origin of phrase, i. 332
Commission of Excise and of Customs, i. 327
Congregationalists (*see* Independents)
Congress of Vienna, ii. 127

DE

Congreve, William :
Complete Edition of Works, ii. 309
Praise of Colley Cibber, i. 233
Continent, struggle for balance of power on, i. 38
Coronation Oath at Queen Anne's coronation, i. 74
'Country Life,' Article on Queen Anne silver, ii. 399
'Coverley, Sir Roger de,' ii. 173, 183
Cowper, Lord Chancellor :
On Marlborough's scheme of retaining command, i. 389, 445
Resigns office, i. 392
Coxe's 'Life of Marlborough,' on Anne's names for William III., i. 65
Cremona, battle of, i. 123, 127
Crimean War, i. 43
Criminal Laws of Queen Anne's reign, ii. 403
Cromwell, Oliver :
Effects of his conquests in Ireland, i. 25
Rule in Wales, ii. 318
Rule of, i. 13
Cromwell, Richard, i. 14
Crown privileges and Parliament, i. 315
Customs, Commission of, i. 327
Duties and Act of Union, i. 320 *seqq.*

'DAILY COURANT' newspaper, i. 258
Darien Company, account of, i. 193 *seqq*
Fate of i. 198
De Rouvigny (*see* Galway, Earl of)
De Torcy on attitude of French towards peace, i. 423, ii. 93

THE END.

PRINTED BY
SPOTTISWOODE AND CO. LTD., NEW-STREET SQUARE
LONDON